Of Rule and Revenue

California Series on Social Choice and Political Economy

Edited by Brian Barry, Robert H. Bates, and Samuel L. Popkin

Of Rule
and Revenue

Margaret Levi

UNIVERSITY OF CALIFORNIA PRESS
Berkeley • *Los Angeles* • *London*

University of California Press
Berkeley and Los Angeles, California

University of California Press, Ltd.
London, England

© 1988 by
The Regents of the University of California

First Paperback Printing 1989

Library of Congress Cataloging in Publication Data

Levi, Margaret.
  Of rule and revenue / Margaret Levi.

      p.   cm.–(California series on social choice and political
economy ; 9)
    Bibliography: p.
    Includes index.
    ISBN 0-520-06750-9
    1. Revenue–History–Case studies.   2. Income tax–History–Case
studies.   3. State, The–History–Case studies.   I. Title.
II. Series.
HJ2250.L48   1988
336.02–dc19   87-28397
                                                     CIP

Printed in the United States of America
        3   4   5   6   7   8   9

For Douglass C. North

GRANDPA: Suppose I pay you this money—mind you, I don't say I'm going to do it—but just for the sake of argument—what's the Government going to do with it?

HENDERSON: How do you mean?

GRANDPA: Well, what do I get for my money? If I go into Macy's and buy something, there it *is*—I see it. What's the Government give me?

Moss Hart and George S. Kaufman
You Can't Take It with You

The revenue of the state is the state.

Edmund Burke
Reflections on the Revolution in France

Contents

Acknowledgments

This project has been many years in the making. Since the initial publication of "A Theory of Predatory Rule" (*Politics and Society,* vol. 10, no. 4) in 1981, I have accumulated innumerable debts.

Administrative and material support for my research and writing came primarily from the Department of Political Science of the University of Washington, chaired by David Olson, and the Social Justice Project, directed by Pat Troy, within the Research School of Social Sciences (RSSS), Institute for Advanced Studies, Australian National University. The Department of Sociology of the University of Essex, the Graduate School Research Fund of the University of Washington, and the Department of Economic History of the RSSS also made substantial administrative contributions.

These affiliations produced criticisms and suggestions from three continents. I hope I am leaving no one off the list of those who offered me detailed comments at one or another stage of the book writing: Lee Alston, Malka Applebaum-Maizel, Ernst Badian, Alan Barnard, Yoram Barzel, George Behlmer, Neil Berch, Paul Brass, Geoffrey Brennan, John Brewer, Mary Brinton, Elizabeth A. R. Brown, William Brustein, Noel Butlin, David Carrell, G. A. Cohen, James Coleman, Jon Elster, Arthur Ferrill, Norman Frohlich, Robert Goodin, Michael Hechter, Carol Heimer, Ira Katznelson, David Kauck, David Lockwood, John McCallum, Michael Mann, William Mitchell, Maxine Molyneux, Kathryn Norberg, Joe Oppenheimer, Elinor Ostrom, Vincent Ostrom, Philip Pettit, Jonathan Pincus, Adam Przeworski, John Roemer, Debra Salazar, Richard Saller, James Scott, Graeme Snooks, Stephanie Todd, and Pat Troy. Patricia Williams and, especially,

Elisabeth Case offered invaluable advice. Ann Buscherfield, Norma Chin, Barbara Gramza, Cheryl Mehaffey, and Carole Mulligan provided superb secretarial assistance. Julie Harrison, Wayne Naughton, Jeanette Ryan, Johanna Sutherland, and Doug Whaite provided first-rate research assistance or technical support.

Robert Bates, Russell Hardin, Philip Hoffman, Sam Popkin, and Michael Taylor read the entire manuscript more than once and were generous with their feedback. They deserve special expressions of gratitude.

My greatest debt is to Douglass C. North. Since 1975, when we established a concentration in political economy at the University of Washington and began to teach a seminar together, we have fought and debated the grand questions of political, economic, and Marxian theory. This book is but one of many products of those conversations. I blame Doug for at least some of what others may perceive as misguided arguments. I am confident that Doug will, as ever, continue to hold me to account—as should the reader—for errors and sloppiness in the text.

CHAPTER I

Introduction

The history of state revenue production is the history of the evolution of the state. As specialization and division of labor increase, there is a greater demand on the state to provide collective goods where once there were solely private goods or no goods at all. The introduction of economies of scale in the production of state-provided goods and services augments the state's ability to provide collective goods. Improvements in state coordination of people and resources further enhance state capacity. Constituents may come to perceive gains from trade. Certainly, they become more dependent on the state. At the foundation of increases in a state's provision of goods and services is its revenue production system.

The state is a complex institution that has undergone numerous transformations in size, function, and organization over the centuries. What characterizes a state is territorially bounded and centralized regulation of important aspects of social life (Mann 1986, 26–27). The object of state regulations changes with time and place. However, all states attempt to monopolize the concentrated means of violence within a given territory.[1] All implement and enforce property rights and other formal rules,[2] including rules concerning the extraction of revenue.

This definition makes it possible to determine where a state exists or, at

[1] This statement is obviously derived from Weber's classic formulation. However, I eschew the word *legitimate,* at least until the term acquires a consensual meaning.

[2] Ostrom (1985, 465) defines rules as "prescriptions about what behaviors (or states of the world) are required, prohibited, or permitted." For an interesting discussion of rules from the constitutionalist perspective, see Brennan and Buchanan (1985). Their agenda is primarily normative, but they make some important points for positive analysis.

least, where it does not, but it sheds little light on variation in state behavior. The institution of the state is the wrong starting place for a theory of state policy in general and of revenue production policy in particular. Many of the differences among states are themselves the consequences of state policy. I propose instead to begin with rulers—actors or sets of actors who perform as the chief executives of state institutions. Monarchs, chiefs, the Senate of the Roman Republic, presidents, and prime ministers all play this role.

Rulers rule. That is, they stand at the head of the institutions that determine and implement state policies and regulations affecting a given polity and the state's provision of collective goods. They both inherit and create policies that allocate state resources. Minimally, rule connotes defense and justice; but over time rule has evolved to include a wide array of collective goods, although with considerable variation from polity to polity.

The power of rulers rests on coercion, but most operate within the rules of the political constitution. A distinction exists between the process of making the rules and the process of making decisions within the rules (Brennan and Buchanan 1985, 6). Rulers participate in both processes. However, they are also responsible for enforcing the rules. They must inhibit free riding and enforce compliance with the laws of the society, especially its laws governing property rights.

One major limitation on rule is revenue, the income of the government. The greater the revenue of the state, the more possible it is to extend rule. Revenue enhances the ability of rulers to elaborate the institutions of the state, to bring more people within the domain of those institutions, and to increase the number and variety of the collective goods provided through the state.

The major arguments in *Of Rule and Revenue* concern the constraints on a ruler's capacity to produce revenue. I hypothesize that rulers maximize the revenue accruing to the state subject to the constraints of their relative bargaining power, transaction costs, and discount rates. Relative bargaining power is defined by the degree of control over coercive, economic, and political resources. Transaction costs are the costs of negotiating an agreement on policy and the costs of implementing policy. The discount rate refers to the time horizon of a decision maker. The more an individual values the future relative to the present, the lower the discount rate.

The model I discuss and evaluate in the chapters that follow consists of two related claims: (1) the relative bargaining power, transaction costs, and discount rates of rulers will have determinant effects on their revenue production policies; and (2) changes in the relative bargaining power, transaction costs, and discount rates will lead to determinant modifications in revenue production policies. My emphasis is on the variation in the constraints that modify behavior.

My hypothesis follows from two paired assumptions. The first is that all the actors who compose the polity, including the policymakers, are rational and self-interested. By this I mean that they calculate the costs and benefits of proposed actions and choose the course of action most consistent with their fixed preferences. The second is that actors who compose the state have interests of their own, derived from and supported by institutional power. Rulers may sometimes, even often, act on behalf of others. Nonetheless, they are not simply handmaidens of the dominant economic class or other influential actors. They will act in their own interests when and if they can.

Following these assumptions and my earlier definitions, I hypothesize that rulers are predatory in that they try to extract as much revenue as they can from the population.[3] They may use the funds to line their own pockets or to promote their personal power.[4] They may use the funds to support social or personal ends. They may have ideological ends they wish to promote. They may be altruistic. Randomness of ends characterizes rational choice models in general, and rulers operate with a wide range of alternative goals. Whatever the rulers' ends, revenue is necessary to attain them. It is by means of the state and its revenues that rulers achieve their personal and social ends.

Rulers are predatory in the sense that they are revenue maximizers. However, sometimes rulers are the principals—that is, the persons who primarily control and benefit from the organization of the state; and sometimes they are the agents—that is, the persons who act on behalf of

---

[3] I hypothesize that rulers are predatory, but this does not imply that they are necessarily exploitative. I distinguish predatory and exploitative behavior. Predatory action connotes a choice of policy based on a calculation of its pros and cons for maximizing revenue. By one definition exploitation refers to the extraction of surplus labor; the exploited individual works more hours than are necessary to produce the goods that he or she consumes (Elster 1985, 167ff.; Roemer 1982, *passim*). In another and related definition, exploitation refers to unequal access to assets (Roemer 1982, *passim*). By either definition the power of the state to enforce property rights underlies exploitation (Levi and North 1982). As heads of the state, rulers can exploit directly, can protect the ability of others to exploit, or can prevent exploitation.

[4] Rulers do not always take all that they legally or forcibly might, nor do they always engage in what Pareto labels "spoliation"—that is, personal gain at the expense of the general welfare (1966, esp. 114–20). The behaviors Pareto characterizes with that label are similar to those some public choice analysts call rent seeking, which is discussed in chapter 2. Pareto's concept is both less universal and more precise. Exploitation and spoliation are real phenomena. However, the extent to which they are undertaken varies considerably.

powerful constituents. In either case they act as the chief executives of the state.

The objection will immediately be raised (and has been raised often in seminars) that not all rulers maximize state revenue.[5] What about those few pious kings of history, or the nineteenth-century liberals, or the twentieth-century monetarists, social reformers, and other rulers whose concern is revenue reduction or a particular social end? I admit at the outset that there are rulers who cannot be characterized as revenue maximizers, but I suspect that they constitute the exception. My argument does not deny these possibilities. Revenue maximization as the source of organizational variation is a hypothesis, not a conclusion. If it is a powerful hypothesis, it will account for most, but not all, behavior.

The fact that rulers often refrain from extracting the greatest amount of revenue they could in principle extract from the population does not mean they are refraining from maximizing behavior. Rulers refrain from extraction primarily because of the constraints to which they are subject. Maximizing revenue involves reduction of the costs of extraction or a trade-off between extraction costs and gross income. This means minimizing rebellion as well as lowering the transaction costs. Revenue maximization can stimulate a desire for a higher return over time. Therefore, rulers may provide incentives to production by permitting the ruled to keep more of what they produce. What follows from my model is that proposals to lower taxes are usually reflections of constraints on rulers imposed by powerful constituents or by the desire to increase revenue over time. One can, in principle, test this claim by investigating the consequences of variations in the constraints on rulers. If the constraints do not explain the behavior, the hypothesis is disconfirmed. As usual, it is most instructive to push the hypothesis as far as possible to test its bite.

The empirical focus of my study is variation across time and place of rulers' choices of revenue production systems, particularly how revenue collection is organized and what revenues are collected from whom. My aim is to explain major policy choices. I am not concerned with incremental reforms of tax systems. Nor do I calculate the amount of revenue collected in a particular society, the amounts lost to tax collectors through pay or corruption, or the amounts personally pocketed by rulers. The records and

---

[5] I am well aware of the critique of maximizing and the preference, among many eminent organizational theorists, for the assumption of satisficing. Yet, on purely methodological grounds, the conventional *homo economicus* (and *femina economica*) assumption remains the most useful for comparative and testable analysis. For a recent and particularly nice defense of this assumption, see Brennan and Buchanan (1985, esp. chap. 4).

other evidence for making such calculations simply do not exist for many of the historical periods I investigate. We do not yet possess adequate tools or theory for evaluating the efficiency of any revenue production system.[6] Moreover, my aim is to account for organizational variation in revenue production systems rather than to evaluate their performance. If my hypothesis is correct, I should be able to explain the form of revenue production chosen, given the constraints of rulers' relative bargaining power, transaction costs, and discount rates.

In *Of Rule and Revenue*, I elaborate my hypothesis and draw out its theoretical implications. I provide case studies (in chapters 4–7) drawn from quite different places and periods of history. Each case presents the state at a different level of development and during a period of large-scale change. Moreover, each case is drawn from a distinct economic organization of society or, in the Marxist terminology, a distinguishable mode of production or stage in a mode of production.

All the material is from Western history. Some critics will argue that my choice of cases reflects the bias of the model I have chosen to apply. However, preliminary research on revenue production in historical China and Japan, for example, suggests that the model applies to non-Western societies as well. And Robert Bates (1987, chap. 2) has successfully used a variant of this model to account for state behavior in African societies. I restricted myself to societies about which I already had sufficient knowledge, so that the research task would not become more overwhelming than it already was. Although the cases are Western, they represent a diversity of cultures, norms, and institutions. Thus, they enable me to affirm (or disconfirm) the generalizability and universality of the arguments I am positing.

Each case presents a distinct substantive problem of revenue production and highlights a distinct aspect of the theory. Together the cases form a picture of state structures evolving to capture gains from trade. Transformations in the state tend to correlate with changes in the relative prices of goods and services and with changes in the specialization and division of labor. The cases provide insights into how rulers go about establishing taxation and other state structures that enable them both to supply publicly demanded goods and services and to benefit in the process.

The first case concerns the rise and decline of tax farming in ancient

---

[6] Analysts continue to disagree on how one should go about untangling this thorny problem, even with the availability of a very large amount of data on contemporary tax systems. For a taste of this debate, see Posner (1975, esp. 93 in 1980 reprint) and Goetz (1978).

Rome; the second, the emergence of national tax systems in medieval and Renaissance England and France, followed by the divergence of what had been similar revenue production policies in the two countries; the third, the development and imposition of the first income tax in late-eighteenth-century Britain; and the fourth, federal imposition of a uniform income tax and subsequent problems of evasion and avoidance in Australia during and after World War II. Relative bargaining power is an important issue in all the cases, but rulers bargain with their agents in Rome; with nobles and then nobles and agents in France and England; with Commons and citizenry in Britain; and with the states and then the citizens in Australia. Transaction costs also contribute to the outcome in all the cases, but the nature of these costs changes as rulers devise more sophisticated structures for measuring and monitoring compliance and as constituents demand more goods from and permit less discretion by rulers.

It would be far fetched to claim that the cases actually "test" the model. Rather, my aim is to demonstrate that the model is consistent with the facts. By choosing a variety of examples, I also illustrate its power to illuminate diverse historical problems in quite different institutional and cultural settings.

I do not believe that such an enterprise, based in a universal theory, does violence to the diversity of the societies discussed here — although it may do violence to the vocabulary that those societies, and the academics who study them, use to describe behaviors and institutions. I persist with the use of terms such as *state, rational, ruler, contract,* and *transaction costs* even when they might be considered anachronistic (by some accounts) or no longer valid (by some accounts). Having defined them, I consider them descriptive and illuminating. Also, they enable me to make more obvious the similarities and dissimilarities among the cases I have chosen. They help make clear what is general and what is not.

My motivations for this project are both substantive and theoretical. All governments have revenue requirements. Rudolf Goldscheid, the founder of fiscal sociology, claimed that "the budget is the skeleton of the state stripped of all misleading ideologies" (quoted in Schumpeter [1918] 1954, 6). Schumpeter argued, "The fiscal history of a people is above all an essential part of its general history" ([1918] 1954, 6–7). Gabriel Ardant (1971, 1972), the author of the major contemporary work on fiscal history, justifies his study in similar terms. With few exceptions political analysts have given scanty attention to the ways in which governments go about producing and extracting revenue. The relatively small, if important, literature tends to be either empirically thin or theoretically vacuous.

Ardant's work stands out for its breadth and its insights, if not its rigor. Webber and Wildavsky (1986) provide a descriptive history of Western taxation but little explanation.

Although Brennan and Buchanan (1980), Mitchell (1983), and other public choice theorists offer some useful arguments and ideas, to which I shall return later, their work can be differentiated from mine in their singular focus on contemporary capitalist democracies and in their assumption that taxation is theft. They are therefore more concerned with possible constraints imposed on rulers by citizens than with actual constraints that exist willy-nilly in any polity. Their project is more normative than empirical. Frohlich and Oppenheimer (1974), Groves and Ledyard (1977), and, most to the point, North (1981, 1985) and Bates and Lien (1985) begin to offer theoretical guidance. They attempt to account for the mix of taxes and the nature of taxation systems given the assumption that most individuals are opportunistic but within a framework of strategic interactions and institutional arrangements. They spin out the argument in relationship to institutional change and apply it to historical evidence.

My theoretical motivation is twofold. The first is to explain state behavior. The second is to make the point that both individuals and institutions matter. My aim is to account for the effects of institutional change on policy, especially tax policy. Such an objective, I believe, requires a microtheory of individual behavior that links one macro-state of policy to the next. I want to emphasize the importance of structures and institutions while bringing people back into the state.[7]

Explanation would be incomplete without an account of the ways in which macro-level variables affect the micro-level ones, and vice versa. However, theorists have tended to do one or the other. The structuralists have linked one macro-state to another, with little regard to the mechanisms that affect the correlations they perceive. Most neoclassical economists and other methodological individualists have generally ignored the state, organizations, and other events and institutions that affect the decisions of individual consumers.[8]

The form of political economy often called rational choice — that is, the

[7] I am playing here on the title of the famous 1964 presidential address to the American Sociological Association by George Homans, "Bringing Men Back In," and on Skocpol's "Bringing the State Back In" (which serves as the set piece and title of Evans, Rueschemeyer, and Skocpol, 1985a). Homans was arguing against and offering an alternative to functional-structuralism. Skocpol is arguing for a historically grounded structuralism. Thus, I find myself reiterating some of Homans's pleas and some of Skocpol's, although with the following difference: I advocate a micro-macro theory that includes both individuals and structures. See the appendix for an elaboration of these themes.

[8] For a review of the relevant literatures, refer to the appendix.

theory of individual strategic decision making—begins to resolve some of the theoretical and methodological dilemmas inherent in attempts to provide causal explanations of policy choices and changes.[9] Of particular influence on me are those writers who attempt to provide the micro-foundations of macro-historical and comparative phenomena (Barry 1970; Bates 1981, 1987; Bates and Lien 1985; Boudon 1979; Brenner 1983; Elster 1978, 1979, 1983a, 1983b, 1985; Emerson 1983; Hardin 1982; Hechter 1983, 1987; North 1981, 1985; Popkin 1979; Przeworski 1985a, 1985b; Riker 1982, 1984; Roemer 1982; Schott 1984; Taylor [1976] 1987, 1982). All use rational choice, and all are concerned with the collective action problem as defined by Mancur Olson (1965). Some draw on game theory. Others emphasize the tools of micro-economics. Most call on Marx at some point in their arguments. By applying their findings to significant political problems, I hope to be able to evaluate the power of the rational choice approach. And that is at least part of my purpose.

Rational choice is committed to methodological individualism but does not reduce actors to antisocial or asocial creatures lacking regard for or influence on one another. It searches for behavioral regularities but does not practice a simple determinism in which the constraints make choices absolutely predictable. There is always a range of alternatives within the structured set.

The rational choice approach recognizes that institutions and structures are the consequences of human actions. It is individuals who act, individuals who think. Individuals create institutions—although, of course, institutions, structures, and other macro-states also influence individual preferences and behaviors. These influences can be modeled as the rules of the game. Given a new set of rules, will people rebel, how will institutions be transformed, what policy changes will occur? Although the current power of rational choice lies in accounting for the ways in which individuals interact with and influence one another within a particular framework, the ultimate goal, the explanation of long-term secular change, may be in sight.

To achieve my ends, I start with a simple and, I believe, acceptable assumption about human behavior—namely, that individuals calculate the costs and benefits to themselves of various actions they are considering and then choose the alternative most consistent with their fixed preferences. I

---

[9] The concluding essay in Bates (1987) is a compelling statement of the advantages of rational choice as I have described it. Bates also clarifies the consistencies and inconsistencies of rational choice with both Marxism and neoclassical economics, an enterprise in which I am also engaged. Also see Przeworski (1985b) on "Marxism and Rational Choice."

then posit that rulers maximize revenue to the state subject to determinant constraints on their behavior. It is these constraints that motivate my hypothesis. It is the effects of the variations in these constraints that I am investigating. Finally, I attempt to construct more fine-tuned arguments about the mechanisms by which the institutions of the state are created and maintained. Ultimately, I hope to demonstrate the process by which state structures evolve in response to changes in bargaining power, transaction costs, and discount rates.

CHAPTER II

The Theory of Predatory Rule

Rulers maximize revenue to the state, but not as they please. They maximize subject to the constraints of their relative bargaining power vis-à-vis agents and constituents, their transaction costs, and their discount rates. These constraints determine the choice of revenue system. That is my hypothesis.

Rulers are predatory in that they always try to set terms of trade that maximize their personal objectives, which, I argue, require them to maximize state revenues. They do not always plunder, pillage, and exploit. However, each will, in North's words (1981, 23), "attempt to act like a discriminating monopolist, separating each group of constituents and devising property rights for each so as to maximize state revenue." Consequently, rulers devise structures to facilitate exchange and increase their marginal rate of return.

Most rulers must offer some return for the revenue extracted. Even rulers who hold nearly all the resources of power—which does occasionally occur in history—are still likely to require agents to enforce the policies. Rulers are chief executives (see, esp., Barnard 1938), who are sometimes principals and sometimes agents but whose administrative efficacy always rests on their ability to manipulate their environment.

The action in my model lies in the constraints on ruler behavior. Relative bargaining power and transaction costs account for the fact that rulers in history do not always rob their subjects blind and are not always running protection rackets. Rulers cannot simply advance any policy that appeals to them. They choose among the feasible set of options, and they can act to change that feasible set. By definition rulers are actors within a domestic and an international context, and they must interact with constituents, agents, and the representatives of other polities. To achieve their ends, they must coerce and bargain, develop their resources, and, often, alter their constraints.

Policies are the outcome of an exchange between the ruler and the various groups who compose the polity.[1] Policies are a function of rulers' terms of trade. Rulers negotiate contracts with their agents and constituents, and each set of actors attempts to attain the best possible terms. Contracts are possible only if they make each party better off. Rulers are providing goods, usually collective goods, that have the attributes of gains from trade. Such gains are possible only if rulers can provide economies of scale in protection, justice, and other sought-after goods or if they can reduce uncertainty and ensure against risk. Of course, over time a contract is likely to prove unfavorable to one or the other of the contracting parties, who will then try to change it. Changes in state policies and organization require renegotiation of contracts.

Although I start with contractual relationships, I do not assume a precontract Hobbesian state of nature, with its equal distribution of power. I follow the contracting paradigm in arguing that the state economizes on resources that individuals otherwise would have to pay for, such as self-defense. There are gains from initial contracting. However, I part company with many neoclassical economists who argue that all economic actors are subject to and benefit from contracting. In my view a group could be so powerless as to be effectively excluded from a meaningful contractual relationship altogether. Nor do all parties benefit equally from the contract. Moreover, when the state itself is the enemy from whom people are buying protection, the state resembles a protection racket rather than an institution that engages in productive activity (Lane 1958; Frohlich and Oppenheimer 1974; Davis 1980; Emerson 1983; Tilly 1985). It is not unusual historically to have both kinds of states exist side by side.

The first determinant of the terms of exchange is the relative bargaining

---

[1] Jensen and Meckling (1976) and Fama (1980) characterized the firm and property rights as a "nexus of contracts." In earlier formulations of my argument, I posited that the state is also a "nexus of contracts" between rulers and agents, rulers and constituents, and, often, constituents and agents. One problem with this formulation, as Douglass North pointed out, is that the ruler or institutions of the state are contractors who can be sued as a whole. Another major problem with the formulation, I have come to realize, is that it provides too trivial a role for the institutions that structure the contracting and exchange process. Such institutions are the heart of the state-building and revenue-producing process. Moreover, they do not develop *de novo* with each new ruler or set of constituents. They are usually givens that must be worked with or around.

power of the contracting parties.[2] Rulers will have more bargaining power the more they monopolize coercive, economic, and political resources. Rulers will seek to control the supply of resources by either ensuring that they are a party to all exchange of resources or by eliminating rival suppliers. As governments increasingly regulate and license economic activities, there will be more rent seeking by those subject to state surveillance. However, from the point of view of rulers, encouraging rent seeking could be an efficient strategy despite its promotion of social waste.

When others possess resources that the ruler needs or when they can successfully resist the ruler's demands, their bargaining power is increased. Since bargaining resources are distributed unequally throughout the population, a single ruler will form different contracts with different groups of agents or constituents. Thus, rulers can use the same state organization as both a productive enterprise and a protection racket.

Given the behavioral assumption that people, or at least most people, are opportunistic and will break contracts when it suits them, and given the high costs of acquiring information about the activities and possessions of others, rulers must devise policies that lower their transaction costs. These are the costs of implementing and enforcing policies. More specifically, they are the costs of measuring, monitoring, creating, and enforcing compliance. Transaction costs include the costs of bargaining — that is, the costs of locating appropriate bargaining partners and the costs of reaching a contract. An increasing stock of knowledge about efficacious administrative practice — knowledge that comes with learning-by-doing, experience, or example — reduces transaction costs. They are increased by increasing demands that rulers must arbitrate, negotiate, and meet.

Rulers occasionally make trade-offs between their bargaining power and their transaction costs. They sometimes choose to use bargaining resources or to alienate powerful allies in order to promote a policy with relatively low transaction costs. Alternatively, they sometimes undertake high trans-

---

[2] My argument is influenced by my reading of power dependence theory in the social exchange literature, especially Emerson (1962) and Cook and Emerson (1978). It also owes a debt to the pioneering work of Robert Dahl (see, for example, 1961) on political resources as well as the more recent contributions of Ilchman and Uphoff (1971, esp. 32–37 and chap. 2) in their important effort to integrate political and economic theory into a method for political economic analysis. My approach is most similar to theirs in our contention that resources are the basis for power. However, Ilchman and Uphoff are more taxonomic than I am. They provide examples rather than case studies to demonstrate the plausibility of their model. More fundamentally, however, they believe that the kinds of resources available to rulers differ from those of other actors; and they include nonmaterial resources — namely, status, authority, and legitimacy — in their analysis. Also, they are considerably less concerned than I am with the relationship between rulers and agents.

action costs in order to avoid policies that would upset constituents or agents on whom they depend. It is trivial to say that rulers consider the costs and benefits and choose the policy that gives them the most advantage. Certainly, they are not always choosing the policy that produces the most revenue, and the reason lies in one additional factor that affects all rulers: the requirements of maintaining power. Holding the office of ruler is the sine qua non of rule. This self-evident fact can be restated in terms of two observable and potentially testable factors: the rulers' discount rates and their need to create and sustain quasi-voluntary compliance. The discount rate derives from the nature of rivalry over rule and is the parameter within which bargaining power occurs. Quasi-voluntary compliance is a mechanism for reducing transaction costs. Without a fairly high degree of quasi-voluntary compliance, revenue production policies are not even feasible. Quasi-voluntary compliance will be the subject of the next chapter.

An important constraint on the policy choices of rulers is their discount rates, that is, the extent to which they value the future relative to the present.[3] The higher the discount rate, the less concern with the future. Two objective reasons for a high discount rate are the likelihood that the future will not come or relatively poor information about the future. There can also be subjective reasons, resulting from weakness of will or *akrasia*, in which rulers succumb to the present moment despite knowledge of the likely future costs. Low discount rates accompany security of rule. High discount rates follow from insecurity and intense rivalries.

What I have outlined thus far are the major constraints on policy formation. Variation in these factors should explain a large part of the variation in policies. However, these constraints are themselves the consequence of other variables. The possibilities are infinite; nonetheless, the most significant can be summarized into three main categories: (1) productive forces and economic structure, (2) the international context, and (3) form of government. Predatory rulers will act to alter these factors to suit their purposes. Nonetheless, at any given point in time, these factors structure rulers' choices.

---

[3] Lance E. Davis (1980), in his Presidential Address to the Economic History Association, picks up the themes of Frederick Lane (1958) and argues for an economic history that recognizes the importance of politics and political analysis. One of the questions he thinks must still be addressed is "the appropriate rate of discount" (9–10). This is exactly the task some game theorists have taken on. In particular, Taylor uses variations in discounting as part of his explanation for variations in conditional cooperation ([1976] 1987). Elster introduces *akrasia* into rational choice considerations (1979, esp. 173–75 and chap. 2). Hardin (1985) has recently brought these and other factors together in an extremely interesting discussion of the role of time in rational choice theory. I rely heavily on his distinctions in my own account of discounting and of dynamic analysis.

What follows from this model is that significant differences in state policies will primarily reflect differences in constraints on the rulers. For example, feudal monarchs are rulers confronted by subjects with comparable political and economic resources. Feudal rulers are likely to make concessions in the form of tax exemptions and services in exchange for loyalty to the regime. In contrast, absolute monarchs are rulers who possess a virtual monopoly over coercive capacity but not necessarily a perfect monitoring ability. Their policies will create a large revenue base for the state while providing only minimal services. However, they will keep only as much revenue as they can prevent their agents from pocketing; they may even have to provide incentives that make it worth the while of agents to collect the revenues in the first place.

The way I have conceptualized ruler, as the chief executive of the polity, means that rulers exist even in modern democracies. Given its connotations, the term *ruler* may be misleading to some. However, in my perspective presidents and prime ministers of contemporary democracies are rulers who face legal checks and balances as well as innumerable pressure groups. Their policies will be contradictory, expensive, and inefficient (for economic growth). There will be, for example, legal restrictions upheld by courts and police, who are constitutionally out of the rulers' jurisdiction. Legislators, who can block a ruler's policies and pass their own, effectively share policymaking power with the ruler (the president or prime minister). Well-organized agents will demand both higher incomes and reduced work loads. And heads of state will have to depend on economically and politically influential subjects for reelection, social order, or the implementation of policies.

Given such constraints, is it, therefore, correct to model presidents and prime ministers as predatory rulers? Is not the state an arena for bargaining and the chief executive the disinterested arbitrator of competing interests and the executor of resulting policy decisions? This is, of course, the world of the pluralists, the vision that neo-Marxists and other neostructuralists have rightly criticized as misleading and wrong.[4] In another, more sophisticated view, there are again no "rulers," only administrators implementing group decisions. They may be opportunistic administrators and bureaucrats, but they remain agents. This seems to suggest to some observers that they cannot be "rulers." Let me now take up each of these perspectives in turn.

---

[4] See the appendix for an elaboration of and the problems with the positions taken in these literatures.

To understand the limits of the pluralist perspective, or what Brennan and Buchanan (1985) label "the myth of benevolence," it is useful to theorize about the nature of policies that would result solely from pressure groups with conflicting claims jockeying for power. Becker (1985) presents such a model. He assumes an equality between taxes and subsidies, and he defines political effectiveness as the ability of a group to control free riding by its members. Under these conditions he finds that deadweight or social cost also influences political effectiveness. He argues, "An increase in the dead weight cost of taxation encourages pressure by taxpayers because they are then harmed more by tax payments. Similarly, an increase in the dead weight cost of subsidies discourages pressure by recipients because they then benefit less from the subsidies received" (Becker, 1985, 343). When he adds to this the "compensation principle" of welfare economics (in which gainers *could* compensate losers), he finds, *ceteris paribus,* that the push by interest groups that benefit from a policy will be stronger than the opposition of those that lose.

Introducing predatory rulers into this model fundamentally alters the findings. First, it adds an additional competitor, which makes the bargaining game more complex. Second, as rulers gain power in the bargaining over policy, the effect will likely be an increase in the use of government for noneconomic purposes and an increase in governmental regulations. Rulers can — and quite regularly do — use government employment and programs to purchase loyalty.[5] Third, rulers influence what pressure groups perceive as the deadweight cost of a policy. Thus, they can influence the outcome of the competition by means of a source of political effectiveness not available to the other claimants.

The second alternative to the model of predatory rule is the analysis of heads of government as agents. In this view they are embedded in a structure that limits their options to such a degree that it is nonsensical to label them rulers. I argue that rulers can be principals or agents. In modern industrial democracies, they are likely to be agents of the citizens. In historical settings the principals may have been dominant economic classes

[5] This need not represent "inefficiencies." As Becker (1985, 338) notes, "If the *intent* of public policies were fully known, I am confident that public sector would be revealed to be a far more efficient producer and redistributor than is popularly believed. . . . These enterprises may only appear to be less efficient because they are used to raise the income of employees (or others). Redistribution should be included among the measured 'outputs' of public and regulated enterprises before one can conclude that they are less efficient than private enterprises." Michels ([1919] 1949, 185–89) made a similar point about the functions of public employment. Reder (1975), among others, makes political outputs part of his model of government employment.

or the nobility. As with Niskanen's bureaucrats (1971), they are maximizing utility subject to constitutional constraints that affect their bargaining power and transaction costs. The difference is that I specify the content of their utility function as maximizing revenue to the state.

It may, however, be more difficult for modern presidents and prime ministers than for their predecessors to design policy according to the requirements of rationality. A recent literature derived from "positive political theory" (Riker and Ordeshook 1973) investigates the character of democracy, especially in the United States. Some writers demonstrate that decision rules and majority voting seldom, if ever, produce Pareto optimal results (see discussions of this literature in Frohlich and Oppenheimer 1978, chap. 1; and Mueller 1979, esp. chap. 3). Others conclude that collective rationality is unstable and that this instability further erodes economic efficiency and the possibility of pluralist political practice (see the review of the relevant literature in Miller 1983). One crucial finding of this work seems to be that the relationship between citizens and policies depends, more than anything else, on who sets the agenda (Plott and Levine 1978; McKelvey 1979; Shepsle and Weingast 1984). This finding reiterates and formalizes the now classic, and once radical, insight of Bachrach and Baratz (1962). Again, this literature is not inconsistent with the theory of predatory rule. Rather, it illuminates the kinds of bargaining resources that emerge from and are necessary to be effective within democratic rules.

The major implication of the theory of predatory rule is that rulers will devise and formalize structures that increase their bargaining power, reduce their transaction costs, and lower their discount rates so as to better capture gains from exchanges of politics. They will design institutions that they believe will be efficient in promoting their interests (which may overlap — but need not — with the general welfare or with the interests of a dominant class). More specifically, within the limits of the constraints upon them, they will design revenue production policies that maximize revenues to the state. However, as relative prices change, institutions that once facilitated exchange may begin to hinder exchange or reduce return. Rulers will then try to redesign state structures and rewrite state policies.

My model is static in the sense that, at any point in time, policy choices are a consequence of a given set of bargaining resources, transaction costs, and discount rates. Nonetheless, rulers can and do act to modify and structure the institutions that facilitate exchange. Establishing domestic and international peace permits rulers — and their constituents — to devote fewer resources to protection and more to production. An increase in bargaining power over a rebellious community not only increases the possibility of favorable policy for rulers but also reduces the transaction costs of achieving compliance with the policy. Over time, arrangements constructed to minimize transaction costs may affect bargaining power; for example, putting workers together in factories or creating bureaucracy facilitates both control and political mobilization. Changes in relative bargaining power, transactions costs, and discounting should lead to new bargains.

This chapter focuses on the factors that explain the choice of a particular revenue policy. The theory of predatory rule is initially an exercise in comparative statics. In the next chapter, I take up the consequences of incremental changes in the contract over the life of the contract. Comprehending shifts in compliance, I argue, is a major component in the development of a dynamic model of state policy.

RELATIVE BARGAINING POWER

The relative bargaining power of rulers is determined by the extent to which others control resources on which rulers depend and the extent to which rulers control resources on which others depend. Rulers will be better able to set favorable terms of trade the less they depend on others and the more others depend on them. Rulers whose power resources diminish will either have to offer more in exchange or give up some of their ends. In my model, rulers always calculate whether the marginal costs of their maximizing strategies will outweigh the expected return.

To keep this formulation from being tautological, I realize one must specify the bases of such a calculation. An outside observer must be able to analytically reproduce the choices confronting rulers. At best, actors (and observers) make rough estimates. Some resources are difficult to measure accurately; even if they were measurable, most decision makers find precise calculations too costly (Simon 1947; March and Simon 1958), if not impossible (Kahneman and Tversky 1984; Simon 1985). Nonetheless, rulers, constituents, agents, and rivals can make fairly good estimates of their own and others' bargaining resources — at least as I define resources. I include only resources that have a material basis and could, in principle, be quantified. I exclude legitimacy, status, and authority (Ilchman and Uphoff 1971, esp. 60–67 and 73–86). Although I do not deny their importance, they are even more difficult to specify than the factors I have chosen. But my major reason for exclusion is that they are, more often than not, a consequence of other resources. I take up this point in more detail in chapter 3.

The major categories of resources are coercive, economic, and political resources. Rule has evolved so that, over time, state officials have come to control a greater proportion of these resources. There has been a reduction, at least by historical comparison, in internal military competition. Dependence on the state for economic resources has increased. Political institutions have developed that contain and channel collective action and pressure and that permit few people to escape the arm of the state. Although this description would hardly capture all contemporary polities, it is a fair characterization of the majority of the most advanced industrialized countries.

The institutions of rule have evolved so that rulers are able to bargain, and bargain on their terms, with a greater number of constituents. Yet the constraints on rulers have far from disappeared. They also have evolved and changed. In particular, the increasing economic power of the mass of the population has led to an increasing political power, which has culminated in the granting of universal suffrage and the formation of popular political parties. The result has been an increase in political pressure groups and the development of legal institutions for containing the power of the ruler. It is an interesting paradox that as the state has increased its control of coercive, economic, and political resources, a ruler's personal command of bargaining resources is more constrained. Over time rulers have become more dependent on others for resources.

In the process of investigating the character of bargaining resources, the nature of their evolution also becomes clear. Historically, military resources have been extremely significant. When particular individuals monopolize the military resources of a society, they are likely to achieve and maintain power as well as accomplish policy ends. When military resources are distributed among several individuals or coalitions, rulers are likely to have rivals or potential rivals. In such instances the dependence of individuals or groups is decreased, and the ruler's dependence may be increased. Consequently, rulers will have to exchange resources for support or use up resources to prevent attack. At the least, rivals' command of military resources reduces the ability of rulers to enforce contracts in areas that rivals control or dispute. Consequently, rulers will have to forgo certain policies, implement them unevenly throughout the domain, or implement them evenly but bear high transaction costs in the process.

Historically, military technology has evolved so that there are economies of scale in centralized armies, with corresponding increases in rulers' control of military resources (Bean 1973; North 1981, esp. 135–42). The development of new forms of property, which were subject to laws governing exchange as well as possession, further increased rulers' control of

coercive resources. State arbitration of property rights, with the conse-
quent creation of more elaborated courts and the institution of the police,
increased the dependence of constituents on rulers.[6]

Even rulers who effectively monopolize military and other coercive
resources also need economic and political resources to obtain their ends.
To the extent that rulers find themselves dependent on the political and
economic resources of constituents and agents, their bargaining power is
reduced. To the extent that constituents and agents have alternative suppliers of economic and political resources, their dependence on their rulers
is reduced. Rulers can improve their terms of trade by increasing the
economic and political dependence of constituents and agents on themselves and by reducing their own dependence on the political and economic
resources of others. The more rulers can monopolize economic and political resources, the better able they will be to negotiate favorable terms of
trade.

Economic resources consist of ownership and effective control of the
means of production, that is, the raw materials and tools (Cohen 1978,
32); the routes and facilities of trade; valued skills and knowledge; the labor
supply; negotiable wealth, that is, money or its substitute; and what
Ilchman and Uphoff label goods and services (1971, 32, 58–60). These in
turn are affected by the economic structure and productive forces, structural conditions to be discussed later.

It is difficult even to imagine a situation in which rulers monopolize all
these resources, although the hydraulic societies probably come close
(Wittfogel 1957). A division of labor has existed in all historical societies,
and this of itself creates interdependence among the individuals in the
economy. In contemporary democracies, where rulers are elected, the
resources that individuals command are seldom adequate. Candidates
depend on those who possess the funds necessary for a modern mass-media
campaign, which is generally big business (Ginsburg 1984; Bates 1976).
Indeed, most rulers, throughout most of history, have had to make concessions to economically powerful actors in return for their support.

Political resources also affect the relative bargaining power of rulers.
Rulers possess political resources to the extent that they can inhibit the
desertion of constituents to competitors or rival states and to the extent that
they can block opposition and promote support, that is, ensure that
collective action is in their interests. People will vote with their feet if they

---

[6] For an interesting account of the development of property rights, see Offer (1981). His
focus is on Britain, 1870–1914. Silver (1967) discusses the development of domestic police
forces in response to changes in property relations.

can flee at low cost (Hirschman 1970). It is a truism that dissatisfaction often causes "flight or fight." Thus, the more rulers can raise the costs of exit while preventing antagonistic mobilization, the more they can increase the prospects for loyalty, that is, compliance with their policies.

The prerequisites of collective action (see, for example, Olson 1965; Lipsky 1970; Frohlich, Oppenheimer, and Young 1971; Oberschall 1973; McCarthy and Zald 1977; Tilly 1978; Popkin 1979; Moe 1980; Hardin 1982; Taylor 1982) include positive selective incentives, negative sanctions, and entrepreneurial skills that enable the relevant actors to locate and manipulate additional incentives. All rulers necessarily possess some positive inducements, negative sanctions, and entrepreneurial skills. The question is how successfully rulers can mobilize their subjects and agents and whether alternative leaders exist who are equally able to mobilize people.

Government-created rights and programs are sources of positive incentives in the form of bribes, patronage, or other material inducements. Governments are also sources of such negative sanctions as social ostracism, exclusion from valued goods and services, and actual punishment. Feudal monarchs rewarded the knights who fought for the crown. Ivanhoe and Robin Hood are the romantic versions of such tales; both men benefited by choosing the winning side in the conflict between John and Richard. In contemporary polities rewards for loyalty include employment or advantageous legislation. Punishments for undependability or disloyalty include job severance or the abolition of beneficial government programs.

Constituents and agents also possess political resources. Sometimes they use government-created benefits to their own advantage. Generals, provincial governors, and all the others to whom rulers have had to delegate authority over history are often able to use these state-provided resources to mobilize against rulers. Moreover, in contemporary democracies government programs sometimes can be used by skilled entrepreneurs to finance the organization of the relatively poor and powerless against the government itself (Piven and Cloward 1971, chap. 10; Lipsky and Levi 1972; Levi 1974; Walker 1983).

Community is another important basis for mobilization. Marx and Engels predicted that the establishment of the factory system, combined with the migration of workers to the city, would facilitate the organization of labor ([1848] 1978, 480–81). They understood that regular interaction and communication among similar individuals promote the capacity for collective action, but they did not specify the mechanisms. Taylor ([1976] 1987, 1982) offers an account of how community—that is, shared common beliefs and norms, direct and multifaceted relationships, and reciprocity — can lead to conditional cooperation, in which individuals cooperate only as long as others do. Combined with the appropriate structural conditions, community underlies revolutionary movements and other large-scale collective actions (Popkin 1979; Skocpol 1979, chap. 3; Taylor 1988). Its variations, due to differences in economic structures, account for regional variation in rebellion (Brustein 1985; Brustein and Levi 1987) and industry variation in pressure groups (Bates 1987, chap. 3).

Political entrepreneurs, be they rulers or rivals, can promote political mobilization by constructing community where it does not already exist and by bringing new incentives and disincentives to bear where it does. In his analysis of peasant movements and collective action in Vietnam, Popkin (1979, chap. 6 and *passim*) stresses entrepreneurial behavior meant to enhance peasant estimates of the entrepreneur's efficacy in securing promised returns (259). Peasants must be made to believe in the entrepreneur's credibility and capacity to deliver. Entrepreneurs encourage this belief by offering rewards consonant with the existing moral code, by understanding and being able to communicate with the peasants they are organizing.

At least initially, entrepreneurs must demonstrate their ability to provide immediate payoffs on locally important issues. Ultimately, entrepreneurs want to mobilize support for leaders and groups outside the local community and to increase peasant participation in nonlocal collective actions. In return for such participation, entrepreneurs must offer peasants private goods in the form of better yields, a higher welfare payment, a lower rent, or insurance against crop failure.

Most of what constitutes entrepreneurial activity is in fact coordination of resources or people. With increasing specialization and division of labor, the need for coordination has increased. The demand by constituents for rulers to perform this role has intensified. Coordination is something constituents want that rulers not only can supply but also, in many spheres, have a comparative advantage in supplying. Increases in both the demand for and the supply of coordination enhance the political — and economic — bargaining power of rulers.

Ideology is often presented as an additional political resource. How else can we account for cases where the material incentives fail to compensate for the hardship experienced? If both positive and negative incentives are insubstantial, arguments based on the assumption of rationality predict a failure of collective action. However, there are many exceptions to this rule. Some — such as the Crusades, where soldiers put up with considerable discomfort because of incentives in the form of promises of future returns in booty or salvation — can possibly be understood within the rational choice framework. Other examples are not so easy to explain: the nationalism that accompanies most wars, the behavior of the people of Paris during the French Revolution, the ghetto residents of Detroit and Watts during the rebellions of the 1960s, and the workers of Poland during the past years.

These may be examples of communities where conditional cooperation applies, or they may represent "moments of madness" (Zolberg 1972). But ideology is also likely to be part of the explanation. Both rulers and revolutionaries use ideology to mobilize support for their regimes. Fidel Castro and Mao Zedung legitimated their revolutions on the basis of justice and equity as well as redistribution. Khomeini used antipathy to the Shah and love of the Islam religion to rally the Iranians. And many monarchs kept both their heads and their crowns by appeals to divine rule. Yet, despite the evidence of the importance of ideology for political mobilization, a theory of collective action that adequately incorporates the role of ideology or norms has still to be written.[7] Without it an analysis of the distribution of political resources must, unfortunately, remain incomplete.

Coercive, economic, and political resources are usually interwoven. Economic resources probably explain a large percentage of the variance in military and other coercive resources. Affluent rulers, such as Elizabeth I of England and Philip II of Spain, tend also to be dominant militarily. Conversely, a militarily powerful ruler can wrest the economic resources needed from those who hold them, as Philip of Macedon did.

Political resources also affect the distribution of other resources. Rulers who have entrepreneurial skills or who perform the central coordination function in political exchange can use the political system to redistribute the flow of economic resources to their advantage. Moreover, political mobilization provides people with group economic power. Given that rulers are economically dependent on the skills, knowledge, and labor of other individuals, their choices will be influenced by the probability of slave rebellions, mutinies, strikes, and other work disruptions. Guilds, craft unions, and professional associations that limit the amount of labor available or monopolize information about or the right to perform a particular task also alter the terms of trade. For example, the success of the medical

---

[7] Marx and Engels ([1843] 1978, 172–75; [1848] 1978, 481), Gramsci ([1919–37] 1971), and their followers provide some clues from within the Marxist framework. Both North (1981, esp. chap. 5; 1985, 394–97) and Coleman (forthcoming) offer promising starting points from a rational choice perspective. Ilchman and Uphoff (1971, esp. 73–80) present an account of legitimacy as a political resource, but it relates less to the mobilization that affects bargaining than to the compliance issues that will be taken up in detail in the next chapter.

profession in protecting its privileges in the United States rests on its past success in winning from state governments a legal monopoly over valued skills and knowledge and control over the number and qualifications of individuals labeled physicians (Freidson 1970; Larson 1977, chap. 3).[8]

Groups that already have significant economic resources can enhance their bargaining power by improving their political resources. For example, the antebellum U.S. Congress was most responsive to pressure on tariffs from industries that were cohesive (Pincus 1977). Bates and Lien (1985) demonstrate that rulers will have a preference for collective agreements on taxation when significant economic assets are mobile. If rulers tax mobile assets, their owners are likely to shift them to the possession of those who are exempt from taxation. Collective agreements solve this problem. However, argue Bates and Lien, collective agreements aggregate already resource-rich constituents who demand concessions in return for tax compliance. The consequence, more often than not, is the establishment of representative and other democratic institutions.

TRANSACTION COSTS

Transaction costs are the positive costs of bargaining a policy and of implementing a policy once it has been bargained. The most important transaction costs are those of negotiating agreements, measuring revenue sources, monitoring compliance, using agents and other middlemen, punishing the noncompliant, and creating quasi-voluntary compliance. A policy is not viable if the transaction costs are too high.

In recent years public choice analysts, particularly but not solely those with a conservative political bias, have emphasized maximizing behavior they designate as rent seeking. Rent is "a return in excess of a resource owner's opportunity costs" (Tollison 1982, 30). Buchanan (1980b, 4) argues that "the term rent-seeking is designed to describe behavior in institutional settings where individual efforts to maximize value generate social waste rather than social surplus." In his view rent seeking is a form of profit seeking but within an institutional setting that hinders the efficient

---

[8] However, the power of doctors may be alterable. To reduce the costs of medical care and decrease the political influence of physicians, some United States government agencies are encouraging the training of nurse practitioners and physicians' assistants as possible substitutes. They are also mandating an increase in the size of medical school classes. At least some politicians and bureaucrats recognize that physician monopoly is not revenue maximizing for the state, and they are beginning to discourage some of the rent seeking that their predecessors made possible. A power struggle is in process. Its outcome is still far from clear.

allocation of resources. According to Buchanan (1980b, 4–15), Tullock (1975 and 1980, *passim*), Tollison (1982, 38ff.) and others, the more the state intervenes in the market, the more rent seeking. Rents are made possible by governmental restriction of entry into a market and by its granting of special privileges through regulation, licenses, legal monopolies, and the like. These actions create an artificial scarcity, which profit maximizers then attempt to capture. In the process, they use up — or, more precisely, waste — resources. Bates (1981, chap. 6) provides a vivid illustration of how African governments, in their desire to promote economic growth and modern agriculture, create artificial scarcities in foreign exchange, agricultural commodities, and the like. The immediate consequence is socially wasteful competition to secure monopoly control of these goods and services. The final result is personal gains, profits, and corruption, which make some people rich but at the expense of the general welfare.

The problem with the rent-seeking approach is that its focus is too narrow. Most of the advocates of rent seeking are obsessed with demonstrating the negative impact of government on the economy. They view competitive markets as the most socially efficient means to produce goods and services. Their commitment to the market tends to blind them to inefficiencies that can occur within the market and, conversely, to efficiencies that can result from nonmarket solutions. They do not treat the effects of government intervention as variable, sometimes reducing and sometimes stimulating social waste. As a result, they seem to suggest the rather silly conclusion that entrepreneurs are wasteful only when governmental intervention gives them the opportunity to be. Nonetheless, the notion of rent seeking does give analytical grounding to a set of behaviors that undoubtedly exist. For example, Bates (1981), who makes no universal claims about government's causing waste, demonstrates that the concept of rent seeking is useful in explaining how African marketing boards can promote an inefficient use and distribution of producers' resources.

Rent seeking is only one source of social waste, and not necessarily the most empirically important. The rent-seeking literature recognizes only the waste caused by government, ignoring the waste entailed in the relationships among firms and among employers and employees. The disjuncture between private costs and social costs is what is really at issue. When does individual maximizing behavior generate externalities or public bads? What is the best means for preventing social waste as well as for promoting the general welfare or Pareto optimality? More crucially, for my purposes, which policies are perceived as most likely to increase and which to reduce the returns to government?

A more general approach is the analysis of transaction costs,[9] a concept derived from Coase's now classic (1937) article on the theory of the firm. As Offer (1981, 2) notes, "'Transaction costs' are like sand in the gears of perfect exchange. They eat into ownership and aggregate into a middleman's interest, which takes on the attributes of a species of property."

The definition of transaction costs includes a vast number of factors, all those variables typically assumed away by micro-economics—that is, "the costs of searching, negotiating and enforcing contracts, and of defining and policing of rights" (Cheung 1978, 24). With the publication of seminal work by Alchian and Demsetz (1972), Williamson (1975), and Jensen and Meckling (1976), economists began to drop the traditional assumption that transaction costs are zero. The revisions of the theory raise serious challenges to neoclassical economics from within the discipline. They also provide the basis for an account of the variation in economic organizations and structures.

The transaction cost approach assumes the omnipresence of contractual relations. It is, in fact, part and parcel of what its practitioners have come to call the "contracting paradigm." Any exchange, be it written or unwritten, connotes a contract. Moreover, and certainly more controversially for non-neoclassical economists, any resource changing hands connotes an exchange. This is the Hobbesian world, where preexisting social relations and norms play little part.

At the heart of the contracting paradigm is the assumption of conflict of interest between the parties to an exchange. But also contributing to transaction costs are the costs of acquiring information.[10] Economists are finally taking into account—if seldom explicitly—the important insights provided by behavioral organizational theorists (see, for example, Simon 1947; March and Simon 1958) regarding the consequences of strategies for coping with inadequate information. However, for the behavioralists the focus tends to be on "bounded rationality."[11] For economists information

[9] See Moe's (1984) excellent survey of the literature. He provides an interesting contrast of the transaction cost approach to organization with the behavioral approach derived from Simon (1947). Also see the review essays by North (1978) and Jensen (1983).

[10] There is now a huge literature on the economics of information, which Moe (1984, esp. 752–58) summarizes quite neatly.

[11] Behavioralists are questioning the very assumption of maximizing behavior. Elster (1979, 1983b) attempts to reconstruct rational choice by using their contribution and the contributions of important contemporary psychologists such as Kahneman and Tversky (1979; 1984).

issues revolve around assessing the quality of the good or service to be exchanged (see, for example, Akerlof 1970; Barzel 1982). In organizations the quality of applicants for a position, as well as the quality of their product once they are employed, must be assessed. However, employers often suffer from asymmetries of information that benefit the employee. Employers are unable to observe an applicant's decisions or actual qualifications and therefore may resort to adverse selection; that is, they may use a rule that ensures against risk but cannot ensure (and probably militates against) the best selection. In addition, employers are not able to observe all aspects of postcontract behavior; therefore, moral hazard—that is, cheating or shirking—may result.

The aim of the transaction costs approach is to build from these arguments about conflict of interest and information costs a model of organizational variation. Coase (1937) asked why firms, with their hierarchical and nonmarket form of organization, exist. He answered that, given transaction costs, they are more efficient than markets for production. Alchian and Demsetz (1972) argue that the hierarchy of the firm can be deduced from the behavior of individuals contracting with each other to derive gains from cooperation through team production. A hierarchy economizes on the costs of acquiring information about shirking by introducing incentives to monitor shirking behavior. Williamson (1975) suggests that the costs of transacting in different sectors explain why some firms choose vertical integration (hierarchy) whereas others choose to purchase goods and services on the market. Jensen and Meckling (1976) provide the first step in a positive theory of agency.[12] They posit that organizations are a nexus of multilateral contracts between principals and agents that specify the rules of performance evaluation, rewards, and decision rights. The problem is to develop organizational structures that lead agents to act consistently in the interest of principals. To do this requires technologies of monitoring and bonding.

The transaction cost framework cannot be imported whole hog from economics to political science and sociology, however. It suffers too much from the limits of economics generally, despite its pioneering elaborations of nontraditional domains. It shares a tendency with public choice and

---

[12] Jensen (1983) differentiates the positive theory of agency, which he is developing with coauthors Meckling and Fama (Fama 1980; Fama and Jensen 1983a, 1983b), from the "other" principal-agent literature (Spence and Zeckhauser 1971, Ross 1973). Jensen characterizes his approach as "positive" because of its attempt to model how the world works, including the behavior of other maximizing individuals. The second approach is less empirical and more mathematical. It centers more on questions of uncertainty and risk sharing.

neoclassical economics to be too mathematical and formal and, thus, too abstracted from the empirical realities it is presumably attempting to explain. Moreover, the definition of transaction costs is still too imprecise. It often remains a residual category for all those variables that economists have neglected. Moe (1984, 759–72) points out the difficulties of applying an approach developed for economic organizations to public bureaucracies. Economic organizations generally have a shared concern for and a standard of efficiency, while the goals of public bureaucracies vary widely. With few exceptions even the best-intentioned economists seem to have an oversimplified and unsophisticated comprehension of power and political institutions.[13]

The potential contribution of the transaction costs approach to understanding variation in state organization should by now be obvious. Although most of the discussion of transaction costs remains within economics, the concept is beginning to have an impact on the other social sciences. Williamson (1985), Cook and Emerson (1984), and Heimer (1985) import the concept of transaction costs into more general organizational analysis. Laumann, Knoke, and Kim (1985) apply the transaction costs approach to participation in state policymaking. Moe (1984) uses it to analyze public bureaucracies. North (1981, 20) uses it to explain the central paradox of the state: "The existence of a state is essential for economic growth; the state, however, is the source of man-made economic decline." He uses the positive theory of agency to investigate the creation of organizations to minimize transaction costs. He then shows that these organizations become inefficient as technological change requires new organizational forms and property rights. North is neoclassical in his assumption of maximizing actors and Marxist in his theorizing about the development and effects of property rights through history.

As mentioned, transaction costs include a wide range of variables. The most important for understanding rule and revenue are the costs of bargaining a revenue production policy; the costs of acquiring information about revenue sources, constituent behavior, and agent behavior; and the costs of enforcing compliance with that policy. These factors are generally interrelated. For example, establishing with whom rulers might strike bargains requires information. What policies rulers will undertake to bargain and with whom are delimited by their capacity to measure revenue sources and to monitor constituent and agent compliance. Monitoring serves both to provide information and to aid enforcement. An effective

---

[13] See, especially, the critique by Cook and Emerson (1984).

system of monitoring enables rulers to identify noncompliant behavior. By increasing the probability that free riders will be caught and punished, increased ruler knowledge is a disincentive to noncompliance. To maximize revenue, rulers will have to design revenue production systems that economize on transaction costs. They must be as concerned with the reduction of expenditures in extracting a tax as with the gross return from the tax.

COSTS OF BARGAINING

Bargaining power rests on resources. Bargaining costs include the costs of acquiring information (specifically, information about what resources will have to be exchanged to reach a bargain) and the costs of negotiating an agreement. The quality and availability of information about bargaining partners are partially a result of past interactions with those partners and partially a result of ruler capacity to measure revenue sources and monitor behavior (to be discussed below). Few rulers operate in a vacuum. Most have dealt, or watched their predecessors deal, with constituents and agents on enough prior occasions to establish a sense of where there is likely to be a high and where a low marginal return. Thus, in stable polities the costs of establishing bargaining partners are relatively low. What raises the costs are major technological changes in measurement or monitoring that alter the relative price of extracting resources from a particular constituency; major political, economic, or military changes that alter the relative bargaining power of rulers in relation to constituents; and major changes in the political and economic system that produce an altered cast of characters about whom reliable information is yet to be acquired.

Bargaining costs also include the costs of negotiating an actual policy. Institutional arrangements can significantly alter these costs. It is far more difficult — and costly — to negotiate with every individual than with a collectivity. It is usually less costly and risky for rulers to achieve agreement to a policy change by discussion in an institutionalized — that is, rule-bound — setting than by quelling rebellions. Technological and institutional change are double-edged, however. For example, although improvements in transportation and communication reduce the costs of ruler access to bargaining partners, they also reduce constituent costs of objecting to or renegotiating policies.

Finally, bargaining involves setting the terms of the contract so that the most revenue can be extracted at the least cost. Again, the limits of measurement and monitoring are crucial to the equation. Equally important are arrangements designed to reduce what Heimer (1985) labels reactive risk—that is, the risks associated with strategic interaction, in which what one party decides to do depends on what the other party chooses. Mechanisms of enforcement are only one aspect of risk reduction. Proper specification of contract terms and appropriate institutional arrangements are also necessary.

COSTS OF MEASURING REVENUE SOURCES

The better the quality of rulers' information about the actual wealth, income, and property produced in the polity, about the behavior of those from whom they extract revenue, and about the behavior of those who do the extracting, the more they are able to extract in revenue from the population. Rulers generally try to act like discriminating monopolists. That is, they attempt to identify the separable parts of the economy and devise a means of measuring the inputs and outputs of each (North 1981, 23 and 26–27).

Measurement is largely a function of the available technology. Historically, one of the first acts of states has been to standardize weights and measures. Money is another mechanism for standardizing the relative value of taxable goods. A tax on income—as opposed to produce, property, or trade—is inconceivable without salary and wage workers. More sophisticated tools of measurement provided by modern technologies permit better evaluations of the quality, quantity, and movement of goods. Even so, a correct estimation of the relevant features of many goods often cannot be obtained through measurement.

Once rulers have established that they will be extracting revenue from a given population, measurement capacity determines what kind of property they can tax and where. Most ancient taxes were on produce and were paid in kind. It may have benefited rulers more to tax land or income, but they had no method for measuring the worth of land or income. Thus, the kind of wealth rulers could tax determined which individuals they depended on for economic resources in a particular society. Measurement problems can also raise the cost of revenue extraction. When areas of rulers' territory are inaccessible or militarily dangerous, land surveys and other normal devices for determining taxable property then become much more expensive.

COSTS OF MONITORING CONSTITUENT COMPLIANCE

Whatever the sophistication of measurement, the problem of monitoring persists. No matter what the dependence of constituents on rulers, many are likely to free-ride, evade taxes, cheat, or shirk if they can do so unobserved and therefore escape punishment. Successful monitoring turns on the capacity to pinpoint as well as to punish those guilty of cheating or corruption. In a tiny and compact polity where everyone regularly scrutinizes everyone else, this is a relatively simple matter. However, in most polities rulers require agents to spy on and punish the noncompliant as well as to collect the actual taxes.

Thus, rulers will try to design political institutions that facilitate low-cost monitoring. For example, the feudal system was based, in principle, on a hierarchy of obligation, which gave monarchs fairly accurate ideas of those on whom they could rely. The political machine of urban America, which worked only to the extent that it could count and control votes, was greatly undermined when the introduction of the secret ballot prevented identification of voters not voting the party line. On the other hand, the post hoc tally of votes tells elected officeholders how many supporters they have and where, something that is far more difficult to determine in a nonvoting system. The roll-call vote has traditionally enabled political parties, constituents, and chief executives to monitor the loyalty of individual legislators. In the responsible party system of Britain, where monitoring capacity was combined with a reward system, the party had considerable leverage in relation to the members of Parliament (Hechter 1987).

The most important contemporary form of monitoring taxpayer compliance is, of course, the audit. There is a huge literature on the most efficient audit procedures, that is, the level of auditing that will deter evasion. Recently several analysts have investigated this question within a principal-agent framework, in which the government is the principal and the taxpayer the agent (see, for example, Graetz, Reinganum, and Wilde 1984; Reinganum and Wilde 1984; Reinganum and Wilde 1985). One ingenious analysis argues for rebates for truth-tellers (Border and Sobel 1985).

What measurement and monitoring capacity rulers have will affect the terms of the tax contract, for they will try to be precise in regard to factors they can subsequently evaluate and will try to specify broadly against other contingencies. Rulers may acclaim their property rights and require a given level of taxation, but their ability to collect those taxes depends on their ability to monitor the compliance of revenue producers.

AGENCY COSTS

Both measurement of revenue-producing activity and monitoring constituent compliance require rulers to pay agents. But agents can shirk and cheat, particularly at the point where they extract revenue and the point where they turn revenue over to rulers. Incentives and disincentives to regulate the behavior of agents, those who carry out rulers' policies, represent a special case of transaction costs, called agency costs. Agency costs are the sum of expenditures by rulers (or other principals) on monitoring and by agents on guarantees that they can be trusted (Jensen and Meckling 1976). Investment in the measurement and monitoring of agent behavior always represents a loss of income to rulers that would not be lost if they could otherwise be certain of receiving all that was defined as their due. Thus, at the least cost and most return to themselves, rulers will try to design revenue production systems that enable them to evaluate agent performance and to incorporate incentives for agent compliance and disincentives for noncompliance.

Weber ([1922] 1968, 963–67) lays out some of the historical forms of agency control — and their pitfalls. In the absence of a money economy, taxes are paid in kind. Often, as in ancient Egypt or China or during the late Roman monarchy, rulers tried to motivate agents by giving them a fixed income in kind as insurance against fluctuating yields. As Weber points out, this "easily means a first step toward appropriation of the sources of taxation by the official and their exploitation as private property" (964). If rulers are not careful, the land itself is transferred to the official, who then takes on more of the attributes of a feudal lord than a tax collector. Rulers still demand revenue, but the nature of the negotiation and, probably, the level of return are transformed. A related form of agency is prebendal organization, in which officials have lifelong property rights to economic rents as payment for the fulfillment of the duties of their office. As Weber notes, "All assignments of services and usufructs in kind as endowments for officials tend to loosen the bureaucratic mechanism, and especially to weaken hierarchic subordination" (967).

An alternative is tax farming, one of the cases to be investigated in chapter 4. This can occur in a monetary or nonmonetary economy. Here the official bids for the right to collect the tax, pays a specified sum before collection, and pockets the surplus that he collects from taxpayers. Rulers can budget and can avoid paying the costs of monitoring tax collectors or measuring the taxable material of constituents. When tax farming is highly regulated, the tax farmers bear the direct costs of measurement (which are, of course, reflected in their bids); incentives for monitoring lie with the taxpayers and the tax collector. If tax farming is not regulated and if a tax farmer's interest is short-term profit rather than economic growth or stability, tax farming carries the risk of endangering the long-run revenue yield and creating political opposition from those who feel they are being overtaxed.[14]

The modern alternative, of course, is bureaucratic revenue collection subject to contemporary accounting procedures. Computerized tax assessment is the logical extension. Although the state is likely to receive more of the gross revenue produced than through other methods of collection and to lose relatively little through agent pilfering, the price tag in technology, salaries, and working conditions can be very high. Nor can any agency contract totally prevent goal displacement, routinized treatment of constituents, or agent discretion (Lipsky 1980). Moreover, bureaucracy is not a single organizational structure. The variation in income tax administration among the United States, Great Britain, and Germany is a case in point. They differ not only in the processes of tax assessment but also in the processes of audit and appeal.

ENFORCEMENT COSTS

Enforcement becomes an issue once the rulers have identified the non-compliant. To punish free riding, shirking, and venality by both agents and constituents, rulers rely on a repressive apparatus composed of police, jailers, and other hirelings paid to uphold the laws. However, coercion is expensive, and its use often precipitates resentments that can fuel the flames of opposition. Thus, rulers will seek to create compliance that is quasi-voluntary. It is voluntary in that constituents pay because they choose to. It is quasi-voluntary because they will be punished if they do not and are caught. (Quasi-voluntary compliance is the subject of chapter 3.)

DISCOUNT RATE

Rulers' discount rates—that is, how much present value future returns have for them—are another major factor in the calculation of the costs and benefits of a policy choice. Rulers with high discount rates care little for the future. They will be less concerned with promoting the conditions of economic growth and increased revenue over time than with extracting available revenue even at the risk of discouraging output. Rulers with low discount rates do have an interest in securing future revenues; they will

---

[14] Weber ([1922] 1968, 968) makes a related point, but he does not recognize the important variable of regulation.

extract revenue up to the point at which further extractions would put future output at risk.

Rulers with high discount rates will encourage agents to extract all there is from constituents but will try to ensure that they get the lion's share of the take. Rulers with considerable bargaining power vis-à-vis agents and low discount rates are likely to rely on some form of bureaucracy.

Rulers' discount rates are always something of a function of personal psychology, of whether they have a short or long time horizon. However, the principal determinant is security of office. Without security rulers are unlikely to be concerned about economic growth. For example, rulers subject to periodic elections and unable to use tax revenue in the campaign are likely to refrain from imposing unpopular taxes on potential supporters.

The most important cause of a high discount rate is military conflict. An embattled ruler who needs to win a war to stay in power will probably extract all there is in the hope of having sufficient resources to defeat rivals. Where risk is high, expensive and sophisticated techniques of measurement and monitoring techniques are likely to prove a waste of resources enough of the time to make preferable a predictable, if lower, return based on a less costly procedure of extraction. Rulers with very few pressures are unlikely to undertake costly bargaining, measurement, and monitoring, and they are unlikely to extract beyond the point at which taxpayers will resist through either decreased production or actual rebellion. Rulers under greater pressure may be compelled to.

Schumpeter ([1918] 1954) and more recently Peacock and Wiseman (1961), Mann (1980), Tilly (1985), and Rasler and Thompson (1985) have emphasized the causal importance of war in accounting for the increased size and power of the state. Military conflict produces pressures that alter rulers' transaction costs and bargaining behavior as well as discount rates.

STRUCTURAL CONSTRAINTS AND VARIABLES

Relative bargaining power, transaction costs, and discount rates are themselves the product of macro-level variables. I am concerned primarily with the effects of macro-level variables on transaction and bargaining costs and on rulers' discount rates, rather than with the causes of the shifts in the macro-level variables. Moreover, I expect to address only part of the variance. The peculiarities of a particular period and of particular minds always have a role to play in explanations of this sort. My more modest purpose is to begin to specify the relationship between major macro-level changes and major policy change. I recognize that each historical situation and each historical configuration of macro-level variables is unique. Nonetheless, it is possible to identify structural factors that occur throughout place and history. This helps us to organize the complex and numerous facts that constitute a historical period.

Theorists working within the Marxist tradition have generally provided the best guidance for determining the most significant macro-level variables affecting a political economic system. Marx himself emphasized the importance of the productive forces and economic structure of a society for understanding nearly everything else about the society. Lenin added an emphasis on the international context, both economic and military.

PRODUCTIVE FORCES AND ECONOMIC STRUCTURE

Following Cohen's (1978) interpretation of Marx's theory of history, I define productive forces as the means of production (including the instruments and raw materials of production) and labor power (that is, the productive capacity of producers). The economic structure of a society refers to its production relations, "the relations of effective power over persons and productive forces, not relations of legal ownership" (Cohen 1978, 63).

Economic structure is an important determinant of the relative bargaining power of different sets of actors. The nature and extent of effective power over persons and productive forces should indicate what groups are likely to have significant economic and political resources. For example, feudal economies empower nobles and inhibit rulers from taxing producers directly.

The organization of work, the markets in which producers are active, and the nature of their living arrangements are further consequences of economic organization. These factors have particular analytical importance in that they provide information on the capacity to engage in collective action. A knowledge of these factors can produce a road map of which groups are likely to organize and with whom they will ally or conflict (Brustein 1981, 1985; Brustein and Levi 1987; Bates 1987, chap. 3).

When we know what kinds of property the members of a class are entitled to own, we have an important guide to the distribution of economic resources and conflict in a society. However, the existence of unequal bargaining resources connotes neither control of the state by the dominant economic class nor a high probability of class political action. First, other classes also exist and — as in the case of the bourgeoisie in late feudalism or the middle class in contemporary capitalism — often have bargaining power of their own. Second, classes do not always act as such. Major conflicts are as likely to be intraclass as interclass.

The level of development of the productive forces determines the economic structure. It also has fundamental effects on the transaction costs of rule. What is produced, how, and by whom delimits what revenues rulers can extract from producers. For example, subsistence agriculture creates less taxable material than industrial production for profit. Moreover, in the absence of a commercial and monetized economy, measurement costs are very high indeed.

Where technological and productive development is low, there will be less to tax and fewer means (and reasons) for measuring and monitoring the extraction of revenue. The growth of technology and increases in the stock of knowledge tend to correlate with a more productive economy, one in which — from the ruler's point of view — there is more to tax. They also correlate with organizational innovations — such as the firm, bureaucracy, or income tax — that make it less costly to tax a larger proportion of the population. Greater ease of taxation promotes government expansion by enabling rulers to supply more goods and services (Riker 1978). More revenue means more extended rule.

As the productive forces develop, there is also an increase in the specialization and division of labor. This has two consequences for transaction costs of rule (see, esp., North 1985). First, specialization increases the number of economic actors and institutions that require coordination. The market provides some of that coordination, but the provision of the infrastructure of transportation and communication is often left to the state. Second, increased specialization results in a larger number of interest groups who make demands on the state. The proliferation of interest groups increases the costs of negotiating and implementing policies. Rulers may come to depend on some of these interest groups, with obvious consequences for relative bargaining power. Yet rulers can often play the various groups off against each other, particularly when rulers gain control of the central place in the network of political exchange.

As the distribution of economic resources changes, so does the cast of characters with bargaining power in relation to rulers. Technological innovation can alter an already existing balance of power, as evidenced by the fate of the Armada. It can also make advantages in economic wealth by competitors irrelevant or secondary. For example, Philip of Macedon introduced the phalanx and reorganized the army when Macedon was no richer and probably poorer than Athens. These innovations enabled him to engage in successful military operations that yielded increased economic resources, especially the gold mines of Amphibolis. The combination of, first, his technological and, then, his economic advantages with his strategic brilliance gave Philip such military superiority that he was able to unify Greece for the first time in history. Subsequently, Alexander was able to carry out his father's plan to conquer Persia, Egypt, and parts of what are contemporary India (Bury, Cook, and Adcock 1969).

Technology is one of the motors of long-term secular change for both Marxists (for example, Cohen 1978) and neoclassical economists (for example, North 1981). It can also be a catalyst to revisions of state policy. A major change in the technology of production, information, or management can make existing property rights inefficient and provide new power resources to old rivals or new actors. The efficiencies of large enclosed estates precipitated state-backed enclosure legislation. Lenin's ([1917] 1975) famous essay on imperialism documents how the growing dominance of monopolistic finance capital over competitive industrial capital led to significant changes in military and colonial policies.

The development of technology and the increase in specialization and division of labor are crucial factors in accounting for the involvement of the state in an ever-widening range of activities. Specialization in the division of labor promotes new demands on the state, and technological and organizational innovations make it possible to supply the goods and services in response to demands.

State structures evolve to correct market failures, but they also evolve in competition with the market. Rulers can manipulate constituent and agent demands to justify extensions of their rule and increases in their revenue. Moreover, increases in the stock of knowledge provide each generation of rulers with tools and strategies often unavailable to their predecessors. For example, the tendency of tax farming to serve the interests of the tax farmers better than the interests of the rulers has been discovered over time and in a variety of contexts. Thus, it is unlikely that even a Reagan or Thatcher would turn to the market solution of tax farming to replace the current government tax collection bureaucracy. On the other hand, a Reagan or Thatcher knows how to use the mass media in ways that even such successful pretelevision politicians as Roosevelt or Churchill did not.

INTERNATIONAL CONTEXT

International trade, overseas colonies, and other such aspects of the international political economy are also important in determining rulers' available sources of revenue and their relative bargaining power. The bargaining power of rulers will be enhanced where producers are dependent on the government for tariff protection, regulated factor markets, and so on. It will also be enhanced when rulers have sources of revenue external to their domestic constituents (Kiser 1986–87). However, the extent to which rulers have a relative monopoly and a relative benefit from international trade vis-à-vis their constituents depends on the extent of international competition, the status of the ruler in that competition, the dependence of rulers on trade for revenue, and the bargaining power of the traders.

The bargaining power of the rulers will be reduced to the extent that subjects can make a better deal with an alternative ruler and to the extent that powerful constituents control external sources of revenue.

Thus, in the international context the important factors are (1) the existence of rival powers to whom constituents can flee or with whom they can bargain; (2) the ability of rulers, constituents, or individuals from other states to profit from the products being traded internationally; and (3) the importance of international trade as a possible source of revenue for the state.

FORM OF GOVERNMENT

Historically, several forms of government have existed. Monarchies, military dictatorships, oligarchies, and representative democracies hardly exhaust the possible list. Even within democratic polities, there is immense variation in electoral rules, power and number of legislatures, relationship between legislature and head of state, and other features. Each of the general forms and each of these distinct features of government have consequences for the decisions and actions of rulers or heads of state. They affect the bargaining strategies and resources available to citizens, the ability of rulers to use the public coffers as their own, the forms of agency that will be permitted or denied, the permissible types of inducements to compliance and punishments for noncompliance, and the nature of the rulers' rivals.

What is crucial for this discussion is that each major change in government has predictable consequences for transaction costs, discount rates, and relative bargaining power.

Rulers will try to alter forms of government to suit their purposes if they can. Indeed, rulers will try to alter all the constraints on their behavior. In the cases presented in chapters 4–7, I shall highlight those instances in which decisions made in response to one set of constraints have enhanced or decreased the ability of rulers to negotiate better terms of trade at another point in time.

CONCLUSION

Variations in state policies over time and across countries are a consequence of variations in rulers' relative bargaining power, transaction costs, and discount rates. But rulers walk a tightrope. The pursuit of personal ends — within constraints — is the sine qua non of predatory rulers. However, such pursuit may antagonize allies and constituents and enhance the appeal of rivals. On the other hand, too many concessions to allies and constituents could undermine rulers' political and economic power. Rulers are always searching for means to increase their bargaining power and lower their transaction costs. However, what leads to one may block the other. Such dilemmas of predatory rule are consistent with the primary contradiction of economic development as put forward by Marx and Engels: The property rights that serve the dominant interests of society come into conflict over time with innovations in technology and economic organization and with the new and powerful classes these innovations create.

The theory of predatory rule differs from the classical Marxist approach in its focus on rulers rather than on the dominant economic class. It differs from the new state-centered structuralism in its emphasis on deductive theory, which simplifies political, economic, and social complexity as a means for better understanding state organization and policies. It differs from public choice and neoclassical economists in its recognition of power and the unequal distribution of power.

There are several advantages to this reformulation. First, by eliminating the emphasis on class as the primary historical actor and by investigating instead individuals or sets of individuals, the theory becomes more general. Class is not eliminated as an important factor, but class becomes a variable rather than a given. History ceases to be an eternal search for the rise of the next dominant class. Second, by focusing on rulers instead of the state, the theory avoids the anthropomorphism prevalent in many contemporary discussions of the state. After all, the state is an institution composed of people. Its actions and behavior are the end result of concrete human actions. Third, the deductive approach permits an identification of significant causal factors in the creation and maintenance of state policies. It simplifies "real world" complexity on theoretical grounds and makes the generation and testing of hypotheses possible. In sum, the theory of predatory rule offers a micro-foundation to macro-processes.

There are also obvious limitations to the model. First, so far it remains in the domain of comparative statics. Another book would be necessary to analyze the transformations in the structural variables that affect transaction costs, bargaining power, and discount rates. In the next chapter, I take up the more tractable problem of the incremental changes in policy that occur over the life of the policy. Second, ideology may turn out to explain a great deal of variation in both ruler and subject behavior. This point will also be taken up in the next chapter. Third, the analysis of ruler behavior becomes considerably more difficult in modern polities or where rulers are a collection of individuals rather than a single individual. I addressed this point earlier and will again in chapter 7.

No theory is interesting unless it can be used to explain actual events and data. This chapter represents only a first step in that process. By laying out the assumptions and the major independent variables in the theory of predatory rule, I hope to have clarified how this theory might be used to account for variations in state policy. But the next step, the application of the theory, will decide the extent to which it can achieve all it sets out to do.

The case studies in chapters 4–7 have been selected from vastly different periods and places in history: Republican Rome, medieval and Renaissance France and England, eighteenth-century Britain, and twentieth-century Australia. By choosing cases from different periods of history and "modes of production," I hope to demonstrate the generality of the model.

The basis of selection was threefold. First, each case occurs in a period of transition, when there was a fundamental change in the structural factors that I posit as the determinants of transaction costs and relative bargaining power. This permits me to explore the influence of changes in relative bargaining power and transaction costs on revenue production policies. If the policies do not change in the expected direction, my model is disconfirmed.

Second, in each case the ruler has different powers and power resources and must bargain with different sets of constituents. Moreover, these powers and power resources change over the course of the period covered by the case. This permits evaluation of the influences of both ruler autonomy and class power on policy outcomes. It also permits me to compare instances where the ruler is the principal or the agent.

Third, each of the cases illustrates a different aspect in the history of transaction costs. Costs of monitoring, measuring, and enforcing policies change with new techniques and with extensions (or contractions) of citizenship and citizen rights. The choice of cases permits exploration of both the influence of transaction costs and the interaction of one kind of transaction cost with another.

My model, if successful, will be consistent with history and will illuminate history. However, before proceeding to the empirical material, I wish first to engage in a brief excursus on state formation. Then I shall take up one additional question for theoretical elaboration: How do rulers create compliance with revenue production policies without constant resort to direct one-on-one coercion?

Excursus on the Acquisition of Rule

Before I proceed to the analysis of revenue production policies, let me take a quick detour to try out the theory of predatory rule on one of the primary issues of political theory: the question of state formation.

Rarely, if ever, in history has a state emerged full blown from society. In general, the term *state formation* refers to the consolidation or takeover of an organization that already performs at least some of the functions of a state. Nonetheless, the analysis of the related processes of formation and transformation remains an important aim of theoretical inquiry, and there are, consequently, innumerable theories of state genesis, ranging from relatively concrete and historical accounts[1] to philosophical exercises on the emergence of government from the state of nature.[2] One common argument is that the state evolves as a specialized agency of justice and protection when the population of a society exceeds that of a community able to engage in face-to-face interactions and generalized reciprocity. Once in place, the state makes it more likely that the society will survive and

---

[1] Anthropological accounts include Carniero (1970), Service (1975), Wright (1977), and Cohen and Service (1978). Sociologists and historians have also explored the question of state formation and transformation. For example, see Bendix (1978), Moore (1966), Anderson (1974a), Poggi (1978), Tilly (1975, 1985), and Mann (1977). While the anthropologists tend to focus on the emergence of an institution that can be labeled a state, these analysts tend to investigate the emergence of the modern state. One theorist who addresses the question across many time periods and countries is, of course, Weber ([1922] 1968).

[2] Political philosophers address the question of state emergence in still another way. The great works in this literature abound, but among the most important older texts are Hobbes ([1651] 1962), Locke ([1690] 1968), and Rousseau ([1762] 1950).

grow without splintering. There is considerable debate about what the relevant size is and what determines it.[3] The focus here, however, is not so much on state formation itself as on how rulers achieve and maintain control over the state apparatus.

What is clear, from Hobbes to modern-day anthropologists, political sociologists, and economic historians, is that the first step in the process of state creation is to build a monopoly of organized violence. Both the provision of protection and the ability to engage in war are crucial aspects of state making, and both depend on the extraction of sufficient resources to pay for organized violence (North and Thomas 1973; North 1981; Tilly 1985). The great economic historian Frederick Lane argued (1958, 402) that "the violence-using, violence-controlling industry was a natural monopoly at least on land. . . . A monopoly of the use of force within a contiguous territory enabled a protection-producing enterprise to improve its product and reduce its costs." Both economies of scale in violence and the use of superior military capacity to defeat enemies enable government to monopolize protection.

But who benefits from this monopoly varies over time and place. So, too, does the ability of rulers to extract a surplus or, alternatively, to extract so much that the payer can no longer maintain production (Lane 1958, 403). The causes of variation lie in the political, economic, and military resources possessed by constituents and agents — that is, as Lane puts it, who "owns" the monopoly or, as I prefer to think about the issue, who can bargain with and/or control the predatory ruler.

Persons who wish to attain and maintain positions of rulers almost always face rivals. Much of history is the story of potential rulers vying for leadership of a state organization, and conflict seldom ceases with victory. Elected officials rarely lack opponents. Monarchs often worry about the Macbeths and Richard IIIs within their courts. Demagogues and charismatic leaders fear that another will prove more compelling than they. The internecine struggles that marked the Middle Ages in Europe, the fourteenth through the sixteenth centuries in Japan, and the nineteenth and early twentieth centuries in China are evidence of the difficulties faced by leaders who attempt to impose their rule in the face of strong competitors with relatively equal resources. Challengers from subjected populations can also put a ruler's position in jeopardy.

Rulers aim to develop sufficient coercive capacity to defeat rivals and maintain control over the countryside defined as their territory. Only in the

---

[3] For a neoclassical economic view of these issues, see Auster and Silver (1979, chap. 2).

instance of a small, isolated community where all are unarmed except for the one person who possesses a six-gun is it possible even to conceive of rulers as able to obtain power without allies and support. This turns out to be a fanciful scenario even for the American West, where everyone, in fact, possessed a six-gun (Umbeck 1981). Rulers always depend on others for some of the resources necessary to acquire and sustain rule. They depend on the generals and even the soldiers of their armies, on the owners or managers of economic wealth, on the church officials who justify their status, or on the scientists or inventors of new technologies of force.

Moreover, few rulers can survive if they plunder all constituents. In Border and Sobel's (1985, 20–22) formal "theory of plunder," it is not in the interest of revenue-maximizing brigands to plunder, which is costly, if all they would get is what they would be offered in tribute. To elicit the most from the peasants in the way of tribute, rulers must make a credible commitment not to take more later. Both to ensure stable rule and to keep their costs down, rulers must offer positive benefits to "a minimum winning coalition" (Gamson 1961; Riker 1962) of the population in return for allegiance.[4]

Taylor (1982, 129–39) summarizes recent evidence on state formation in primitive societies where coercion is distributed relatively equally. One determinant is the presence of some strain—due to ecological pressures, external enemies, or both. Another determinant is limitations on emigration from or on fissioning of the existing community. Under the combined conditions of strain and high opportunity costs of exit, the population may agree—or be compelled—to trade some degree of liberty for state-provided benefits. The result, however, is the creation of an organization specializing in violence, an organization that benefits some more than others. In contrast with Engels's account ([1884] 1973), economic inequalities seem to follow rather than precede the concentration of coercive power into an organization with the characteristics of a state.

The transformation of a state that is able to make and enforce few property rights into a state that exercises considerable control over its population is also a function of strain and high opportunity costs of exit— although here economic inequality may well be a factor in causing strain. For example, Hechter and Brustein (1980; also see Kornmesser 1981) attempt to account for the pattern of state development in sixteenth-century western Europe by modifying Engels's argument that the state

---

[4] Emerson (1983) neatly develops this point with reference to state formation in Baltistan.

"arose from the need to keep class antagonisms in check" but that "it is, as a rule, the state of the most powerful economically dominant class" (Engels [1884] 1973, 231). They observe that an absolutist state is necessarily based on a landed aristocracy but that in the sixteenth century there were three major modes of production in western Europe, and only in the feudal regions did the conditions exist for the emergence of modern centralized states. For them class competition is indeed the catalyst to state transformation, but only where the property rights of an economically dominant class are threatened by an encroaching class. In these circumstances the members of the stronger class will form a coalition to establish a state to enforce property rights beneficial to them. Their aim is to force their ruler on the rest of society while they still possess the military superiority that comes with economic and political dominance.

Whatever the catalyst, individuals will consider joining with others in a state organization only when they face a common enemy or problem. In the early stages, the benefit may merely be coordination into larger groupings. A state organization becomes necessary to prevent recurring competition among the members of the group. The underlying choice is between loss of economic advantages and the chance to protect or even improve these advantages. Groups develop only where the individuals who participate receive a larger benefit from joining than from abstaining. The benefit to each participant is a state capable of securing property rights, of minimizing the strains on the contracting population, and of enforcing the compliance of the others to a mutually beneficial policy. Generally, it is only through collective action that these ends can be achieved at all, for seldom does a single individual have sufficient resources to win the battle alone. Rulers tend to be heads of coalitions, to whose membership they are initially accountable.

The stability of the state organization, once it is formed, requires a mechanism for enforcing compliance with its rules and ruler. Otherwise, individuals who oppose the concentration of force in general or in the hands of a particular ruler will resist, and those individuals who seek the benefits of the state will free-ride. Over time, even the members of the ruling group may be distracted from their common purpose by the conflicts that arise among them. The concentration of coercive capacity in the hands of rulers is at the root of all mechanisms to ensure compliance, for rulers must have sufficient power to prevent shirking from and breaking of the most important contract terms.

One stunning example of several elements of this process was the agreement made by all rulers of the independent, nonunified, and often competitive heads of the Greek kingdoms when they sought the hand of the most beautiful woman of her time, Helen, in marriage. Each wanted her enough to fight for her. Helen's father, fearful of making enemies of the rejected suitors, accepted the solution proposed by the "brilliant" Odysseus, who sought the hand of Helen's sister Penelope. The young king of Ithaca suggested that an oath be sworn by all the suitors to bear arms against any who subsequently tried to harm Helen's father or bridegroom and any who tried to abduct the bride. Agamemnon, brother of the husband chosen for Helen and a chieftain eager for power, became head of the coalition, and Helen became a property right protected by law and by the institution of an organization of defense, a metastate, to enforce the law. However, by the time Paris stole her off to Troy, several of the previous suitors no longer wished to honor the agreement they had made. Among these was Odysseus, whose famous wile had led him to seek the contract in the first place and to attempt to break it in the second. The agents of Agamemnon had to make the reluctant honor their agreements. All the kings sailed off to Troy and the infamous war that followed. The issue was no longer Helen but the invasion of property rights represented by her abduction.

This little story tells a tale of state development. Individual, self-interested actors are united in the face of threats to their individual and common property rights. The threat can be internal, external, or both. They form a coalition aimed at dominating the state apparatus, as a means not only to combat their common enemies and delimit their own destructive rivalries but, equally important, to enforce each individual's agreement to cooperate. However, they are successful only if they themselves give up power to a leader who then controls the apparatus of violence, is able to coordinate the members of the ruling group, and can ensure compliance through a selective use of rewards and coercion.

The victory of the ruling group does not signal the end of its members' problems with external competitors or with one another. Groups are unstable over time, with the members tending to revert to their original status as distinct and conflicting individuals. Most rulers have to exert considerable energy to hold a group together. Usually they must direct attention to new issues and threats that will invoke a recommitment to a contract of mutual support. Rulers often manipulate wars and crusades to this end.

Nor do all rulers prefer to maintain the coalition that helped them achieve power. Some rulers perceive the members of the coalition as their potential rivals and so practice a strategy of divide and conquer while seeking to develop support elsewhere, perhaps in the people as a whole. Louis Bonaparte is the classic example of a ruler who broke with the coalition that put him in power (Marx [1852] 1974). The candidate of an uneasy alliance between the two major factions of the capitalist class, he played the factions off against each other while he appealed to the mass electorate, the peasantry. The success of this strategy was largely due to the conditions of peasant life, which prevented peasants from engaging in coordinated action on their own behalf; their only hope for economic improvement lay in the aggregation of votes, each an individual act, for a leader who represented their interests. Despite his initial success, this second Bonaparte was doomed to failure. Ultimately, his rivals, in this case the class that had gotten him elected in the first place, had sufficient resources to overthrow him, particularly given the failures of his military policy.

Because the interests of rulers differ markedly from those of their backers, tensions inevitably result, even when they do not take the extreme form of Bonapartism. Rulers are often agents whose principals seek to ensure the promotion of their own interests. While the victorious coalition will use the state organization to extract from the populace a disproportionate share of society's wealth, the original grant of power to the coalition's agent-ruler has created a rival. Similarly, while rulers will use control of the state organization to achieve personal ends, they are dependent on those who help them maintain their position. If rulers fail to deliver and fail to create an alternative base of support, they are likely to be overthrown.

A process of collective action underlies the acquisition and maintenance of rule. To become ruler requires first coordinating a group of individuals who face a common enemy or problem, but rule ultimately rests on control of resources necessary to enforce participation in the dominant group by the individuals who agreed to become its members. Successful rulers are those able to maintain the group, able to maintain its relative dominance over the opposition, and able to build sufficient coercive power to block rivals.

Such a view makes scholastic the distinction between conflict and contract theories of state genesis.[5] All rulers are part of a contract, yet all

---

[5] Bates (1987, chap. 2) makes a similar argument in his discussion of state formation in Africa through the process of political centralization. Using historical and ethnographic data on thirty-six African societies, he arbitrates competing claims of those who believe that the state promotes collective advantage and those who argue that the state is a mechanism of expropriation. He concludes that the "literature has offered a false choice" (41). The state is an instrument of those who seek private advantages, but to hold power requires concessions to followers.

engage in conflict. The contract is with those who agree with the selection of a particular individual as ruler; the conflict is with those who do not. The contract is with those who gain from the trade of revenue for protection and other services; the conflict is with those who are plundered or victims of a protection racket. The form of government — whether it be tyranny, oligarchy, or democracy, to use the classic three — reflects what percentage of the population is part of the contract every ruler must make. Bargains made with the constituents and agents on whom rulers depend underlie the acquisition and maintenance of rule. Rulers are always predatory, but they cannot always do as they please.

CHAPTER III

Creating Compliance

The establishment of revenue production policies, the subject of the last chapter, is a problem in comparative statics. Within a given set of constraints, rulers have a given set of options. Rulers bargain a tax policy at one point in time for future points in time. They are establishing the rules of the game. However, over time taxpayers may begin to feel their taxes are too high relative to what is received in return. Compliance becomes increasingly problematic among those who feel that they are not getting as good a deal as they bargained for. No compliance procedures will work forever. Knowledge of gains and losses, acquired over time, can alter choices. So can the transformation of relative bargaining power, which makes possible another, better contract.

The focus of this chapter is on what Brennan and Buchanan label "in-period" rather than "constitutional" choices (1980, 2–3). The emphasis is on the dynamic element in revenue policy, that is, variation in compliance with an existing tax contract. Tax evasion has become a major issue in the United States, Australia, and other advanced industrial democracies, but it has always and everywhere been a problem. My purpose is not to join the debate as to whether evasion is on the rise. My purpose is to investigate tax compliance as a strategic interaction between rulers and constituents and among constituents.[1] I hope to understand the means by which rulers can encourage as well as the conditions that increase or decrease compliance.

---

[1] There is an extensive economics literature on tax avoidance and evasion. Much of it is quite formal. For less formal analysis, see, for example, Kay (1979) and Feldman and Kay (1981).

A polity's rules and procedures for extracting and collecting revenue comprise its "fiscal constitution." The bargaining of this fiscal constitution establishes the operative definition of a fair revenue production policy. It also enhances expectations that compliance will be widespread. The creation of the initial revenue policy is usually a quite public event, accompanied by a high degree of negotiation from a wide range of potential taxpayers. The institution of tax farming in ancient Rome, of the national tax systems in France and England, of the income tax in Britain, and of the uniform income tax in Australia are all examples of such extraordinary events.

Once a policy is understood as a contract between ruler and agents or ruler and constituents, compliance with the contract becomes problematic. Immediately, the free-rider problem raises its omnipresent head. It is in each person's interest to make a contract and then break it, thus receiving the benefits without incurring the costs. No contract is ever perfectly specified. Enforcement is nearly always imperfect. Even with considerable coercive power and effective techniques of measurement and monitoring, a ruler cannot achieve total compliance unless there is a policeman on every corner, a fed under every bed. There is always room for shirking and cheating.

The problems of achieving compliance are exacerbated by the slow but steady transformation of the terms of exchange that accompanies the return of politics as usual. Special interest groups negotiate alterations in the contract favorable to themselves. Some people find ways to avoid and evade taxation. At the same time, the revenues collected by government enable it to grow in both scale and scope. It takes on more employees and new tasks. The defense establishment increases in size, or welfare programs expand beyond what they were when taxation was publicly discussed and established.

The ordinary taxpayers may not be attentive at first to the effects of these changes on the return they receive for their revenue, but at some point they are likely to come alive to any deteriorations in their situation and to government expenditures of which they strongly disapprove. It is then that noncompliance should increase,[2] thus setting the stage for a renegotiation of the tax contract.

In effect, rulers can reduce the costs of compliance in three ways: through the use of coercion, the establishment and maintenance of norms

---

[2] Heimer (1985, 209–14) raises some similar issues in her discussion of insurance fraud and outdated contracts.

of compliance or ideological compliance, and the creation of quasi-voluntary compliance. I shall take up each in turn, but my emphasis will be on the last. My major argument in this chapter is that rulers take advantage of or seek to create institutions that promote cooperation.

COERCION

Coercion, the Hobbesian solution to the social contract, underlies taxation policy. It is illegal to evade taxes. People who do not pay their taxes or who underreport taxable material face sanctions, often serious sanctions. Despite coercion and monitoring, individuals still cheat. No ruler eliminates noncompliance altogether.

It is costly to use coercion to enforce compliance. However, some technologies of enforcement are more expensive than others. One critical factor in the cost is the effectiveness and efficiency of monitoring. The easier it is to identify the noncompliant, the less costly is enforcement. Using communal institutions to collect revenue—for example, the Roman gens (see chapter 4)—makes coercion unnecessary; no one can hide. Withholding taxes on income achieves the same end in a large polity. The affected taxpayers have no means of evading and avoiding payroll taxes.

Monitoring is not always effective or cost-effective, however. For example, seventeenth- and eighteenth-century Britain was plagued by smugglers escaping customs and other taxes. The excise tax, on the other hand, was a model of effective monitoring—but at a very high price in surveillance of the excisemen (see chapter 6).

To lower, let alone prevent, tax evasion and avoidance, rulers seek cheaper and improved means for obtaining tax compliance. Government officials, past and present, have searched for alternative means of promoting compliance.

IDEOLOGICAL COMPLIANCE

Coercion induces compliance out of motivations of self-interest. However, individuals do sometimes act out of a strongly held normative or ideological conviction. Certainly, some proportion of behavior is nonrational, irrational, or imperfectly rational, or can be accounted for only by extrarational motivations. Such behavior is outside the model of rational choice. Nonetheless, ideologically motivated compliance is one important source of variation in compliance.[3]

[3] Discussions with Lee Alston helped me considerably in my formulation of ideological compliance.

The problem with reliance on ideology (or norms) as a causal variable is that the concept still remains insufficiently specified and, therefore, difficult to separate from other factors.[4] A better theory of the emergence of norms will represent a major step in providing social scientists with a useful concept.

There are attempts to do just that.[5] One of the most promising is North's (1981, chap. 5; 1985). For North "Ideology consists of the set of individual beliefs and values that modify behavior. It can be measured by the premium people are willing to incur not to free ride" (1985, 394). North argues that ideology is most likely to influence choice where the costs of its use are low. For example, he points out, the independence and lifelong tenure of U.S. Supreme Court justices and the insulation of complex committee structures in which U.S. legislators operate account for why these two sets of actors are as likely to vote their consciences as their interests (North 1985, 394–95). Democratic rules in which citizens perceive their vote as having little consequence for the outcome may also promote ideological expression (Brennan and Lomasky 1985; also see Brennan and Buchanan 1984).

North makes a strong case that ideology matters. He begins to clarify the conditions under which ideology causally influences behavior independently of self-interest. He does this—as do I in my model—by treating ideology as a residual category for those situations in which self-interest is clearly not explanatory. However, ideology does not always promote compliance. Institutions that make ideological expression relatively cheap may elicit expressions of ideological dissatisfaction with the tax system. Moreover, North does not acknowledge that ideology also may intensify or confirm self-interested behavior.[6] One would expect—with North—that where normative concurrence is costly, compliance will decline. However, one would also expect that compliance should be highest where ideology and self-interest reinforce each other. For example, an ideological convic-

[4] A review of the best of the literature makes clear the difficulties with its use and definition. For example, Wilson (1973) and Moe (1980) are convincing in their argument that purposive incentives motivate some individuals, but they fail to offer observable measures of when and in what amounts such incentives exist. Hechter (1987, esp. chap. 2 and in his discussion of socialization theory in chap. 4) offers a useful critical perspective on the reliance on norms in social science explanations.

[5] Ullman-Margalit (1977) makes an interesting, if not wholly successful, attempt to conceptualize norms from games. See the critique by Hardin (1980). Axelrod (1984) offers some insights. Hardin (forthcoming) and Coleman (forthcoming) promise progress.

[6] North (1985, 394) explicitly states that he is "not concerned here with ideology when it *merely* justifies self-interested behavior" (my emphasis). However, the fact that many people may be doubly motivated by self-interest and by ideology makes that "merely" quite an important category for investigation.

tion in favor of a welfare state is at least part of the story of some contemporary compliance with taxation.

Rulers can promote institutions and structures that make compliance relatively cheap. Moreover, they can — and do — invest in rituals, symbols, and propaganda meant to encourage compliance. The problem analytically is to determine how much of the variance in compliance is due to ideology as opposed to positive inducements or the effectiveness of monitoring and coercion. From a ruler's point of view, however, promoting ideology *may* reduce the costs of enforcement. Certainly, rulers throughout history have believed that it does.

North's framework raises the question of the extent to which rulers can construct or take advantage of institutions that make it cheap for taxpayers to comply out of public-spiritedness or normative conviction. It is a tricky problem, for not complying can put more money in one's pocket while compliance most certainly takes it out. What kinds of institutions promote compliance is the subject of the next section. Here my concern is with the fact that ideology exists.

In the area of taxation, ideology affects compliance by defining existing norms of fairness. Rulers may try to socialize the population or mold the conception of fairness or justice to fit their policies. The factors affecting a ruler's ability to promote a particular ideology is beyond the scope of my text. I argue below that it is possible to model how the failure of rulers to live up to the prevailing norms of fairness undermines compliance. However, I am offering no theory on the emergence or transformation of the norms that underlie an existing tax contract. I attempt to specify the role ideology plays in the explanation of compliance, but I am not attempting to explain the source and content of the ideology itself.

QUASI-VOLUNTARY COMPLIANCE

One way that rulers can reduce the costs of enforcement is to create or encourage situations where taxpayers engage in quasi-voluntary compliance. It is *voluntary* because taxpayers choose to pay. It is *quasi*-voluntary because the noncompliant are subject to coercion — if they are caught. The fact that compliance is not only a matter of principle distinguishes quasi-voluntary compliance from ideological compliance. Taxpayers make a calculated decision based on the behavior of others. Nor is quasi-voluntary compliance purely self-interested behavior. It cannot be accounted for solely by coercion and only rarely by positive selective incentives.

Quasi-voluntary compliance will occur only when taxpayers have confidence that (1) rulers will keep their bargains and (2) the other constituents will keep theirs. Taxpayers are strategic actors who will cooperate only when they can expect others to cooperate as well. The compliance of each depends on the compliance of the others. No one prefers to be a "sucker."

Quasi-voluntary compliance requires rulers to behave like political entrepreneurs (Frohlich, Oppenheimer, and Young 1971; Popkin 1979, esp. 259–66). To create and maintain quasi-voluntary compliance, rulers search for noncoercive strategies that produce a high level of constituent cooperation. They must create confidence in their credibility and their capacity to deliver promised returns for taxes. They must convince taxpayers that taxpayer contributions make a difference in producing the desired goods. They must coordinate the actions of taxpayers so that each perceives others doing their share, too.

I argue that rulers can increase compliance by demonstrating that the tax system is fair. A perception of exploitation—that is, an unfair contract—promotes noncompliance. Presumably, those who are "exploited" will resist paying if they can. Gains from trade and exploitation are not mutually exclusive, of course.[7] However, if individuals are not getting the gains they bargained for or if they feel they are being "suckers," they will try to withdraw from the contract.[8] Favoritism toward special interest groups, programs that they disapprove of, declining return for their taxes, the failure of some to comply can all violate taxpayers' norms of fairness. The consequence will be a decrease in quasi-voluntary compliance.

Dissatisfaction with the contract will have only a slight initial impact on compliance, especially among those whose only motivation for compliance is coercion. However, as dissatisfaction increases, more people will con-

---

[7] Roemer's theory of exploitation (1982) as an unfair contract hinges on such a distinction. Also see North and Thomas (1973), who make this point in relation to feudal arrangements, and North (1981, 50). Brenner's (1982, 76–84) description of the deals between French peasants and kings in the sixteenth century demonstrates historically that gains from trade can exist side by side with exploitation.

[8] Although taxation is a common enough historical rationale for rebellion, passivity is a more common response to taxation, even among those who would count as the most exploited—by any definition. Moore (1978, 455–57) recognizes this when he discusses exploitation as nonreciprocity that can exist even when people do not react to it. Moreover, people vary in their ability to resist. The same group can fluctuate over time, developing, losing, and then rediscovering its capacity to fight back (Shorter and Tilly 1974; McCarthy and Zald 1977; Levi and Hechter 1985; Scott 1985). Outright rebellion reflects improvements in the rebels' organizational capacity as often as it reflects changed relationships between rulers and ruled. However, resistance can take forms other than outright rebellion; for example, it can take the form of high productivity, individualistic tax avoidance, or even free riding. What causes resistance, I argue, is not only the recognition of exploitation but also, and more important, the ability to act. Resistance is as likely—indeed more likely—to come from those with resources as from those without.

sider noncompliance. As people break the law and get away with it, more people are likely to begin to break the law. Becker (1968), Stigler (1970), and Posner (1981) claim that government tries to find an efficient level of enforcement that suffices to deter most offenders while keeping costs down. In these models individuals use marginal utility analysis to calculate the expected net utility of committing a punishable offense. If, as Becker, Stigler, and Posner claim, effective coercion rests on a sufficient supply of deterrence to dissuade those considering lawbreaking, the coercive apparatus may be inadequate to deal with sharp shifts in noncompliance. In other words, quasi-voluntary compliance bolsters mechanisms of monitoring and enforcement. For that reason, if for no other, it is in the interest of rulers to act consistently with prevailing norms of fairness.

Quasi-voluntary compliance rests on the effectiveness of sanctions when enough constituents are already cooperating. Rulers can then focus scarce resources on those constituents most likely to be noncompliant. Most rulers calculate that the marginal cost of universal enforcement is too high. Most are willing to tolerate imperfect enforcement as long as they can ensure that there is relatively general compliance, which, I argue, requires quasi-voluntary compliance.

Quasi-voluntary compliance can work with or as an alternative to ruler-provided coercion. Those engaging in quasi-voluntary compliance are complying not out of fear of punishment; they are not being deterred in the Becker-Stigler-Posner sense. Indeed, in many instances they are choosing not to free-ride in situations where they are fairly certain of escaping detection. The decision to comply quasi-voluntarily has a normative root in that the compliant would prefer to promote the social good the tax bargain represents. But the decision also has a strong element of rational calculation. The importance of deterrence is that it persuades taxpayers that *others* are being compelled to pay their share.

Quasi-voluntary compliance is one aspect of what is generally labeled legitimacy. However, my formulation permits me to separate analytically (although not always empirically) the elements of legitimacy that rest on strategic calculations and gains from trade and those that rest solely on ideology, that is, norms and beliefs. Quasi-voluntary compliance can decline even if the ideological views of taxpayers stay constant. What changes is the bargain or the perception of the bargain rather than ideas about what a good or fair contract is.

My conceptualization of quasi-voluntary compliance is consistent with the logic of game theory and the logic of collective action. I am neither engaging in game theory here nor arguing that the game theoretic applies neatly to the complex and *n*-person situations I am investigating. Rather, I am identifying empirical versions of mechanisms that game theorists have suggested are effective for resolving problems of conflict, coordination, or cooperation. In particular, I argue that rulers try to establish or take advantage of institutions that transform problems of zero-sum conflict into matters in which individuals are best off when there is coordination or mutual cooperation.

Collective action generally has the structure of an *n*-person prisoner's dilemma (Hardin 1971, 1982). The returns from individual defection are higher than the returns from mutual cooperation. For Player X (whose choices are on the left), the payoffs in a game with Player Y (on the right) are:

$$
\begin{array}{cc}
& X\ Y \\
1. & D,C \\
2. & C,C \\
3. & D,D \\
4. & C,D
\end{array}
$$

where C = cooperation and D = defection; and where 1 is the highest and 4 the lowest payoff.

This is the collective action problem as posed by Olson (1965). It is also the Hobbesian world. In a one-play prisoner's dilemma, the dominant strategy is defection. The outcome is payoff 3. Individual rational action leads to both an individually suboptimal and a Pareto inferior outcome. Each defects, and everyone is worse off.

Tax payment to produce collective goods is, at least initially, a collective action problem. Individuals will always calculate whether they are better off complying or not complying. In many instances the dominant strategy is to avoid or evade payment even if the best social outcome is universal payment. Thus, rulers will try to alter individual calculations by changing the costs and benefits or the nature of the game.

MANIPULATING GAINS FROM TRADE AND THE NATURE OF THE COLLECTIVE GOOD

Revenue extraction represents an exchange with the rulers by those people who have some say in establishing its terms: citizens in ancient Rome, lords and nobles in medieval Europe, voters (through representative institutions) in modern democracies. Exchange requires gains from trade, and gains from trade are the prerequisites of quasi-voluntary compliance. Unless there is a material benefit, the question of compliance becomes moot. But gains from trade are not the cause of quasi-voluntary compliance. Their very existence, particularly in the form of collective goods, is what makes the free-rider problem a dilemma.

Rulers offer constituents private as well as collective goods. In some cases this may be a direct exchange, in which free riding is not an issue. The sale of offices for revenue is an example. Protection rents are another. However, there are also many instances where one group pays while another benefits. This is a common complaint about the tax systems of all the advanced industrial democracies. It was also the concern of nobles whose monarchs could not tax the church and of colonials who watched their countries drained of resources to support a luxurious lifestyle in the imperial center. When those who do pay feel exploited—that is, feel they are in an unfair contract—they are less likely to comply quasi-voluntarily. Underlying quasi-voluntary compliance are norms of fairness as well as material benefits.

The potential for free riding is obvious when rulers offer collective goods in return for taxes. The most common collective goods are protection from internal and external enemies and the administration of justice, both of which presume the institution of property rights. However, these are the minimum a state provides. Even Adam Smith admitted that "the invisible hand" might leave some important areas of social life untended. In consequence, he argued, government would have to provide military defense, the administration of justice, and certain public works and institutions that no individual would have an incentive to fund (Smith [1776] 1937, 653–768).

It is to the advantage of most rulers to offer positively valued goods as well as sanctions that taxpayers wish to avoid. Frohlich and Oppenheimer (1974, 59) conclude a highly formal analysis of taxation policy, "Even when the taxer is only interested in maximizing the profit of a tax operation, they will not specialize in either coercion or the supply of positively valued goods. They will supply some mixture of the two for each level of expenditure." Rulers will seek the "optimal mix" of threats and offers. It turns out that the kinds of positive goods provided, and the amounts provided, also affect quasi-voluntary compliance. Groves and Ledyard (1977) have demonstrated mathematically that the proper mix of collective goods reduces free riding.

Without a perceived benefit, there is absolutely no reason for a rational actor even to consider assuming the costs of taxation. War, the threat of war, depressions, wide-scale poverty, and natural disaster are among those events that demand cooperative behavior. Throughout history rulers have used or even manufactured such events as a way to raise additional revenues — although, as we shall see in chapter 5, monarchs who regularly posed war threats that came to nothing found it increasingly difficult to convince revenue-paying constituents of their veracity or need. A more common theme in contemporary politics is the promise of economic improvement through expensive and expansionary programs. The deterioration of public school systems, the increase in crime and the breakdown in services despite major social programs, and, perhaps most important, the failure of Keynesian programs to prevent recession fueled the flames of tax revolts.

The existence of positive benefits increases the probability that taxpayers will comply quasi-voluntarily, without direct coercion. However, as long as the benefits are collective goods, they are more likely to produce than to solve free-rider problems.

There are some exceptions to this rule. The nature of the collective good may affect the level of quasi-voluntary compliance. The prisoner's dilemma flows most clearly from collective goods that can be modeled with a linear production function; that is, each contribution produces more of the good. Following Schelling's (1973) typology of binary choices with externalities, Frohlich and his colleagues (1975) demonstrate that strategic individuals may develop contingent, as opposed to dominant, strategies when the collective goods have either S-shaped or step production functions. What each does depends on what others do.

Protection in a small polity often has an S-shaped function (Emerson 1983, esp. 430–33). A contribution to a little protection is a waste of the contribution. A contribution to the "right" amount of protection can make all the difference in the world. If there is "enough" protection, contribution once again makes no difference.

Lumpy goods are represented by step functions (and are often called step goods). They require a certain level of contribution before any of the good is produced — for example, before a bridge is built or a polluted lake cleaned. In these cases taxpayers calculate that they receive a greater payoff from contributing than from defecting, if they are certain that others will also contribute. There is some question about whether the prisoner's dilemma characterizes the provision of lumpy goods,[9] but lumpy goods certainly affect individual strategy. For example, Hirschman's description

[9] Hardin (1982, 55–61) thinks that it can, but he admits that the application is not simple. On the other hand, Taylor and Ward (1982) think that many lumpy goods are best represented as chicken rather than prisoner's dilemma games.

of public education (1970, 45–52) exemplifies a lumpy collective good that rests on the contributions of a critical number. Once too many exit, decline will set in. It must be noted, however, that education, the environment, and other collective goods whose quality can be improved with increased contributions are lumpy goods with sloping risers. They have a linear production function after the initial production threshold is crossed. Thus, once minimum production is achieved, they may again take on the form of the prisoner's dilemma (cf. Hardin 1982, 59).

For many taxpaying is a binary choice: to pay or not to pay. Furthermore, it is a choice with externalities, for one's decision affects the amount of collective goods that are available to others — and, even, whether the good will be provided at all. Where there is a binary choice with externalities, the decision of whether to contribute may hinge on whether the good is lumpy or continuous, whether one values the good enough to pay for it oneself individually or as part of a coalition, and how many others are contributing.

There is one sort of lumpy good that clearly provokes contributions. Indeed, it poses no free-rider problems. All contribute, and the good is provided. If some do not contribute, the good will not come into being. Such a case is Hirshleifer's (1983, 371) mythical island where floods will wipe out everyone if even one property owner — and even the smallest landowner has access to the sea — does not build an adequate dike. Such collective goods have the structure of an assurance game (Taylor and Ward 1982, 353–54). Its payoffs to Player X (left-hand column) against Player Y (right-hand column) are as follows:

$$X \ Y$$
1. C,C
2. D,C
3. D,D
4. C,D

where C = cooperation and D = defection; and where the highest payoff is to 1 and the lowest to 4.

This is a game with two equilibria and no dominant strategy. Each will cooperate with the "assurance" that others will also cooperate, and each will defect in the absence of such assurance (see discussions in Elster 1979, 20ff. and 146; Elster 1983b, 29; Sen 1967).

In the prisoner's dilemma, the highest payoff is for individual defection as long as others cooperate. In the assurance game, it is for mutual cooperation. Assurance games most clearly apply to disasters that can be prevented only with reciprocity practices. There will be no protection unless everyone contributes. Each has an effective veto over the provision of the good. Each perceives herself as making a difference, as being the "weak link" who can make or break the chain.

The socially optimal provision of the good is more likely to occur in this situation than where the situation resembles a prisoner's dilemma.[10] Because it is an assurance game, disasters provoke heroism and self-sacrifice. However, the effective veto of the "weak link" also raises the possibility of blackmail.[11] One person can hold all the others up for ransom. The only protection against possible blackmail is a situation where the marginal benefits of a ransom would be less than the marginal benefits of cooperation. Either the potential blackmailer will lose too much should the ploy fail or depends too heavily on the future cooperation of the other players.

The achievement of mutual cooperation in an assurance game situation requires perfect information. Perfect information is possible only if it "is supplied from the outside (e.g. by the rulers acting as a coordinator) or if the community is sufficiently small and stable so that everyone can really come to know everyone else" (Elster 1979, 22). Information and coordination can also affect the outcome in large-number prisoner's dilemmas (Frohlich and Oppenheimer 1970, 119). If taxpayers sufficiently value the collective goods whose provisions are made possible, they may want to consider paying rulers for their services as coordinators. Certainly, rulers tend to claim coordination as an important task that justifies a charge beyond the cost of the collective goods.

It is not always clear how assurance games are established, nor are there obvious collective goods whose creation and maintenance depend on the contribution of all, or even most, of the population in large polities. Nonetheless, this brief excursus on assurance games highlights both the important entrepreneurial role of the rulers and the contingent calculations of taxpayers. These factors, I argue, affect taxpayers' behavior even when they are not players in an assurance game.

Assuming that taxpayers seek the goods and services for which taxes are being collected, the payment of taxes often has the structure of a prisoner's dilemma, in which the payoff from defection is higher than the payoff from payment. Rulers can alter this calculation by manipulating the nature of the collective goods so that an individual's strategy becomes contingent on

[10] See Hirshleifer's (1983) discussion of the "weakest-link social composition function" as opposed to either the "best-shot" or the "summation."
[11] Philip Hoffman raised this point.

what others do. In the process, rulers may have changed the game from one of exchange (or cooperation) to one of coordination. Rulers coordinate taxpayers to assure them that others are also contributing. Rulers also coordinate sanctions. Indeed, they may need relatively few sanctions if they use them effectively, so that each individual calculates the likelihood of punishment to be high. One basis of ruler power lies in such coordination, particularly in the absence of organized protest.[12]

Even so, some taxpayers will not benefit at all, and others will always prefer to free-ride. For these people direct coercion is the sole cause of compliance. To ensure their cooperation is clearly a prisoner's dilemma problem.

Quasi-voluntary compliance affects those who desire a collective good enough to consider paying. These are the individuals who have ideological motivations for complying, that is, who believe the revenue production bargain is fair. Their cooperation is more a coordination than a prisoner's dilemma problem. With coordination rulers can increase the likelihood of compliance by those with a "taste" for compliance. The argument here is that such taxpayers will comply quasi-voluntarily only as long as they are confident that others are also contributing and only as long as they are relatively certain that the good will be provided once paid for. Thus, their quasi-voluntary compliance requires assurance not only about other taxpayers but also about the actual delivery of the perceived benefit. Before rulers can coordinate the expectations of cooperation, they must first become credible in regard to their own commitments. I shall take up this question next.

GAINING CREDIBILITY

The first task of predatory rulers in their efforts to create or maintain quasi-voluntary compliance is to provide reassurance that they will deliver the promised goods and services. Taxpayers will not voluntarily pay taxes if they expect to be duped by their rulers. Precommitment strategies are a principal means by which rulers provide this assurance, especially in large polities. Conditional cooperation can also be effective, especially in small polities or for small groups within a larger polity.

[12] In a recent paper, Hardin (forthcoming, p. 6) states, "The gunman theory might well be called the coordination theory of state power. It depends on coordination at the level of government and on lack of coordination at the level of any potential popular opposition. The state need not compel everyone at gunpoint, it need merely make it virtually in everyone's clear interest to comply with the law."

Precommitment   Precommitment is a device for ensuring that individuals will carry out decisions in the future that were agreed to at an earlier time, that they will not succumb to "weakness of will." It provides "causal machinery that will add force to your inner resolution" (Elster 1979, 37). Precommitment involves a choice by the actor to submit to rules and punishments that make it impossible to act otherwise than previously committed (Elster 1979, esp. 37–47).

Since rulers, like other individuals, will be tempted to use tax money for nonspecified, often personal, purposes, rulers precommit themselves to spend it as contracted. In modern democracies presidents and prime ministers submit budgets, to which they are then bound. The rulers have the "right to be sued" (Schelling 1960, 43; Hardin 1982, 211–13). They put themselves in a position to be sanctioned — or at least legally and publicly rebuffed — if they overstep the precommitted limits. Precommitment by the rulers can also involve abdication from power (Elster 1979, esp. 89–103). For example, Renaissance kings legally bound themselves to ask for taxes only for certain purposes. The result of these partially self-imposed restraints on their power is, in principle, an increase in the ability of rulers to collect the taxes they do impose.

A further precommitment strategy is for rulers to make themselves the residual claimants. They behave like self-policing entrepreneurs (Barzel 1983). The rulers bear the major and, often, the initial costs of providing the good or service and are the residual claimants of any surplus from the charges for its creation, maintenance, or use. Thus, rulers have a double incentive to come through on their promises. Entrepreneurs in general (Popkin 1979, 263) and rulers in particular are demonstrably likely to front the start-up costs of the construction of silos, dikes, public buildings, and other public works, as well as the costs of providing protection and administration. Alternatively, rulers can make "credible commitments" by standing to lose valuable resources if they renege, by forfeiting "hostages," either literally or figuratively.[13] The result of such strategies is an increase in ruler credibility and, presumably, an increase in quasi-voluntary compliance.

When rulers are clearly the principals, as were many traditional monarchs, they will design precommitment mechanisms that maximize their revenue in two ways. First, reassured by "credible commitments," constitu-

---

[13] See Williamson (1983; 1985, chaps. 7–8) on the use of hostages in structuring incentives in the principal-agent relationship. Williamson claims that the hostage strategy is one of many ways around the prisoner's dilemma, which, in his view, is an overrated problem.

ents are presumably more willing to pay without direct coercion, thus minimizing ruler costs. Second, rulers will ensure that they receive significant rewards for fronting the necessary revenue or coordinating the necessary effort.

Rulers are sometimes the agents of constituents, however. This is arguably the case in contemporary democracies. The agent-rulers will still engage in precommitment that reassures their principal(s) yet maximizes their benefits. For example, a prime minister will threaten to resign if he does not receive parliamentary support on cherished legislation. On the other hand, the principal(s) will be trying to design incentives that provoke the best effort by the agent-rulers on behalf of the principals. The major problem is uncertainty about the future and lack of information about the extent of the actual effort, let alone what would constitute a "best effort." Periodic elections represent one such attempt to subject rulers to reevaluations that are meant to induce high performance.

Conditional Cooperation Between Rulers and Constituents   Rulers also can achieve credibility by promoting conditional cooperation between themselves and constituents. The decision by constituents to comply quasi-voluntarily is reversible. Tax payment is an ongoing contractual relationship in which the decision to comply is continually being made and remade. Taylor ([1976] 1987), Hardin (1982), and Axelrod (1984), among others, have shown that with iteration defection may no longer be the dominant strategy. What each individual does becomes contingent on what others do.[14] Moreover, if players have sufficiently low discount rates so that they care about future payoffs, the benefits of cooperation can outweigh the costs of defection. It then becomes rational to engage in a tit-for-tat strategy. The result is the evolution of "contract by convention" (Hardin 1982, chaps. 9–12)—that is, a tacit agreement to comply—or conditional cooperation (Taylor [1976] 1987, *passim*), in which one individual's compliance is conditional on the compliance of others.

Both contract by convention and conditional cooperation depend on the acquisition of information, although not necessarily perfect information, about the other players and on sanctions imposed by players on each other. A capacity to monitor is crucial (Hechter 1987). Repeat transactions provide such sanctions and information and enhance monitoring. These transactions can occur in the reciprocal relations of a community (Taylor 1982, esp. 25–38 and 91–94), the overlapping memberships of a larger polity (Hardin 1982, esp. chap. 11), or repeat market transactions.

---

[14] This was Frohlich and Oppenheimer's point in their 1970 critique of Olson.

Conditional cooperation presumes sanctions that are neither centrally coordinated nor centrally provided. Within a group of people who share some common beliefs and norms and have multifaceted and reciprocal relationships, each person will cooperate only as long as others do. Conditional cooperation depends on the establishment of institutions in which the players not only engage in repeat transactions but actually perceive that they are engaging in repeat transactions with other actors. For conditional cooperation to be viable, each actor must have confidence that the others are indeed cooperating.

These factors enhance "common knowledge" (Schofield 1985) about the past behavior and preferences of the relevant actors and permit intelligent guesses about future behavior. A monarch with a reputation for reneging will have a harder time getting nobles to pay taxes quasi-voluntarily than will a monarch with a reputation for keeping bargains.

Some historical parliaments were institutions that made conditional cooperation viable (see chapter 5). Parliamentary procedures tend to reveal both rulers' and members' preferences, and they can provide a forum for repeat transactions. Parliaments have evolved in all constitutional democracies as institutions that help keep rulers to their bargains. They also are important in ensuring that all the constituents who have agreed to comply (or are bound by the agreement to comply) actually come through. Members of parliament must continually meet each other again. In the Renaissance they depended on each other for defense and "good" (read profitable) marriages. In modern times they depend on each other for support of legislation, especially pork barreling and logrolling.

Conditional cooperation requires public discussion and public actions from time to time. The contributor then acquires and reacquires knowledge of both the current terms of the contract and the behavior of others. Parliaments fill this role neatly.[15]

However, not all parliaments—historically or contemporaneously—promote conditional cooperation. Military dictators and other rulers who monopolize most of the significant bargaining resources can bend parliaments to their wills. The consequence may be compliance, but it is hardly voluntary. It rests straightforwardly on coercion. On the other hand, the establishment of institutions that link potential contributors rather than keep them atomized can pose dangers to a ruler. The other side of compliance is defection, individual and collective. Should rulers break their

---

[15] My analysis of the development of institutions within the state bears some similarities to Keohane's (1984) analysis of international institutions and regimes.

pacts, they face already organized resistance. Parliaments are both bulwarks for legitimacy and hotbeds of rebellion, a seemingly contradictory but nonetheless logical conclusion.

ENHANCING EXPECTATIONS OF COOPERATION

Quasi-voluntary compliance requires taxpayer confidence that other taxpayers will keep their side of the bargain with the rulers, that is, pay their taxes. I have already argued that conditional cooperation among parliamentary members provides one device for promoting and monitoring the compliance of others. Rulers can also enhance the expectation of taxpayer compliance through the use of selective incentives, the promotion of conditional cooperation through communal responsibility for taxes, and more general coordination.

Selective Incentives   The most straightforward way for rulers to provide assurances that others are paying is to get them to pay. The Olsonian solutions to noncompliance are, of course, side payments, other selective inducements, and coercion.

Side payments in the case of taxes generally go to already privileged groups. The relationship between mobile assets and bargaining power (Bates and Lien 1985) has already been noted. Contemporary corporations may threaten to leave one state for another if their taxes are not kept low. A monarch might offer a position in the court in exchange for tax compliance. Merchants and industrialists engage in rent-seeking behavior that wins them protective tariffs. These and other examples suggest that side payments are most effective for appeasing those with significant bargaining resources—especially those constituents from whom it is better to get some tax than no tax. Relative bargaining power can determine the kinds of tax reductions, cutbacks, extra services, or other concessions a constituent receives. It is difficult to imagine cases where rulers use positive inducements to obtain quasi-voluntary compliance with tax payment among ordinary citizens.

The fear of coercion obviously increases compliance. Auditing and other monitoring devices that increase the probability of being caught make the threat of sanctions more effective. However, if coercion is straightforwardly the reason people pay their taxes, then they are simply complying. Quasi-voluntary compliance is not at issue.

Conditional Cooperation Among Constituents   Historically, rulers have promoted communal institutions as a means of administering a polity indirectly and with low cost. This in effect creates conditional cooperation among the members of the community, who then produce social order or enforce a policy among themselves.

A modern example that has little to do with revenue production but everything to do with promoting conformity, encouraging self-sacrifice, and enforcing discipline is the institution of the Committees for the Defense of the Revolution (CDRs) in Cuba.[16] Developed during the Bay of Pigs, the CDRs were organized as local military units. Each neighborhood had its own CDR, and everyone in the neighborhood belonged. By 1974 the members of the CDRs were supervising each other's behavior; that is, they saw to it that everyone kept to the rationing and other rules. The CDRs also were organizations for discussing any proposed new laws. This feature enabled people to voice objections, which would then be carried through the organizational network to the center. It also ensured that everyone understood the provisions of the laws and could monitor each other's behavior. Compliance became quasi-voluntary in that state coercion and monitoring were seldom needed.

Relatively small units have similarly benefited historical revenue collection. The gens, tribes, and centuries, connected by family and ethnic ties, were responsible for the collection of certain revenues in the Roman Republic (see chapter 4). The manor was the locus of revenue production during the medieval period. Root (1987) provides an account of the resurrection and use of communal institutions to collect taxes for the king in *ancien régime* France. Such arrangements lower the transaction costs of measurement and monitoring by creating or maintaining small groups. If the groups are small enough and their members have overlapping activities, they may promote conditional cooperation.

The state can use such groups to its advantage. Olson's federal solution is one in which the central government provides sufficient incentives to its constituent units so that they mobilize the individuals in the smaller group to contribute to the provision of collective goods (Olson 1965, 62–63). In other instances the state, an encompassing organization, may "piggyback" its aims on extant and more narrowly focused organizations (see Hardin 1982, 43–44).

In the cases cited, the constituents monitor and enforce policies among

---

[16] This discussion of the CDRs, organizations built around where people live, is based on my own observations in Cuba in 1974. Taylor (1982, 125–26) discusses moral incentives, a similar policy in Cuba.

themselves. They control each other, not the rulers. The use of a hierarchical federation of gens, villages, or even states and provinces as a device for overcoming the collective action problems of revenue production evolved in response to complex problems of monitoring and control in relatively primitive technological and political economic conditions. As central governments develop sophisticated techniques that enable them to control and monitor individuals more easily, the device of federation is superseded.[17] Decentralization occurs frequently enough, but few decentralized units qualify in size as small groups where there is regular face-to-face interaction and a strong sense of mutual interdependence. Where decentralization is established as a means to reduce free riding, my argument implies that alternative forms of control and monitoring are too costly.

Nonetheless, rulers can use one of the principles that underlies conditional cooperation — namely, the necessity of a low discount rate — to their advantage. The discount rate will vary with the kinds of collective goods taxes are meant to pay for. War encourages people to exploit resources in the present; otherwise, there will be no future about which to be concerned. Education encourages long-term planning among people with children or among employers who benefit from the skills an education imparts. National parks are not everyone's idea of recreation but are priority for protection by those people who highly value the preservation of a natural environment as their playground. Despite all the differences among people and among goods, it is possible to imagine, nonetheless, that many taxpayers will have a low discount rate relative to at least some bundle of goods their taxes are meant to cover.

This suggests that rulers who want to promote quasi-voluntary compliance should offer collective goods that take time to provide and that their constituents are likely to continue to value over time. Rulers who rely on wars as the primary means to gain consent to taxation often find themselves in serious fiscal difficulties once the war is over. Urban development, industrial planning, and competition to produce superior weaponry are more likely (but hardly certain) to promote continuing quasi-voluntary compliance.

Coordination and Loyalty   Another means available to rulers for promoting quasi-voluntary compliance is to coordinate the populace by providing information and assurances that others are in fact cooperating. Most

---

[17] I thank Russell Hardin for this observation.

important, rulers must coordinate sanctions in such a way that the potentially compliant are convinced the sanctions can and will be directed at others.[18] Even when people prefer to pay, they still require assurances that others also are paying. Otherwise, they will feel like "dupes" and "suckers" who must reconsider their own willingness to contribute. Thus, rulers invest in deterrence that constituents perceive as directed toward others.

In addition, rulers spread the knowledge that noncompliant individuals are being punished. Specifically, they publicize accounts of high levels of compliance and quash publicity about outbreaks of evasion and avoidance. They also make speedy, effective, and, again, public reprisals against tax rebellions and resistance.

Part of the purpose of ruler coordination is to promote loyalty to the regime. By clarifying their role in producing and promoting contributions to valued collective goods, rulers enhance their own value to the taxpayers. Rulers are most successful at such self-promotion when there is uncertainty that enough people will contribute to make provision of the collective good viable. When there is certainty, the rulers receive little credit for achievement. Only in conditions of uncertainty will their role receive the kind of appreciation that promotes loyalty and what Emerson (1983, 433–37) labels "authority-validating coalitions." The "function of loyalty," as Hirschman (1970, chap. 7) points out, is to maintain a level of compliance and contribution when noncompliance becomes most attractive — that is, in the face of competition, deteriorating collective goods, or exit by others.[19] Loyalty, as defined here, contributes to quasi-voluntary compliance and results from the coordinated and contingent contributions of taxpayers to valued goods. It is a strategic decision based on the calculation of costs and benefits.

CONCLUSION

Unless they are coerced, induced, or otherwise motivated to pay, constituents will minimize their tax payments or, should the circumstances permit, try to get out of paying them altogether. My claim here is that some of the variation in compliance is accounted for by the extent to which, given a belief that they are benefiting from the tax contract, taxpayers are assured that both other taxpayers and the rulers will live up to the contract. If the

[18] This is one of Emerson's (1983) important insights in his discussion of state formation in Baltistan.

[19] Frohlich and Oppenheimer (1974, 53–56 and 60) offer an interesting formal analysis of the "loyalty function."

terms of the contract shift without the consent of the taxpayers or if taxpayers can negotiate a better bargain, noncompliance should increase. If there begins to be evidence that rulers are not delivering promised goods and services or that others are not paying their share, defection should increase.

The argument is often made that rulers or government can reduce the transaction costs of enforcing a contract by an "ideology" in which people are duped into believing that it is in their interest to comply; by concerted "socialization" of people into feeling a responsibility to comply; or by "legitimization" of a policy, so that it appears to be offering what people expect is their due. The terms *ideology, socialization,* and *legitimization* have come to mean almost as many things as the people writing about them, but the definitions usually include a strong dose of what Marxists call "false consciousness" or what rational choice theorists might label irrational behavior. It is uncontestable that people sometimes act contrary to their own interests, but my claim is that people generally understand their situation.[20] They either have no choice, or there are incentives to comply. One of the incentives may be ideological, that is, a taste for compliance with a fair contract. However, without assurances that the contract is indeed fair, compliance will decline.

By conceptualizing quasi-voluntary compliance as a rational act responsive to certain specified factors, I have attempted to clarify what part of variation in compliance is due to quasi-voluntary compliance, as opposed to coercion and norms. Strictly normative compliance occurs in the absence of either coercion or assurances of fairness. It is nonstrategic voluntary compliance. It is neither coerced nor quasi-voluntary. Quasi-voluntary compliance, on the other hand, combines strategic interactions and norms.

Quasi-voluntary compliance is a way to reconceptualize legitimacy. If legitimacy means generalized consent to rules of conformity enforced by rulers on the polity, the concept of quasi-voluntary compliance is, I believe, a first step in developing a more precise model of how consent is manufactured and achieved.

Quasi-voluntary compliance rests on norms but is backed by material incentives and by coercion.[21] The material inducements with which I am concerned include but are wider than financial rewards, standard of living,

---

[20] Several sociologists have made similar arguments although they have reached their conclusions by quite different methods than mine (see, esp., Moore 1978; Abercombie, Hill, and Turner 1980).

[21] I concur with Stinchcombe (1968, 160) that "A legitimate right or authority is backed by a nesting of reserve sources of power set up in such a fashion that the power can always overcome opposition." However, I think this definition is too narrow.

and working conditions, the kinds of incentives Przeworski (1985a, chap. 4) discusses in his elaboration of consent in advanced capitalism. They include the sanctions, incentives, and reciprocity practices that produce social order and conditional cooperation without central state- or ruler-imposed coercion (see, for example, Taylor 1982). Laiten's description (1985) of the resurrection of tribes and tribal authorities by the English colonial authorities is a nice case in point.

There are, of course, other definitions that share with this one a primarily material, as opposed to normative, basis. One of the most common, derived from Weber, is that what is legitimate is what it is legal for rulers to do. Legitimacy then becomes a resource of rulers.[22] The focus tends to be on what attributes rulers possess and manipulate rather than on how the rulers find or manufacture the appropriate means to achieve consent.

To minimize the costs of enforcement and to maximize the output that can be taxed, rulers have to create quasi-voluntary compliance. Quasi-voluntary compliance rests on reciprocity. It is a contingent strategy in which individual taxpayers are more likely to cooperate if they have reasonable expectations that both the rulers and other taxpayers will also cooperate. The key lies in what rulers and other government officials do to create mutual expectations of tax payment. They might establish institutions that promote conditional cooperation or contract by convention. They might emphasize collective goods that have the structure of assurance games or that have S-shaped supply functions. They certainly have to provide coordination, whose costs they may use to justify even more taxes. Moreover, increased dependence by constituents on coordination by rulers tends to enhance the power resources of rulers. The empirical chapters of this book (chapters 4–7) investigate some of these possibilities.

The achievement of significant quasi-voluntary compliance within a population is always tenuous, however. Individuals will be less likely to continue to comply quasi-voluntarily if they suspect that others are not complying. If multiple defection makes it unlikely that the valued collective good will actually be provided, the benefit of compliance is even further reduced. On the other hand, the continued provision of the collective good, despite considerable noncompliance, would make contributors wonder

[22] Ilchman and Uphoff (1971, 73–89) discuss legitimacy in relation to taxation and, as I do, note that it requires an exchange between the taxer and taxed. However, they then proceed to argue that legitimacy is a resource of statesmen derived from their authority and political prestige. Przeworski (1985a, 141) argues, "Legitimacy thus refers here not to any states of mind . . . but merely to the correspondence between the uses of force and the rules which specify when it can and should be used." Although this formulation makes legitimacy a resource of the rulers, their major concern is consent formation.

why they are the ones bearing the burden. In either scenario, free riding, once begun, is likely to increase. Once quasi-voluntary compliance has declined, it is extremely difficult to reconstitute. Its reestablishment often requires an extraordinary event—such as war, revolution, or depression— that makes people willing to negotiate a new bargain.

Consequently, rulers or governments must try to keep benefits derived from defection low and the advantages of compliance high. A failure to make clear the gains from trade, a change in tax law that encourages (or at least does not adequately discourage) individual defection, or publication of the extent to which free riding is taking place will all have the effect of increasing noncompliance.

The cost to the rulers of occasional defections lies less in the loss of revenue than in the possibility of massive free riding. Therefore, Axelrod argues, government will overinvest in deterrence and punishment in order to secure its reputation for toughness (1984, 155). But does this action constitute "overinvestment" if the alternative is massive noncompliance?

There is one other aspect to the creation of compliance, a social consequence that should not be overlooked. Even in the Hobbesian formulation, rational, self-interested actors prefer cooperation. Hobbes advocated imposition of a strong state to enable people to achieve the peaceful and cooperative social order they actually wanted. The prisoner's dilemma is the war of all against all. However, once peace or, in this case, the benefits of mutual cooperation are secured through precommitment, conditional cooperation, and coordination, people will be able to operate according to the golden rule—but only as long as they believe that others are doing the same.

CHAPTER IV

Revenue Production in Republican Rome

The motives that had restrained dreams of personal glory
(and enrichment) and of the aggrandizement of the Roman
People in accordance with the censor's ritual prayer, had
largely been social and political ones. They had gradually
ceased to operate. . . . After Sulla, men could seek power and
profit without fear of really firm opposition.

> Ernst Badian
> *Roman Imperialism in the Late Republic*

The story of taxation during late Republican Rome exemplifies the institutional responses of a simple state to an increasingly complex political and economic environment. Territorial expansion and growing specialization and division of labor led to realignments in the traditional distribution of power. Experiments with new techniques of taxation occurred within a context of intense rivalries for rule and new economic and political resources. The costs of achieving compliance increased with the transformation of the institutions of governance and with the imposition of taxes on non-Roman peoples. This was a period of transition in both the economy and the government. The constraints on rule were transformed.

This chapter has two goals. The first is to demonstrate that changes in relative bargaining power, transaction costs, and discount rates have determinant effects on the choice of the form of taxation. The second is to demonstrate that changes in the constraints on rulers[1] will determine how likely they are to use revenues to promote the general welfare or to advance personal ends.

The case study focuses on the rise and demise of tax farming and on the variation in opportunism (or what Pareto labels spoliation) by tax farmers and rulers. Tax farmers purchase contracts to collect revenue in a given area

---

[1] Although Roman historians generally contend that the concept of ruler is meaningless for the late Republic, particularly with the rise of the Gracchi, there were few years that could be designated as lacking in rulers by my definition.

and time period. The government receives the funds in advance of their actual collection. The tax farmers, if they have calculated correctly, also benefit, for they recoup their investments and make a profit on what they are legally entitled to collect — and often on what they can get away with collecting beyond that. They are profit maximizers engaged in a business proposition and will not seek contracts if they are not reasonably certain of gain from them. Usually, tax-farming contracts are given out through auctions. Rome began to use tax farming in the third century B.C. Augustus started abolishing tax farming fairly early in his reign.

The Roman Senate, before 133 B.C., was an institution with considerable bargaining power relative to that of groups with an interest in profiting from taxes. The theory of predatory rule suggests that rulers will choose the form of revenue production that has the lowest transaction costs relative to the alternatives, *ceteris paribus*. The alternative to tax farming was a state bureaucracy. Therefore, it follows from the model that:

> *The choice of tax farming was a consequence either of Rome's inability to construct an elaborated state bureaucracy or of the calculation that tax farming was more efficient than a state bureaucracy in securing revenue.*

After the rise of the Gracchi in 133 B.C., effective rule passed from the Senate to powerful consuls and tribunes. According to the theory, rulers will sometimes tolerate high transaction costs, or at least will not minimize transaction costs, if a change in policy would alienate powerful actors on whom they depend or if it would threaten their continued hold on power. In other words, rulers sometimes make a trade-off between relative bargaining power and transaction costs. As the empire grew, so did the transaction costs of creating quasi-voluntary compliance and monitoring tax farmers in distant territories. Thus, one would expect to observe that:

> *An increase in the dependency of rulers on tax farmers for political and economic resources would lead to the maintenance of tax farming even when it no longer minimized transaction costs.*

In the post-Gracchi years, particularly after Sulla left office in 79 B.C., rule became increasingly unrestrained and increasingly unstable. Most of the institutions and arrangements that had kept rulers in check eroded. Rivalries intensified, and there was even civil war. Rule increasingly devolved on a single individual, whose tenure depended on continual military victory. This produced a high discount rate — which, the theory suggests, will compel rulers to emphasize short-term returns over long-range benefits. One would expect those defending their rule to become more willing to sacrifice quasi-voluntary compliance for immediate revenue. Rulers would still maximize revenue to the state, but they would pocket more of the funds to finance their campaigns. Therefore, one should observe that:

> *An increase in opportunism by both rulers and tax farmers would correlate with a decrease in the security of rule and a decline in institutional constraints.*

The material presented in this chapter provides evidence that these expectations are fulfilled. Moreover, by using the theory of predatory rule to analyze the historical record, one can arbitrate among some conflicting claims within the literature on Roman taxation.

Some scholars argue that tax farming developed in the Republic as a means of extracting revenue by a government lacking an elaborated civil service or bureaucracy (see, for example, Badian 1972; Fowler 1916, 72; Hill 1952, 52 and *passim;* Weber [1924] 1976, 61). Ernst Badian (1972, 15) argues that "the early Roman Republic did not regard economic operations as, in principle, in its sphere at all—even though, for reasons that nobody bothered to expound in theoretical form, some were traditionally exercised." The state delegated to the publicans, private entrepreneurs who handled the public property of Rome, the supply of public works, provisions to the army, and collection of certain revenues. The implication is that a state providing so few collective goods had no need of a bureaucracy.

A. H. M. Jones (1974, 151–85) takes a different position. He begins with two significant observations. First, throughout ancient history and within the same economies, some taxes were the responsibility of private entrepreneurs, particularly tax farmers, and others were the responsibility of government agents. Second, tax farming was not a substitute for a complex government organization. The Greeks, Egyptians, and Romans were capable of devising complex censuses and assessments for one tax while using tax farming for another. From these observations Jones concludes that the choice of a tax system is determined by the uncertainty of return plus the costs of supervising both tax collectors and taxpayers. Where the return is predictable and where deviations from the required payments can be detected relatively easily and cheaply, the state uses its own agents. Otherwise, it resorts to contracts with tax farmers. For both Jones and Weber ([1922] 1968, 965; [1924] 1976, 62), tax farming provides a ruler with secure and predictable revenue, so that the ruler is able to "budget."

Tenney Frank (1927, 186) raises a different set of theoretical issues. He points out innumerable inefficiencies in the revenue production system — particularly during the heyday of Republican tax farming — and argues that democratic governments, where there are numerous and diverse claimants and beneficiaries, tend to be more inefficient than despotic governments, where the kingdoms are perceived as the private possessions of the ruler. Weber also contrasts the ancient monarchies with the more democratic city-states. He claims that capitalist practices, among which Roman historians count tax farming, are more regulated in monarchies ([1924] 1976, 64–65).[2]

Weber's major argument, however, is that the amount of profiteering by tax farmers will vary widely "depending upon the distribution of power between the lord and the farmer, the latter's interest in the full exploitation of the paying capacity of the subjects or the lord's interest in the conservation of this capacity may predominate" ([1922] 1968, 965–66). One of the major findings of this chapter is that Weber has underspecified this relationship. He is correct as long as "political lords" are concerned with future returns. When they are not, they too may engage in "full exploitation" even if their power vis-à-vis the tax farmers is great.

Before proceeding to a more detailed evaluation of these arguments, I first present a short economic history of Republican Rome to illuminate the changes in structural factors that affected the constraints on policymaking.

A SHORT ECONOMIC HISTORY OF REPUBLICAN ROME

Rome is often designated as one of the paradigmatic cases of the ancient mode of production (Marx and Engels [1848] 1978, 471–79; Engels [1884] 1973, 118–27, 140–43; Weber [1924] 1976; Anderson 1974, 18–28, 53–103). The fact that it was basically agricultural and used slaves (although to varying degrees and in various ways) throughout its history disguises its diversity regionally and over time.

During the early Republic, from 509 B.C. until the middle of the third century B.C., Rome was still a city-state with increasing control over the villages of Latium. Subsistence agriculture was the dominant economic activity; markets were relatively insignificant. Land was either privately owned, leased from aristocratic landlords, or leased from the government (Rome owned lands throughout Italy, the *ager publicus*). Most landholdings were small and worked by peasants as owners, tenants, or sharecroppers. The fertile land around Rome supported its peasantry. Indeed, there seems to have been some underemployment of labor (Hopkins 1978, 19–25).

Disparities in wealth appear to have had less import than disparities in

---

[2] However, he concludes that this "monarchical regulation, though beneficial to the great mass of subjects, spelt in fact the end of capitalist development and everything dependent on it" ([1924] 1976, 65).

power and political privileges based in family background (Brunt 1971, 42–59; Loewenstein 1973, 21–39). Originally, only patricians could be considered for the Senate, but the long struggle by the plebeians for political parity finally achieved success around 286 B.C. What developed after was a timocratic and gentilian organization of politics. Eventually, richer and more industrious plebs from the equestrian order—those entitled to membership in the cavalry—gained access to the Senate.

By the end of the third century B.C., the economic organization of Rome began to change drastically (see, esp., Frank 1927, chaps. 4 and 6; Rostovtzeff 1960, chap. 8; Toutain 1930, Part 3, chap. 4; Hopkins 1978, chap. 1). Small peasant holdings gave way to large latifundia, dedicated to sheep and cattle herding, olive groves, and vineyards, activities that required more capital and less labor than grain production.

The city of Rome became a market for the products of the latifundia owners, whom the state provided with grain (Hopkins 1978, 74). Rome grew, attracting immigrants from the provinces as well as displaced peasants and freed slaves. The city of Rome became the major market of the growing empire. It was a huge urban agglomeration, "one of the largest preindustrial cities ever created by man," with a population of approximately one million by the end of the first century B.C. (Hopkins 1978, 2). It was not the only city, however. The town was the administrative unit throughout the territory under Roman control.

The transformation from small-scale subsistence agriculture to market-oriented latifundia was one consequence of Roman empire building. The first campaign to conquer Italy (280–275 B.C.) and the First Punic War against Carthage (264–241 B.C.) marked the beginning of more than two centuries of military campaigns, both for defense and expansion. Military obligations in conditions of constant warfare made it harder for peasants to maintain their farms. Conquest brought in slaves, opened up large new tracts of land and trade routes, and often provided the state with revenues from booty sufficient to finance many of its campaigns as well as aid the landless citizen (see, esp., Hopkins 1978, chap. 1).

Rome increasingly depended upon its provinces, particularly Sicily and Africa, for its grain, usually acquired through taxes. Despite its many victories, Rome had only six provinces in 146 B.C. The number grew to ten by 88 B.C. and fourteen by 62 B.C. (Stevenson 1932, esp. 438–43).[3]

---

[3] There is a scholarly consensus that the Roman nobles sought *dignitas* (honor) through military service and that Rome was organized as a military society, but there is considerable debate about Rome's imperialist intentions. The evidence points to long senatorial resistance to expansion. The opponents of expansion were concerned about the effect of empire on Rome's internal structure and about the costs and headaches of administering territory.

After 133 B.C. the citizen population became increasingly dependent on the government and especially the army for its bread. The ruling oligarchy, based on landed wealth, faced a landless proletariat, a growing slave population, and rising discontent. In the first part of the first century B.C., Marius began to create a paid, volunteer army, which provided employment and prospects for some of the dispossessed. Payment for military service was land in Italy and, after Julius Caesar, in the provinces.

Class divisions became far more extreme. The rich became richer as they profited from the exploitation of the provinces and the growing market for their agricultural products. The rich were expected to contribute disproportionately to military campaigns and religious festivals, and the acquisition of high office was an increasingly expensive undertaking. Nonetheless, the distance between rich and poor continued to grow.

Throughout most of the history of the Republic, the locus of policymaking remained the Senate. However, the definition of property rights required laws, which had to be passed by one of several important assemblies with both legislative and judicial functions.[4] The centuriate assembly declared war, confirmed the power of the censors, and elected consuls and praetors. The tribal assembly was responsible for all other legislation and for the election of lower magistrates. The plebeians within the tribal assembly, the *concilium plebis,* elected tribunes. After the passage of the Lex Hortensia (287 B.C.), most legislation was in fact proposed by the tribunes and passed by the tribal assembly of plebeians (Taylor 1966, 6).

Executive power constitutionally resided in a series of elected magistrates. The highest ranking of these magistrates were two consuls, who served jointly for one-year terms. The sharing of office, the short terms, the required waiting period before eligibility for reelection to the same office — all served to reduce executive power and enhance the power of the Senate, whose members enjoyed lifelong tenure.

Citizenship was transmitted from parents or from ex-masters to freedmen. It was restricted to males who lived within the territory of the city of Rome and its citizen colonies, which were relatively fewer in number and size than other colonies. Moreover, not all citizens were equal, either de facto or de jure.[5]

From the time of the Gracchi in 133 B.C. until the founding of the

[4] My discussion of the assemblies is drawn from Taylor (1966). See, especially, the chart following p. 4.

[5] Taylor notes (1966, 59), "The essential difference in voting between the assemblies of tribes and centuries was that in the former all citizens within each tribe had a vote of equal value, while in the centuries the upper income groups within the tribe voted separately and had a favored vote."

Principate in 27 B.C., powerful consuls and tribunes began to wrest the cloak of rule away from the Senate, which continued to play an important but not necessarily decisive role in policymaking. The economic situation of the landless citizens and their migration to the city of Rome created citizen mobs, able to vote but just as liable to riot.

After Sulla's reforms (82–79 B.C.), the Senate could no longer be said to rule. Strong military leaders emerged, but their hold on power was tenuous at best. They could maintain power only as long as they won military campaigns that provided the troops with the bread and land that bought their loyalty and only as long as they could control internal conflicts and rivals. Conditions in Rome during this period often approached social anarchy.

In sum, Republican Rome went through three distinct periods: (1) the early Republic, characterized by subsistence agriculture, the political dominance of the patricians, and relative peace; (2) the pre-Gracchan late Republic, characterized by the emergence of latifundia,[6] a ruling oligarchy within a politically powerful citizenry, continual external warfare, and senatorial rule; (3) the post-Gracchan late Republic, characterized by the entrenchment of latifundia and the growing importance of trade and markets, strong magistrates and a politicized army, both internal and external turmoil side by side with considerable territorial expansion, and the erosion and ultimate destruction of senatorial rule. Earlier I argued that these major changes in structural conditions should lead to significant changes in the relative bargaining power, transaction costs, and discount rates of rulers, with predictable consequences for tax policy. I shall now turn to an exploration of the propositions laid out at the beginning of this chapter.

EVOLUTION OF TAX FARMING:
A TRANSACTION COST PROBLEM

Tax farming is as much a banking as a taxing system.[7] Tax farmers give rulers a loan secured by the revenues they then are authorized to collect from taxpayers. Tax farmers possess sufficient capital and organization to enable them to advance funds and to collect taxes. What tax farming provides, particularly if the contracts are allotted through auction, is the greatest possible loan for the price. Rulers avoid having to build alternative

6 As Richard Saller has pointed out to me, land was certainly concentrated in the hands of the wealthy, but few had a latifundium at this point. They tended to own scattered and modest-sized farms.

7 Vincent Ostrom pointed this out to me. I later discovered that Weber ([1924] 1976, 61–62) makes the same point.

tax-gathering apparatus, and they do not have to engage in direct monitoring of agents.

THE PREREQUISITE: AVAILABLE CAPITAL

Tax farming is possible only where a group of individuals possess sufficient funds so that they can front revenue to rulers and cover the costs of collecting the taxes that will repay them. The prerequisite of tax farming is capital, and better-off Roman citizens possessed the kind of wealth that made capitalist enterprise possible. Even so, the capital requirements of public contracts were too high, particularly toward the end of the Republic, for individuals. Consequently, they had to create rather complex associations, *societates*, composed of several investors in a kind of partnership (Badian 1972, 67–81).

The *publicani* (or publicans) — that is, the leaders of the large companies that took on the major tax-farming contracts — were drawn from the order of *equites*, second in status only to the senatorial order.[8] Badian (1972, 103–104) believes that senators were not shareholders in the companies until the 70s (B.C.). He argues that the Sullan reforms of the Senate, "flooding it with a majority from a non-senatorial background, had done much to obliterate the difference between the orders, helping to eradicate the stigma that attached to non-landed wealth" (1972, 99). The economic interests of the senators led them to invest in the publican companies, especially as the costs of higher office increased and the profits from tax-farming contracts grew. The newly elevated *equites* were not eager to give up their source of wealth. Although Rome was a highly stratified and oligarchical society, wealth increasingly could help a newcomer penetrate its highest ranks.

In sum, there existed in Republican Rome, at least in its last two centuries, sufficient capital to support a tax-farming system.

However, capital is a prerequisite, not a cause, of tax farming. Capital and capitalist organization exist today in far greater magnitude than in Republican Rome, but tax farming appears to be a technique of the past.

COSTS OF MEASUREMENT, MONITORING, AND AGENCY

Three factors in Republican Rome affected the transaction costs of revenue production. The first, the absence of a market and therefore of a

[8] For the history and analysis of the equestrian order as such, see, especially, Nicolet (1966).

money or exchange economy to facilitate determination of the value of the item to be taxed, affected measurement costs. The second, physical inaccessibility due to poor transport, poor communication, and generally dangerous traveling conditions, affected both measurement and monitoring costs. The third, uncertainty about the likely return from a tax, sometimes because of social instability and warfare, sometimes because of lack of a technology to predict yield, affected the choice of agency. Uncertainty motivated rulers to secure a guaranteed return.

The early Republic solved its measurement problems with the census, an institution designed to assess the property — and moral worth — of each citizen in order to assign him his place in the military and political hierarchy.[9] Property was defined as land, real estate, and movable assets. The census was a complicated and thorough procedure carried out every five years by two senior magistrates. It initially depended on the physical presence of the citizens to provide oral testimony and to attend the ceremonies at the conclusion.[10]

The census definition provided the basis for the tribute, a direct tax levied as a given percentage of net worth and used for military expenses. The censors were responsible for supervising the assessments. They had to find means both to equate property, a problem of measurement, and to ensure that people told the truth about what they owned, a problem of monitoring. The relative homogeneity of land and the relative simplicity of life in the early Republic made the first task easier than it would become later. Monitoring also turns out to have been relatively straightforward. First, the population of the city itself was small enough to survey easily. Second, it was organized into gens, tribes, and centuries, in which certain members were made responsible for overseeing compliance (and punishable if they failed to do so). Third, there were few incentives for hiding property; indeed, there were greater incentives for exaggerating its worth. The tribute was small and essentially a loan. Since it was a fixed percentage, it hurt the rich less than the poor. However, it did not hurt the rich all that much financially, and a high property assessment brought the right to seek high military and civil offices. The more property, the greater the possibility of honor.

The tribute was probably not collected by the censors but either by the tribes, cities, quaestors, or, what now seems most likely, the *tribuni aerarii,* a

---

[9] Loewenstein (1973, 63–69) and Hill (1952, 32–38) but especially Nicolet (1980, chap. 2) provide lengthy descriptions of the census.
[10] After citizenship was extended to the allies, the requirement of physical presence was waived.

small number of people within the tribe assigned the task by virtue of their place in the hierarchy. It was neither a voluntary nor a paid position. They forwarded what was owed to the state out of their own pockets and then collected from the members of their tribes who had to pay. They were the precursors of the publicans in both function and status. Nicolet (1976, 46–55) argues rather persuasively that what distinguishes these men from tax farmers is that both they and the state knew ahead of time precisely what would be collected.[11]

By 167 B.C. Rome had abolished the *tributum* with the understanding that it could be reimposed. However, citizens were not exempt from all taxation. There was a whole series of *vectigalia,* indirect taxes that included dues and fees on customs, tolls, concessions, and monopolies. There was also a tax on the manumission of slaves. Moreover, the exemption from the tribute applied only to *ager Romanus* and later (89 B.C.) to the soil of all Italy but not to properties held by citizens elsewhere (Nicolet 1976, esp. 19–26; Brunt 1971, 39; Frank 1927, chap. 11; 1933, *passim;* Hill 1952; Badian 1972; Jones 1970, 118–19).

By the middle of the second century B.C., the acquisition of additional provinces, particularly Macedonia, encouraged the Senate to determine how best to administer its territory. The physical inaccessibility of these provinces, the fact that they continued to be battlegrounds for years after their annexation, and the status of the inhabitants as provincials rather than citizens militated against the use of the expensive and complicated census. Outside of the Roman *polis* and its small internal communities, the costs of agency were too high. How could one create the proper incentives and disincentives for truthful reporting when social standing was no longer so clearly tied to income or, for that matter, so valued? How could the person assigned to collect the tribute guarantee the specified amount or be assured that he would receive it back from those from whom he had to extract it? The census did not even exist in the allied states from which Rome collected taxes. After all, its raison d'être was to assign citizenship rank by timocratic criteria, not to assess taxes. Its basis was quasi-voluntary compliance, not coercion. Without quasi-voluntary compliance, the agency costs of the census rose significantly,[12] especially in contrast to the alternatives of plunder or delegated collection, often through tax farming.

---

[11] Nicolet (1976, 50–51) claims, "Il n'y avait donc pas de jeu possible entre son estimation et sa réalité. Or, c'est l'existence d'un tel jeu qui est à la base de tout système de perception fondé sur la ferme, c'est lui qui permet la spéculation des publicans."

[12] Augustus reintroduced the census, but it was transformed into a tool of the central government for surveying the resources of the empire and providing "the basis for fair taxation" (Scullard 1976, 269).

Booty, taken by the troops under the direction of their general, was a major source of income for the state from 200 B.C. to 157 B.C. and a major means for supplying its troops (Frank 1933, 126–41). However, the maintenance of social order in the new territories required the creation of quasi-voluntary compliance. Plunder as a means of revenue extraction was replaced by more orderly and acceptable tax collection procedures.

For most of the revenues extracted from allies and provincials, Rome initially adopted the administrative practices already available and developed in the provinces. It thereby reduced transaction costs by eliminating the costs of searching for and negotiating alternatives. It also facilitated retention of quasi-voluntary compliance created on behalf of the policies of defeated rulers.

The idea of tax farming arrived when Rome acquired Sicily, the first "foreign" province — that is, the first province outside the Italian peninsula. Rome did not interfere with the democratic constitutions of Sicilian cities (Scramuza 1937, 231, 236). It adopted the Hieronic tax system, which it later adapted for use in other provinces:

> According to Hiero's system the officials of each city-state drew up a yearly list of all who actually raised a crop under their jurisdiction, whether owners or renters, taking account of three things: first, the extent of the property involved; second, the area of each crop under cultivation; third, the amount of seed planted. These records were then inspected by the prospective contractors (*decumani*). This information, together with a study of the weather, the quality of the soil, and the competence of each cultivator, made a safe basis for their bids. The collection of the tithes was put at auction before the governor. Having secured the contract, the successful bidder made the round of this district to obtain a contract from each farmer as to the amount each ought to contribute. This agreement was made in triplicate and signed by both parties. One copy remained with the contractor, another with the farmer, and the third was transmitted to the city officials for the protection of both parties. If no agreement was reached, the amount due was settled at the threshing floor. The *decumanus* who took more than was lawful could be sued in the governor's circuit court and, if found guilty, was bound to an eightfold restitution. A cultivator who delivered less than his due was sentenced by a similar process of law to four times the original amount. An official of the city-state involved carried out the governor's decision.
>
> (Scramuza 1937, 237–38)

What is most interesting about this system is how complex it was and how constrained the tax farmers were. Tax farming was also highly regulated in Egypt under the Ptolemies (Ardant 1971, 85–101; Weber [1922] 1968, 966).

The argument that tax farming developed in the Republic as a means of extracting revenues by a government lacking an elaborated bureaucracy begs the central issue. Sicily's Hieronic taxes could have been collected by state agents rather than agents of private companies. Indeed, it is clear from Scramuza's account that state agents existed and did much of the paper-work involved in tax farming. Adequate state machinery to collect certain taxes existed side by side with tax farming.

The only distinction between the initial Hieronic form of tax farming and state-run tax collection was the advance of revenues prior to tax collection. This was a significant advantage in a period that predates government budgeting. Tax farming had several other advantages over the use of state officials. First, it was a system of agency with guarantees and monitoring devices already built in. The efficacy of both the Hieronic officials who supervised the *decumani* and the Roman censors rested on the fact that they represented a small group of people operating under the close scrutiny of their principals. Second, their official performance had conse-quences for future rank. Thus, their self-interest tended to overlap with the promotion of the rulers' interests. Third, the use of local officials for tax collection in faraway and very different places required no new or heavy investment in learning about local conditions.

One final factor determining the choice of tax farming is that it already existed. A large bureaucracy did not, and the idea of a salaried civil service was still centuries away. Bureaucracy was in the process of evolving, but it was not yet an obvious solution to the problem of administering a large and diverse territory. Nor could it evolve until there was stability of rule. Its construction was a long-term project whose benefits would emerge only over time.

Initially, all publicans were provincials. Reliance on Roman publicans followed the expansion of the empire. Their use reduced the transaction costs of administering more numerous, distant, and foreign provinces. Frank (1927, 136) writes:

> The collection of Asiatic tithes by contract, though like all work done by public contracts it led to much corruption, brought in a larger and more dependable revenue than could have been procured through the agency of local authorities, usually unfriendly, and too far distant to watch. Naturally a well organized civil service bureau, such as the empire finally provided, would have been much more considerate of the taxpayer. . . . To Caius Gracchus the introduction of the contract was a step towards efficiency.

The Roman publicans acted as middlemen between the Senate and the provincial tax farmers or, what was more common in the East, the cities.

The Senate and the censors wrote up complicated contracts with the publicans and attempted to protect the provincials by a series of laws passed at the end of the second century B.C. (these arrangements will be discussed later).

The use of Roman publicans ensured the government of a specified amount of revenue. The increasing reliance on Roman as opposed to local publicans may even have been a means of monitoring local tax collection in conditions where municipalities were most likely and able to resist making their contracted payments, for in at least some provinces the publicans did no more than supervise authorities.

Keith Hopkins (1980) argues that the imposition of money taxes on the provinces increased the volume of trade in the Roman Empire from 200 B.C. to A.D. 400 and forced those who had to pay in money to engage in occupations that earned money. If Hopkins is correct, measurement costs should have been reduced, at least at the ports and for the evaluation of property. But, even if measurement costs for some taxes were lowered, monitoring costs remained high. For example, the sales tax, a very efficient form of revenue production in modern times, was still difficult given the dispersion of markets and the problems of surveillance (Ardant 1971, 69–70). The population itself was dispersed, outside the reach of the census (which, anyway, became more and more erratic during the last years of the Republic) and of the small civil administration of Rome.

The provincials were often quite hostile to Rome and its taxes. They had greater reason to shirk the obligations imposed on them than citizens, who had seen their fiscal obligations as a duty to family and state — and who, by and by, were enriched by general compliance. Only among citizens was widespread quasi-voluntary compliance possible, and only among citizens could ideology reinforce the behavioral dicta of self-interest.

Further factors contributing to high costs of measurement and monitoring were uncertainty and risk — or, more specifically, (1) uncontrollable and unknown variables affecting trade and agricultural production, most notably, piracy and weather; and (2) the lack of social stability resulting from wars and rebellions. On products affected by the first and in locations affected by the second, it is hypothesized that the government of the Roman Republic probably would choose a revenue production system that required others to take the risk and yet ensured the government a return.

Indeed, the publicans tended to get contracts for revenues whose collection involved uncertainty and risk. Harbor dues, tolls, and customs were fairly easy to measure and monitor, given their central locations and the growth of a money economy and market for ship cargo, but their yield was uncertain. Presumably, they were introduced as soon as there was enough trade to warrant a taxing system; the first mention of such revenues occurs in 199 B.C., during the early years of Roman expansion. Not until almost the end of the Republic, when Rome gained command of the Mediterranean and Pompey cleared the seas of pirates, was sea trade, the major form of trade, relatively safe. Even then bad weather and poor harvests made the amount of trade and custom unpredictable.

The publicans also won contracts for mines and for the salt and oil monopolies. Yields from all three sources were unpredictable because of a lack of technical knowledge about productivity. However, a flourishing market in both minerals and oil, which were relative luxury goods, may have somewhat countered the effects of poor knowledge.

Collection of the tithe also traditionally belonged to the publicans. The tithe was a function of the harvest, an unknown quantity almost everywhere.[13] The *scriptura,* or grazing taxes, one of the major sources of revenue on the lands belonging to Rome (including those inhabited by citizens), were also probably collected by the publicans (Frank 1933, 150; Hill 1952, 52–53).

In most provinces the state required security of return in the form of contracts from municipalities, local tax farmers, or Roman publicans. As the anticipated revenues became larger, only the Roman publicans had capital sufficient to purchase the contracts. The problems of collecting taxes during the last century of the Republic in these embattled and occasionally rebellious regions gave rulers a further incentive to seek a guaranteed return. Social unrest also raised the capital costs and risks of undertaking collection. Again the Roman publicans were the only ones with enough capital to afford such risk.

In sum, there is evidence that high measurement, monitoring, and agency costs led the Roman Senate to search for alternatives to the use of communal institutions or a bureaucracy in revenue collection. The fact that reliance on Roman publicans increased with the acquisition of provinces suggests the causal importance of measurement costs and the need of the state to budget. Yet tax farming was not the sole means of accurately predicting revenues. The *tributum* also was collected in advance. Tax farming represented an improvement only when the territory and population to be taxed grew in size and heterogeneity.

[13] Egypt, with its relative homogeneity of soil and predictability of weather and irrigation, was a partial exception. Perhaps more important, Egypt became the grain basin for Rome; its administration could not be left to the increasingly powerful publicans. When Augustus annexed it as a province, he seems to have made it the personal property of the emperor. Consequently, it was never farmed out (Wallace [1938] 1969).

High transaction costs, due to physical inaccessibility and to uncertainty and risk, contributed to the choice of tax farming, as Jones (1974) has claimed. However, uncertainty and risk due to weather and lack of technical knowledge persisted into the Principate, suggesting that these factors do not by themselves account for the choice of tax farming. The decreased reliance by the Principate on tax farming demonstrates that preferable alternatives exist, especially if the aim is to win the allegiance of the taxed population. Roman officials increasingly found themselves confronting the serious danger of tax farming—namely, that a tax farmer "will not have the same long-run interest in preservation of the subjects' ability to pay as the political lord" (Weber [1922] 1968, 965). Reports of murdered agents of the Roman publicans and of tax rebellions are evidence that tax farming became very unpopular among the taxed. Yet it continued to be maintained.

MAINTENANCE OF TAX FARMING: PUBLICAN BARGAINING POWER

The relative bargaining power of any group of actors rests on at least two crucial variables: (1) their ability to organize sufficiently to exert pressure and (2) the dependence on them of the individuals or groups at whom they are directing their demands. The first is a collective action problem. The second reflects a combination of the resources and discount rates of rulers. Interest groups will have the most influence when they possess resources that rulers need and when rulers' discount rates are high. This was exactly the situation of the publicans—that is, the leaders of the large companies— as the Roman Republic transformed itself into the Roman Empire.

The Roman publicans were drawn from the order of *equites*. Scholars contend that the equestrian order was heterogenous. They also claim that an oligarchy of wealth composed of both the senators and the richest *equites* emerged in the late Republic (see Nicolet 1966; Shatzman 1975). Although the *equites* did not form a united pressure group, over time the *publicani* did achieve this status (Brunt 1962, 118; Badian 1972, 96–98). They all came from the same tiny stratum and were intertwined by family connections. Such social similarity and interaction must have aided their ability to act collectively.

The capital requirements of tax farming not only excluded certain persons from the occupation but also led to the creation of the *societates*. Each investor depended on the cooperation of the others; the withdrawal of one meant that no one would make the desired profit (each person's private incentive) out of the hoped-for contract (the collective good). The fierce competition that seems to have existed among the companies until about 170 B.C. (Badian 1972, 35–44) limited joint organizational activity, but these arrangements ultimately facilitated collective action in the political sphere. As capital requirements increased, the companies got bigger, fewer, and more oligopolistic.

The publicans became a distinct group within a diverse social order and even within the ruling oligarchy. They had a clear goal: control of all lucrative revenue collection. They also were able to exert considerable influence within the order of *equites* and, thus, within the polity as a whole, for elections were weighted on behalf of those with the most property and those who were resident in Rome.

Initially, however, the publicans had relatively little bargaining power. In regard to Sicily, for example, the Senate resisted pressure from the Roman corporations when it let the tithe to local publicans (Scramuza 1937, 237–40). Roman publicans were also initially excluded from the contracts for the lucrative Spanish silver mines (see, esp., Richardson 1976, 139–44; also see Frank 1933, 154–55).

When publicans were offered the right to bid for tax-farming contracts, it was for contracts with the strict regulations of the kind imposed by Hiero. Unable to change the rules, the publicans indicated little interest. By 184 B.C. Cato and his co-censor "sold the collection of the public revenues at the highest prices, the contracts for goods and services (*ultro tributa*) at the lowest" (Badian 1972, 35). The first type of contract required the publicans to pay the government; the second required the government to pay the publicans. Cato obtained these prices by linking the two kinds of contracts, making acquisition of building and maintenance contracts contingent on revenue contracts. Tax farming was not yet profitable, but competition for *ultro tributa* was keen enough to enable his pricing mechanism to prevail.

That the publicans had begun to achieve some power by this time is evidenced by their ability to persuade the Senate to compel the censors to let new contracts—which, the publicans hoped, might be more favorable to them. The Senate did agree to new contracts, but censorial immunity permitted Cato to keep the winners of the first round of bidding out of the second round. Cato's ploy failed, however. The publican companies lacked the political power to prevent the linking of the contracts, but they possessed the oligopolistic power necessary to lower the price of all contracts in the second auction (Badian 1972, 35–37).

The increasing organizational capacity of the publicans was not sufficient to win them what they wanted until the rulers – that is, the Senate and later the policymaking magistrates – depended on them sufficiently to concede contracts in return for other valued resources. The publicans became increasingly important in funding the constant warfare and in building the administrative apparatus of the emergent empire. Dependence on the publicans increased further with the changes in constitutional arrangements that followed the tribunates of the Gracchi. These changes led potential rulers to seek the publicans as allies in their constant power struggles as well as to seek the resources they had to offer.

The publicans initially gained recognition with the war against Hannibal. Their first major contract was for military supplies in 215 B.C. Even so, the companies of publicans were not yet very important (Frank 1933, 102; Badian 1972, chaps. 1–3). The reliance on them by the Senate began to grow at about the time of the censorship of Cato in 184 B.C. When the tribute was discontinued in 167 B.C., fiscal pressures created even more dependence on tax farming. Provincial tithes became an increasingly important source of revenue, and, as has been discussed, the contracts for their collection ultimately were given to the Roman publicans, who could provide the substantial capital required for administering the tithes.

The pressures on rulers intensified further during the last century of the Republic, when power began to rest with powerful magistrates who had but a tenuous hold on their positions. They maintained their power only through appeals to the mass citizenry and to one or another of the factions of the oligarchy. Ultimately, maintenance of power required delivery of grain to the urban proletariat and of pay and land to the veterans. The booty of war was an important source of both land and wealth, but initial financing was essential for warfare. Thus, all rulers increasingly became dependent on the wealthy publicans and their already existing companies expressly designed to extract revenue from the provinces.

C. Gracchus, tribune from 123 to 121 B.C., was one of the first and most spectacular of such rulers to court the publicans. In return for their backing, he granted them the Asian tithes as well as control of the extortion courts.[14] They accepted his offer but turned on him in the end. Sulla (82–79 B.C.) proscribed approximately 1,600 *equites*. At the same time, he put 300 into the expanded Senate and gave the publicans the Sicilian tithes they had sought for well over a century. In 67–62 B.C. Pompey extended the number of provinces open to the publicans, but Julius Caesar reduced them again only a few years later. During the last hundred years of the Republic,

---

[14] Gruen (1968) offers the best discussion of the role of the courts in politics.

the bargaining power of the publicans fluctuated with their usefulness to the rulers. Nonetheless, these turned out to be the years of their greatest activity and profits, in part because every ruler ultimately needed their votes, capital, and organizational resources.[15]

It is obvious that tenuous rule and short-term fiscal pressure, brought on by war, contributed to the growing power of the publicans. Under such conditions rulers had neither the time nor the means to devise alternative or more economically efficient revenue production schemes that would have increased the return to the state. Their high discount rates stimulated an already growing dependence on the Roman publicans. Consequently, the publicans won better and larger contracts, particularly during the last years of the Republic. Tax farming became a form of rent seeking, in which otherwise productive resources were used to win contracts and in which services were produced according to political rather than economic criteria.

INCREASE IN VENALITY

The maintenance of tax farming may have contributed to social inefficiency, but did it necessarily have to lead to corruption?

When the Senate was the undisputed ruler of Rome, the role of the publicans was small—largely because there were few administrative pressures until the expansion of the Empire but also because of the nature of the Senate itself. First, the Senate made decisions in a relatively small community with which its members had repeat and overlapping transactions. It was not particularly susceptible to outside lobbying. Second, the Senate was organized in a way that promoted conditional cooperation, which, the theory of predatory rule suggests, will help ensure that revenues are actually used for the specified ends. Finally, during this period the opportunities for profit making were small and the ideology of honor, *dignitas,* was emphasized.

Even as publican power increased and senatorial rule declined, Hieronic-inspired regulations on tax farming could have prevented corruption. However, the rulers had no interest in restraining tax farmers. The creation of empire, the destruction of the small Roman community, constitutional changes, and social disorder led to a breakdown of constraints on senators and even more so on the rulers who succeeded them. Moreover,

[15] For the best descriptions of these tumultuous years, see Badian (1972, chaps. 3, 5), Gruen (1974), and Hill (1952, chaps. 4–5).

tumult and rivalry raised their discount rates. They worried less about what was most productive over time and more about how to survive in office (or at all) another year. To the extent that they profited from tax farming, they were unlikely to control its excesses.

It was the search for *dignitas* that underlay the militarism that catalyzed the expansion of territory and the change in personal incentives and disincentives:

> Military success and the holding of office: these are the chief claims to *virtus*. Within the aristocracy, as we all know, Roman politics, especially in the second century B.C., was a constant struggle for prestige (*dignitas*), pursued with single-minded ambition. It was a highly competitive society. But this prestige, as we have seen from contemporary evidence, found its chief support in the holding of office and in military success. This requisite glory had to be gathered somewhere. And since in the second century major wars, and wars against civilized states, were (as we have found) on the whole against public policy, it had to be gathered on the barbarian frontier.
>
> (Badian 1967, 13–14)

The militarism of the senatorial order led to an emphasis on individual success, often at the sacrifice of the collective good. The end effect was personal ambition and greed. By the first century B.C., the Roman ideal of public service had pretty much disintegrated. Sulla, Pompey, and Julius Caesar became rich during their ascendancy, largely through the rewards of conquest. However, they were also large shareholders in the publican companies and thus benefited from illegal tax profits in the provinces (Badian 1972, chap. 5).

The Senate had ultimate reponsibility for ensuring that tax farming was carried on according to regulation. This task became more and more difficult as the publicans gained relative bargaining power and, consequently, access to new provinces or provinces previously denied them. The opportunities for profiteering increased. The resources of the Senate were insufficient for the amount of monitoring required, particularly in later years, when both the incentives for monitoring decreased and the incentives for collusive venality by senators and governors increased. Equestrian control of the extortion courts after the tribunate of C. Gracchus made it even harder to restrain the publicans.

As late as 129 B.C., an adverse decision against the publicans in their dispute with the city of Pergamum indicates that the Senate was still capable of supervising the tax farmers (Badian 1972, 59–61). By 104 B.C. instances of abuses by publicans became more common and the ability to control them more difficult, although still possible. The Roman publicans began to engage in illegal slaving in allied states outside the borders of the provinces in which they had contracts. Badian (1972, 89) claims that the publicans still felt themselves constrained almost twenty years after C. Gracchus. They preferred "to act beyond the frontiers in order to act unobserved; when found out, they had to submit to prompt control on the part of a Senate not in the least afraid of their reaction."

Only a few years later, the publicans could act with relative impunity. In 92 B.C. the extortion court convicted P. Rutulius, whose only crime had been to restrain extortion by the publicans in Asia! The publicans did exercise some internal control but primarily when the corrupt practices of one of their own interfered with company profits. For example, in 54 B.C. they engineered the exile of a provincial governor, A. Gabinius, who had used the system to line his own pocket. Certainly, little of what he collected reached the publicans, but it is also unclear how much reached the Treasury (Badian 1972, 109).

One possible reason for the breakdown in the monitoring and enforcement of compliance to the *pactiones* (contracts between taxpayers and tax farmers) was that huge profits could be made from the provinces.[16] I have already discussed the fiscal pressures on the rulers of the late Republic— once they became rulers. Military success and the acquisition of office also required funds. Governors and senators began to seek money as a means to or substitute for *dignitas*. The wealth was there to be taken, and they were in the most advantageous positions for acquiring the bulk of it.

By the time Pompey attained his consulship of 70 B.C., the ability of the publicans to make illegal profits rested on collaboration with provincial governors and senators, who also profited—sometimes to the actual detriment of the publicans themselves. The case of Verres in 70 B.C. is the most famous example because of its documentation by Cicero. Verres imposed extra charges on both publicans and taxpayers, and he took a large cut of publican profits in return for failing to prosecute them for extortion. Other governors were just as extortionate. Indeed, many seem to have taken the post because they expected to make the fortunes that would help them achieve even higher office.[17]

The senators also increasingly colluded in and profited from the excesses of the publicans. Pompey's annexations in themselves created vast new capital demands on the publicans, while intense competition raised the price for the lucrative new revenue collection contracts. As a rule, senators

[16] See Broughton (1938, chap. 2, "The exploitation of Asia Minor") for one example.
[17] For discussion and documentation of this period, see Hill (1952, chap. 5) and Badian (1972, chap. 5).

possessed more individual capital than members of the order of *equites*. By 61 B.C. it is likely that the senators were often the dominant, if hidden, shareholders in the companies. They influenced policy and grew rich off the profits. Not surprisingly, they neither prevented the formation of cartels among the companies nor actively enforced the *pactiones* in the provinces. The division between state business and private business had totally broken down (Badian 1972, 98–118).

Weber's opposition of the political lord's interest in protecting the tax-paying capacity of the subject and the tax farmer's interest in exploiting the subject to the fullest seldom existed in the last years of the Republic. Both lord and farmer tended to seek as much as they could get. Publican venality was restrained only as long as provincial governors monitored the *pactiones* between tax farmers and taxpayers (Badian 1972, 79–80) and only as long as the Senate was willing and able to monitor the governors. With empire, particularly with the significant increase in annexations after 100 B.C., the difficulties of administration and the temptation of huge profits made surveillance of the publicans more difficult and, at the same time, less desirable. The most intense activity of the publicans as tax farmers correlated with the period of their greatest venality.[18] Certainly, the state as an institution and the taxpayers lost revenue — as evidenced by the increase in the Treasury and the reduction in taxes after Julius Caesar's abolition of tax farming in Asia (Badian 1972, 116). However, rulers and agents gained considerable personal income.

The deterioration in the power of and constraints on the Senate led to a divergence of the interests of rulers from those of the state in late Republican Rome. A corresponding breakdown in restraints on the tax farmers followed. The publicans, rulers, and other government officials all benefited financially.

Profit making certainly encouraged the breakdown in restraints, but profit making on this scale had long been a possibility, as the lobbying of the publicans for provincial contracts attests. An equally important impetus was social disorder and civil war. The various rivals for power were less concerned with promoting quasi-voluntary compliance among the provincial populations or ensuring long-term returns than with acquiring adequate resources to win the battles that would enable them to become recognized rulers. To the extent that they sought cooperation, it was among their armies. Such cooperation was best achieved through payment of

---

[18] An interesting question at this point is whether the magistrates, senators, and governors or the publicans profited more. The data are not sufficient to tell.

salaries during service and of land on retirement. The contenders for rule were constantly embattled. They had little concern with building stable sources of revenue. They took what they could get when they could get it. Only Julius Caesar acted differently, but it was only Julius Caesar who achieved some semblance of stable rule and thus sought quasi-voluntary compliance as a way to reduce the costs of governance. Not surprisingly, then, it was he who discontinued tax farming in Asia and elsewhere, and it was Augustus who, in the process of stabilizing and legitimizing rule, significantly reduced the role of tax farming.

CONCLUSION

From the founding of the Republic in 509 B.C. until the demise of the Empire (variously dated from the late fifth century A.D. through the early seventh), Rome experienced several major shifts in its revenue production system. Indirect taxes, imposts, fines, and other charges were relatively constant, in kind if not in amount, throughout most of this period; but the form of direct taxation changed significantly. The Republic imposed a tribute on citizens, which it sometimes repaid after wars; it also relied on booty and provincial tithes. A specified stratum dealt with the first, the military with the second, and the provincial cities with the third. However, after 167 B.C. the citizen tribute virtually disappeared, and the Republic increasingly relied on provincial tithes, taxes on trade, revenue from the mines, and tribute from the provinces. Tax farming became the principal means of collection. Initially, tax farmers were regulated. By the end of the Republic, both principals and agents were pocketing an unauthorized share of the tax revenues. The Principate reduced tax farming, built a bureaucracy, and instituted a whole series of new taxes on trade and sales as well as an inheritance and a head tax. The land tax was the principal source of revenue, but the rates tended to be fixed rather than the proportional levies of the Republic. During the course of the Dominate, founded by Diocletian toward the end of the third century, feudal dues and prebendal forms of tax collection increasingly became the norm.

To understand the evolution in Roman tax collection, one must begin by analyzing the conditions that promoted the use of tax farming and the factors that caused variation in opportunism by agents and rulers.

The first finding of the chapter is that tax farming minimized transaction costs relative to the available alternatives. Increases in measurement and monitoring costs and in risks associated with extracting revenue from conquered subjects necessitated changes in the form of agency that existed prior to Roman expansion. This finding is consistent with the arguments of Jones (1974).

The second finding is that the growing relative bargaining power of the Roman publicans vis-à-vis that of the Senate and other key Roman officials is the key to explaining the maintenance of tax farming. Transaction costs are crucial to understanding the introduction of tax farming. However, the costs and risks of tax collection that made tax farming an attractive form of agency were also significant in the Principate when tax farming began to disappear. Moreover, tax farming in the late Republic was so unpopular in the provinces as to be the raison d'être of rebellion and resistance to the regime. Arguably, tax farming raised transaction costs in this period as much as, if not more than, it lowered them.

The third finding of the chapter is that variation in the opportunism of agents can be caused, as Weber ([1922] 1968, 965) claimed, by tax farmers holding the balance of power in their relationship with "political lords." The dependence of the Roman rulers was a crucial reason for both the persistence of tax farming and the failure to monitor the tax farmers on behalf of the taxpayers.

The fourth finding is that when rulers do not have an interest in maintaining the long-term revenue-producing capacity of taxpayers, they, too, will engage in opportunism unless sufficient institutional restraints exist to prevent them. This finding modifies Weber's argument ([1922] 1968, 965–66), which seems to rest on the assumption that "political lords" always have a low discount rate. Roman rulers of this period, in fact, had very short time horizons. Military generals confronted by numerous rivals were concerned primarily with winning the battle the next day, with defending their rule against continual onslaughts. They needed funds immediately and at the lowest short-term cost of extraction. Because these rulers began to make personal profits off the tax-farming system, they would not even try to build an alternative revenue collection procedure. Until Augustus established stable rule, future returns had no meaning in comparison to present value. Ensuring a better tax yield over time and promoting quasi-voluntary compliance are part of a ruler's calculus only when rule is stable.

The discount rate is only part of the story, however. Another key to variation in opportunism is precisely what Weber implies it is: the nature of control mechanisms. However, the controls on the rulers are just as important as the controls on the agents. When those break down, both the rulers and the tax farmers engage in plunder and corruption.

Although socially inefficient, the tax farming of the last years of the

Republic was efficient for rulers and agents devoted to lining their own pockets. This conclusion seems to make hash of Frank's (1927, 186) observation that despotism is more socially efficient than democracy. The policies of Augustus's immediate predecessors and successors were not socially efficient, although they, too, were despots—even if some of these rulers were, in fact, sanctioned by voters. For approximately 450 years, Republican Rome, a democratic government by Frank's standards, had a revenue collection system that achieved its ends at what seems to have been the lowest marginal cost. At the heart of social efficiency seems to be quasi-voluntary compliance, which both the pre-Empire Republic and Augustus were able to achieve.

Does this conclusion suggest that a model based on a predatory ruler is wrong? On the contrary, the case of Roman tax farming illustrates that rulers maximize but within constraints. As those constraints change, so do their tax policies and degree of opportunism. Constitutional factors and relative peace made the transaction costs, bargaining power, and discount rate of the senators such that they did not seek even to expand the state coffers, let alone seek personal gain. When these constraints broke down, as they most certainly did in the last years of the Republic, rulers maximized their own immediate revenues—to the detriment of both the state and the people.

CHAPTER V

France and England in the Middle Ages and the Renaissance

In a sense, the history of taxation is the history of the slow
construction of actual states, of their efforts to disengage
themselves from the mechanisms of dependency and bondage
of the feudal regime. It is the history of rulers overcoming the
obstacles in their path, of the resistance they face to their
ambitions.

Gabriel Ardant
Histoire de l'Impôt

The kings do not wish and cannot afford to provoke excessive
opposition; the social power of the royal function is clearly
not yet strong enough for this. On the other hand, they need
for their function and self-assertion, above all to finance the
constant struggles with rivals, continual and gradually
increasing sums of money that they can only obtain by such
aides. Their measures change. Under the pressure of this
situation the royal representatives grope for one solution after
another; they shift the main burden now onto this urban or
other class, now that. But in all this twisting and turning the
social power of the monarchy is constantly growing, and with
this growth, each furthering the other, taxes gradually take
on a new character.

Norbert Elias
Power and Civility

In this chapter I explore changes in lay taxation by French and English
monarchs from the Middle Ages to the early modern era. In tracing
taxation over this period, I am able to perceive the processes that underlay
the evolution of the modern state. By comparing decisions made in two

countries, I am able to illuminate the causes of variation in state policies. I focus specifically on lay taxation, although I recognize that rulers had available a variety of other revenue sources.[1]

The theory of predatory rule suggests that increases in the bargaining power of rulers will lead to increases in taxes, *ceteris paribus*. Thus, given the growth in the power of the monarchy between 1200 and 1700, it is consistent with the theory to discover that Renaissance and early modern rulers succeeded in instituting a greater range of taxes and at higher rates than their medieval predecessors. However, this is hardly a new finding or one that requires the model of predatory rule to perceive. Where my model does illuminate the historical record is in understanding the role of war in promoting the development of national tax systems from the Middle Ages to the Renaissance and in explaining the subsequent divergence in French and English tax policy.

A national tax system could not have been instituted without the consent of powerful constituents. According to the theory, a ruler can secure compliance by manipulating the gains from trade or the nature of the collective good. In the Middle Ages, there was no concept of a common good provided by the monarch. The common good had to be constructed and the relevant constituents convinced that they gained from its provision and maintenance. As argued in chapter 3, persuasion of the populace is best accomplished with a collective good that is lumpy or S-shaped. War and national defense were the public goods that rulers used to justify taxation. Thus, one would expect to observe that:

> *Changes in the format of war making occurred that increased its costs. These changes should correlate with an increase in the ability of rulers to convince constituents that their contributions were necessary to the provision of defense. Subsequently, tax levies should correlate with incidences of war.*

The theory also suggests that divergences in tax policy over time and between countries are caused by significant variations in the bargaining power of constituents vis-à-vis the ruler. This leads to the following expectations:

> *Given the relatively greater bargaining power of French than English monarchs in relation to nobles, French monarchs would be able to impose a greater range of lay taxes than English monarchs.*

[1] For example, I am not addressing the use of dynastic marriage, an important form of revenue production. I am also neglecting taxation of the church, which was very important in France throughout this period. However, a discussion of taxes on the church is a research project in itself. Moreover, it is closely tied to the Reformation and other exogenous factors that I do not wish to introduce at this point in the text.

The greater reliance on taxes on movables in England should correlate with a greater dependency by English monarchs on a relatively few powerful constituents, which in turn should make the English monarchs more likely than the French to acquiesce to constituent demands for representation in taxing decisions.[2]

However, information about what taxes can be imposed and at what rate reveals little about what taxes can actually be collected and at what costs. The theory suggests that, because transaction costs affect net revenue, variation in transaction costs between countries will account for significant differences in tax policies. One should therefore expect that:

Given the considerably larger size of France in a period of poor communications and expensive travel, the costs of negotiating tax policies would be greater in France. Thus, there should be more regional variation in the French than in the English tax system. Also, France should have greater agency costs, unless there is evidence of economies of scale.

More centralized bargaining should correlate with lower transaction costs of negotiation in England relative to the costs borne by French monarchs.

This chapter addresses one final implication of the theory: The creation of quasi-voluntary compliance significantly lowers the transaction costs of enforcement and, thus, raises the net revenue. The centuries discussed here are periods of experimentation and learning. Rulers try out different taxes and different forms of agency. They search for more efficient means of negotiating and enforcing the taxes they wish to impose. They experiment with justifications for taxation and with representative assemblies as forums for negotiation. Thus, the following proposition derives from the theory:

The development of a strong central representative institution, Parliament, in England and the absence of such an institution in France facilitated quasi-voluntary compliance in England relative to France and, thus, increased the proportion of net revenue to the state.

If this is the case, and I shall demonstrate that it is, then the theory produces an interesting finding and paradox: The relatively weaker bargaining position of English monarchs vis-à-vis their constituents led to concessions that French monarchs did not have to make. However, the Parliament that evolved ultimately enhanced the ability of English monarchs to tax. Parliament provided a forum for conditional cooperation. It engendered quasi-voluntary compliance and reduced transaction costs.

---

[2] This last hypothesis is drawn from Bates and Lien (1985) but is also derivable (and in part was derived) from my model.

The monarchs of France may have been "stronger," but their real taxation power was more constrained.

FORMATION OF THE MODERN STATE IN FRANCE AND ENGLAND

By the thirteenth and fourteenth centuries, the nobles, bourgeoisie, clergy, and peasants increasingly turned to the central state for protection and resources. The efficient size of political units had grown enormously, and monarchs began to enhance the power and revenues of rule. Although controversy exists over the causes of this transformation, demographic pressures, expansion of markets, and new military technology were among the important causal variables.[3]

The state played a crucial role in unifying the polity and in redefining and enforcing property rights more appropriate to the new economic realities. The modern state emerged side by side with the modern economy. Thus, it is not surprising that this period, often labeled as the transition from feudalism[4] to capitalism, has received extensive attention.

Those who follow the classic position of Marx and Engels treat rulers as either instruments of or pliable allies of a particular class. Anderson (1974), among others (Hechter and Brustein 1980), argues that the early modern states were created by the threatened nobility rather than as tools of the bourgeoisie, the more traditional Marxist claim; but the state is still conceived as an institution to be captured rather than as an independent actor. The hypothesis that rulers acted in their own interests — although within constraints — is only just beginning to receive attention again (see, for example, Elias [1939] 1982; North 1981; Ekelund and Tollison 1981; Quinlan and Fisk 1982; Kiser 1986–87).

Despite some differences of detail (which will become crucial to this analysis), the emerging modern states of both France and England faced "common political, economic, and social forces" that provoked similar

---

[3] Among the various explanations offered are the importance of population growth and other demographic changes (North and Thomas 1973); of technological, particularly military, change (Bean 1973; North 1981, 135–42); and of the international state system (Modelski 1986; Zolberg 1980). Wallerstein (1974) and Anderson (1974) also make important contributions to this debate, but they are more concerned with the rise of capitalism than with the evolution of the state. Also see the "Brenner debate" concerning the importance of agrarian class structure relative to demographic factors in accounting for the differences in economic development among Western European nation-states (Aston and Philpin, 1985).

[4] After reading Brown's (1974) informative and compelling denunciation of the term, I am eschewing references to feudalism.

institutional responses (Lyon and Verhulst 1967, 81). The defining characteristics of the new state forms were the integration of territory under a single ruler, the centralization of coercion, laicization of power, and the elaboration of administration (Guenée 1981; Strayer 1971). William the Conqueror had achieved centralization of power in eleventh-century Britain (Snooks and MacDonald 1986), but he was the exception. A more modern state did not really begin to emerge until the thirteenth century. Economic growth produced surpluses to be captured both from peasant production and from trade. At the same time, the revolution in military technology made war more costly just as competition for territorial control increased. Warfare accompanied the centralization of power and the new benefits of office. Monarchs fought each other over territory, rivals struggled to win the crown, and rebellions against the centralizing state were relatively common.

Constituents became more dependent on rulers as victory required larger armies and new weaponry, as the expansion of markets created demand for protection of both internal and foreign trade, and as social disorder in the countryside required improvements in the administration of justice. Monarchs became the purveyors of privilege and employment as well as the founts of justice and punishment. For each of these services, they attempted to extract payment. The taxpayers granted them revenues but usually at the cost of concessions that often carried long-term consequences.

In nearly all the emerging modern states, the creation of national taxation systems followed these other changes. It involved a fundamental redefinition of the role of the monarch in society. During the medieval period, a monarch was expected to "live of his own" (*vivre du sien*). That is, funds for the monarch were to come from royal lands and customary dues. In both France and England, revenues were derived from personal domains, from profits of the administration of justice (Miller 1981), and from clerical tenths, often negotiated with the pope. Taxes on Jews, dowries secured from royal brides, dynastic marriages, and loans, especially from Italian bankers, produced additional revenue. Should monarchs need more, even if it was to fund a campaign on behalf of the country as a whole, they had to obtain assent to some form of "extraordinary" taxation. They could neither expropriate property at will nor rely on a regular levy (see, for example, Hariss 1975, 16–17, 47–48; Wolfe 1972, 9–10).

By the Renaissance taxes had broadened from "extraordinary" payments to finance wars to regular payments to fund security, peace, and justice through a system of courts, religious unity, and eventually social and economic policies (Stone 1947; Elton 1975, 45–46; MacCaffrey 1981, chap. 17; Wolfe 1972, esp. chap. 3). Nonetheless, the nature of government remained private in the sense that it belonged to and was paid for by the crown rather than the people (Hirst 1986, 28–29).

If my model is correct, as long as constituents were convinced that in return for their contributions they were getting the collective goods they sought (that is, rulers were keeping their side of the bargain), and that others were making comparable contributions, then a monarch's revenue production policies could also produce quasi-voluntary compliance. Moreover, as long as rulers provided the collective good and asked only the contracted payment in return, they could make themselves residual claimants and apply additional revenue collected toward their own ends.

GROWTH OF TAXATION IN FRANCE AND ENGLAND, 1200–1700

Between the thirteenth and sixteenth centuries, the administrative structures and financial apparatuses of the French and English states underwent major changes as strong, centralized states emerged. It is not my purpose here to determine the ultimate causes of the evolution of a more modern state. Rather in this section I aim to trace the broad outlines of the interrelationship of the changing social contract between ruler and ruled, war and the development of national taxation. In the next section I explore the reasons for the distinctiveness of the tax systems that subsequently arose in the two countries.

CHANGES IN THE SOCIAL CONTRACT

To create a fiscal system adequate to the new pressures confronting monarchy required regular taxation and, therefore, a new conception of royal power. Changes began in the twelfth century and were solidified and intensified in the fifteenth and sixteenth. According to Strayer (1971, 254–63), the major break with the medieval past occurred as early as the end of the eleventh century and the beginning of the twelfth. However, it was in the thirteenth century that two important aspects of modern states appear: the representative institutions of Parliament in England and general assemblies, both provincial and central, in France;[5] and well-organized

---

[5] These institutions predate this period (Villers 1984, 94), but it is in the thirteenth century that they begin to take on the form that characterizes contemporary legislatures. However, Taylor (in Strayer and Taylor 1939, 109–200), in a detailed study on the role of assemblies in the war subsidies of 1318–19, claims that the French evolution was more interrupted than the English. He argues that the legislative and consensual functions were neither as clearly nor as well established as they were in England. Bisson (1972) "recon-

financial systems in the Flemish, Capetian, Norman, and English territories (Lyon and Verhulst 1967, esp. 11).[6] Mitchell (1951, 1) argues that for England "the years from the accession of Henry II to the death of Henry III, about a century and a quarter (1154–1272), are marked by definite and striking changes in the system of taxation employed by the Angevin princes in England." Hariss (1975) dates the first national lay subsidy in England as 1207 and dates the conclusion of the process this began as 1369. As for France, Wolfe (1972, chap. 1) argues that the medieval principles of taxation still flourished under Saint Louis (1226–70) but were gone by the reign of Francis I (1515–47).

As soon as monarchs and princes began to ask for new or greater taxes, people began to resist. Medieval sovereignty was built on mutual obligation and a long tradition of consent to royal demands (see Guenée 1981, 173, 244–63, and *passim*). Most observers comment on popular recalcitrance toward new taxes (see, for example, Finer 1975, 96; Zagorin 1982). All the detailed monographs of this period emphasize the amount of negotiation and bargaining that taxation involved.

One of the best examples of this process was the early fourteenth-century campaign by Philip the Fair (Philip IV) of France to extend one traditional form of taxation, the levy of a marriage aid. Strayer (1971, 195) describes the reign of this king as "the culmination of the medieval French monarchy," while Henneman (1971, 27) claims that he put "into practice the legal theories of royal sovereignty."

Brown (n.d.) presents the most complete account of Philip's policies, if policies they can be called, and concludes that he avoided clear definitions of the ruler's rights in favor of political compromise.[7] Faced with considerable resistance in both Paris and the provinces, he decided to maintain traditional rights instead of demanding new ones. He feared that definitions of sovereignty would result in restrictions on his practice, and he

---

sidered" the character of these and other assemblies under Philip the Fair. He finds that assemblies existed prior to Philip's reign in the form of five kinds of general assemblies "other than the large gatherings of men from the estates" and that they served to inform particular constituencies and win approval of the king's policies (541 ff.). Moreover, his account clearly demonstrates that Philip was searching for mechanisms by which to achieve representative consent to taxation. For a general and comparative discussion of the development of representative institutions, see, especially, Fawtier (1953) and Guenée (1981, Book 2, chap. 2, pp. 244–63).

   [6] Ardant (1971) dedicates a whole section of the first volume of *Histoire de l'impôt* (sec. 2, pp. 493–569) to the political solutions of the fiscal problems faced by the centralizing rulers.

   [7] Strayer (in Strayer and Taylor 1939, 90) makes a similar claim: "Expediency, not constitutional forms, determined the methods used in obtaining the acceptance of a tax by the country."

decided that he was better off manipulating custom. The conclusion that one infers from Brown's analysis is that the extension of taxation required noble and popular consent, or at least acquiescence, but that a skillful monarch could accomplish quite a bit within that framework (also see Bisson 1972). The traditions of consent and negotiation were also extremely strong in England.[8]

Public debate is an indication that contracts were being renegotiated and that the parties were trying to establish both gains from trade and assurances of compliance. Central to the discussion were two questions: First, did new obligations on behalf of the common good entitle monarchs to demand revenues from the general public? Second, what constituted acts on behalf of the public good; that is, when was the ruler's "need" for revenue justified? Even before the fourteenth century, there was considerable quid pro quo bargaining (Brown 1971). By the seventeenth century monarchs actually provided extended services to their constituents; writers such as Thomas Hobbes and Jean Bodin had enshrined the notion of a "social contract," and extended taxation had become generally accepted.

By the beginning of the fourteenth century, royal legal advisors were invoking Romano-canonical theory, which held that the role of the sovereign is to represent and serve the common welfare. It was an idea that had to be reconstructed (see, for example, Henneman 1971, 22–23; Schumpeter [1918] 1954, 10–11). Feudal arrangements were based on mutual obligation, but the exchange was direct, the obligations clearly defined. More modern notions of obligation of rulers to their people involve some sense of a nation, of something more than the constituent parts. It is the ruler's task to see that this larger polity is protected, that its greater good is achieved. In Roman law rulers are guardians of the public interest rather than slightly stronger lords. They do not make law and provide justice because they are the strongest; they do so because it is their job.

Even in absolutist France, Keohane argues (1984, 54), "It would be hard to exaggerate the importance of the concept of the French monarch as the representative of the common interest, the source and embodiment of the good of all. This image had deep roots in medieval France, and retained its power until the eighteenth century." Bodin in the sixteenth century in France and Hobbes in the seventeenth in England built on these notions and developed theories of sovereignty that relied on contractual relations between rulers and subjects to produce public goods rather than the more

---

[8] Dowell (1888), Willard (1934), Mitchell (1951), Hariss (1975), and Prestwich (1980) cite example after example.

limited private benefits of the earlier era.[9] The more democratic versions of social contract theory appeared later in the work of Rousseau and Locke.

The fact that the monarch derived authority from the embodiment of the common welfare rationalized extensions of the monarch's power and justified revenue production policies that constituted a radical break with the past. No longer was there a simple exchange between lord and vassal of private benefit for private benefit. Rulers contributed to the production of the public good through their administration of the tax system and its translation into armies to be used for the protection of the realm. These were public goods whose actual costs were difficult for most constituents to estimate. It became easier for rulers to pocket more of the revenue for themselves. An explicit struggle developed over the right of the ruler to spend public revenues as private income (Miller 1981, 349).

Considerable debate and discussion revolved around the question of how monarchs could be both above and below the law. Monarchs were after all human beings, subject to human whims, passions, and interests, but they were credited with the ability to act for the good of all. Fear that the private interests of monarchs would cause them to free-ride, engage in extortionary practices, or use the public coffers for private ends underlay the famous notion of "the king's two bodies": "the body natural" and "the body politic." This Tudor solution was best stated in Plowden's *Reports,* written during the reign of Elizabeth:

> For the king has in him two Bodies, *viz.* a Body natural and a Body politic. His Body natural (if it be considered in itself) is a Body mortal, subject to all Infirmities that come by Nature or Accident, to the Imbecility of Infancy or old Age, and to the like Defects that happen to the natural Bodies of other People. But his Body politic is a Body that cannot be seen or handled, consisting of Policy and Government, and constituted for the Direction of the People, and the Management of the public weal, and this Body is utterly void of Infancy, and old Age, and other natural Defects and Imbecilities, which the Body natural is subject to, and for this Cause, what the King does in his Body politic, cannot be invalidated or frustrated by any Disability in his natural Body.
> (quoted in Kantorowicz 1957, 7)[10]

There was no exact parallel in France to this formulation. The French conceived the monarch as "a personal unitary will above the state, providing order by means of laws" (Keohane 1984, 81). The monarch was "the

---

[9] For an interesting elaboration of this notion, see the discussion of Bodin in Keohane (1984, esp. 67–82).

[10] Kantorowicz (1957, 20) describes how political theorists evolved this concept, first from the notion of a two-natured God or Christ, then the relationship between Justice and Law, next the interconnection of People and Polity, and finally the duality in man himself.

supreme judge" (Mousnier 1984, 27). Bridles on monarchical power were an issue nonetheless.

The differences between French and English notions of sovereignty proved extremely important by the seventeenth and eighteenth centuries. The emphasis in England was on the monarch within and transcending the person, so that rule could be passed on without interruption. In France the person was the monarch. Thus, Parliament could execute the natural body of Charles I "without affecting seriously or doing irreparable harm to the King's body politic—in contradistinction with the events in France in 1793" (Kantorowicz 1957, 23).

Despite their differences both countries witnessed the development of a theory of rule emphasizing a social contract in which the monarch was owed obedience and taxes in return for enhancing the public good. However, in both countries there was also serious concern about how to constrain the power of rulers who stood atop increasingly invasive administrative and military states.

Distrust of the monarch was part of what lay behind resistance to the extension of taxation. It also was a motivation for actions by Parliament and other institutions to control the monarch's excesses. The end result, according to one observer, was "a view of the state as both a territorial unit and a community in which ruler and ruled were bound by mutual obligations to act for the common profit" (Hariss 1975, vii). A more accurate description is a view of the state in which the ruled sought to protect their private, or at least local, interests against an increasingly centralizing government whose power was limited by the cooperation it could expect. In this view the state was the primary institution of military and civil power within a territory but an institution with which negotiations and exchange took place.

The debate over what constituted sovereignty was also a debate about taxation. By the seventeenth and eighteenth centuries, the monarch clearly had a right to demand taxes in return for services. A monarch still had to "live of his own" to some extent, but the notion of a common good obligated the public to support them and obligated monarchs to serve the public. Therefore, agents and constituents developed an expectation of gains from the trade of their taxes and other contributions, as well as an expectation that monarchs would uphold their end of the bargain and keep others to theirs (although it was far from apparent, short of outright rebellions, what the people could do if the monarch broke a contract). In many ways the discussion shifted to what constituted service on behalf of the public good. It was in this context that war became so entwined with the justification of taxation.

THE ROLE OF WAR

Medieval French and English monarchs lacked the right and the power to impose taxes at will. They had to find reasons why those with financial resources should turn them over to the monarch. By the fourteenth century, rulers proposed new or extended forms of revenue extraction on the basis of "evident necessity" (see, esp., Willard 1934, 18–26 and *passim;* Strayer and Taylor 1939; Prestwich 1980, *passim;* Henneman, 1971, 17–27, 322–23), but the taxpayers did not always agree with the necessity of the so-called necessity. It took several centuries for the concept of the monarch as protector of the common good to take root.

The most acceptable justification for taxation was war. However, the notion of the realm was lacking until nearly the fourteenth century, making even war problematic as a justification. For example, in the mid-thirteenth century, Henry III of England tried to raise taxes for what he claimed were national war expenditures. His barons rejected his pleas—largely because his expeditions tended to be overseas, aggressive rather than defensive, and not very costly (Hariss 1975, 34–35). In his excellent monograph on late-fifteenth-century and early-sixteenth-century lay taxation in England, Schofield (1963) shows that "each of the acts granting taxes to the crown was prefixed by a preamble elucidating the circumstances which made a grant of taxation necessary" (23) and that "Up to and including the act of 1523, the preambles to the taxation acts justified the grant of taxation entirely in military terms" (24). Henneman (1971) explicitly studies the "war subsidies" of fourteenth-century France, where war was routinely used to justify revenue extraction.

War had always been waged by monarchs, and their subjects had contributed to the enterprise; but changes in the technology of warfare and in the size and nature of the military apparatus transformed the political and economic relationships between monarch and subjects.[11] Indeed, the advance in military technology after the early thirteenth century affected

---

[11] Finer (1975) offers the most complete account of the relationship between military format and state making. My discussion of changes in war making, as well as its effects, borrows heavily from his superb article. Also see Prestwich (1980, esp. 62–72) and Henneman (1971, 19–22).

the optimum size and organization of efficient political units.[12] Armored knights and a heavy reliance on cavalry gave way to an increased emphasis on infantry armed with the longbow and pike. The navy developed correspondingly, especially in England.

In a justly famous article, Schumpeter ([1918] 1954, 13–16) emphasized the growing expenses of warfare as the foundation of the modern state. First, they motivated princes to seek new sources of revenue. Second, they led to the argument that wars were no longer the private affairs of princes but a common problem whose costs should be shared. Finally, and most important, once this argument was accepted by the institutions that provided consent, "a state of affairs was acknowledged which was bound to wipe out all paper guarantees against tax demands. . . . Out of the 'common exigency' the state was born" (15).

Successful war making increasingly required contributions by a critical threshold of potential taxpayers. It became a lumpy collective good.[13] The reliance on a paid, standing army rather than on noble knights, the use of the pike and the longbow, the revolution in the architecture of fortifications, a modern navy, and other such changes not only raised the costs of war but also required centralization of war-making power. Monarchs needed more funds to win battles and were the obvious persons to organize war. These facts gave them considerable ammunition in the claim that taxpayers gained from contributing. The monarch's central role in the network of exchange of services and revenue further enhanced central power. Each sector of the realm came to depend directly on the government for national defense, protection, and the administration of justice. Each increasingly recognized that its contribution was critical to the production of the desired collective goods.

Centuries of experiment and controversy preceded this outcome. As the monarchs of the late thirteenth and early fourteenth centuries came to rely more on experienced mercenaries and later on paid volunteers, they began to use feudal military obligations as a basis for raising revenue rather than armies. Vassals could pay — and were encouraged to pay — to commute their service. Commutation was a source of revenue that avoided many of the political pitfalls of direct taxation until rulers were able to overcome the political obstacles to more straightforward taxation. Strayer (in Strayer and Taylor 1939, 9–10, 56–57) discusses the discontent created by Philip the Fair's attempt to adopt a new principle that the obligation of everyone in the

[12] Bean (1973) and North (1981, 135–38) make this claim. Tilly (1985, 177–78) disagrees with Bean's argument but applauds its logic if "stripped of its technological determinism."

[13] It can be argued that war making sometimes took on an S-shaped function. However, it was extremely difficult to determine the point at which additional contributions would no longer increase the probability of success.

realm to contribute to defense could take the form of government extraction of a percentage of property rather than military service. The compromise was that the government called for military service, which individuals paid to commute. The need to precede war taxes with the summons of the *arrière-ban* continued until the reign of Philip V and the war subsidy of 1319 (Henneman 1971, 26–33). English monarchs were regularly able to levy direct war subsidies by the end of the thirteenth century (Prestwich 1980; Hariss 1975).

Even with the right to demand war subsidies, rulers were restrained in what they could request, and in how they could spend what they collected, by the dictum of *cessante causa, cessat effectus* — "when the cause ceases, the effect also ceases" (see, for example, Brown 1972). In other words, taxation had to be linked to actual wars, and taxes had to be paid back if the war failed to materialize or cost less than anticipated. A ruler who attempted to manufacture a war threat might not succeed in winning acquiescence to the next demand. Constituents considered misrepresentation of the circumstances of warfare a breach of faith by the ruler.

When in 1294 Philip the Fair refused to return a subsidy even though war was forestalled, there was significant protest. Subsequently, he had to actually summon soldiers before his need for funds was believed (Brown 1972, 571; Henneman 1971, 323). Consequently, in 1313, after a truce with Flanders, Philip "however reluctantly . . . eventually canceled and ordered restitution of the subsidies pledged by those who had elected to pay rather than fight" (Brown 1981, 111). The following year he issued another general summons, but when a truce forestalled war again, he nonetheless demanded payment of the sums that had been pledged. He and his advisors may have felt justified, given that "the government was particularly hard-pressed for funds, and in view of the many expenses incurred in sincere expectation of conflict" (Brown 1981, 112). His demand provoked considerable opposition in the form of regional and interregional alliances throughout the kingdom, and the subsidy ultimately was canceled (Brown 1981, *passim*). English rulers experienced similar political difficulties whenever they attempted to extend their power of taxation beyond the traditional limits (Elton 1975, 35).

The principle of *cessante causa* operated as a precommitment mechanism on rulers. It was a self-enforced moral obligation. Its existence seems to have been an essential basis for tax negotiations between constituents and rulers.[14]

---

[14] Monarchs sometimes even evoked it against rivals who were also subjects. For example, Philip IV used *cessante causa* to subvert the resource base of the Duke of Gascony, Edward II of England (Brown 1972, 575–76).

Although the attempts by monarchs to establish peacetime taxes were rarely successful, rulers began to link peacetime to wartime expenses by arguing for revenues to ensure preparedness and improvement of military technology (see, esp., Hariss 1975, 474–81). However, Henry VIII and Elizabeth I were still facing problems in this regard (Schofield 1963; Elton 1975), and in 1532 Francis I's efforts to create a war chest in France were only partially successful (Wolfe 1972, 87–91). Increasingly, however, peacetime expenditures did not return to prewar levels (see, esp., Mann 1980).

Rulers probably did not, on the whole, create wars as a means for justifying and regularizing taxation, but they did use the wars to enhance their power and to justify their demands for revenue.[15] The provision of protection from the enemy was the benefit taxpayers could point to as their gain from trade.

There was an additional advantage to war as the initial justification for taxes. War is an extremely public activity. Monarchs who engaged in wars that did not benefit the populace through booty or protection were not keeping their side of the bargain and were going to have difficulty extracting revenues in the future. Cynicism about the need for a tax, or about the effectiveness of a ruler entrusted to implement the policy for which the tax is collected, was expressed in centuries much earlier than the twentieth.

I have tried to show the importance of war in justifying the development of national lay taxes, the foundation of the modern state. As wars changed character, monarchs waged war on behalf of a nation. In administering the war-making apparatus, they were perceived as acting in the common good. Once they had established that there was a common good and that they were able—indeed best suited—to act in its behalf, rulers were able to justify an ever-increasing array of taxes. Moreover, they had created the prerequisite of quasi-voluntary compliance.

However, war explains only one aspect of the development of national taxation. In itself it cannot account for the subsequent variation between France and England, both of which experienced near constant war from the end of the thirteenth century. To that end I now turn to the internal characteristics of the two countries.

DIVERGENCE OF FRANCE AND ENGLAND

During the late medieval period, French and English national tax systems took the forms that were to distinguish them for centuries into the

---

[15] Thus, in some respects my argument is consistent with Tilly's (1985).

future. The procedures for obtaining a grant of taxation and the methods of collection markedly diverged. English monarchs received grants of taxation through a central Parliament, while French monarchs negotiated with a vast number of localities and individuals. By 1334 England had a standardized and regularized system of assessments for lay taxes. France established a relatively huge bureaucracy fairly early but not a standardized system. France relied more on venality of office and on tax farmers, and there was more regional variation in how taxes were collected.

The two countries also diverged in terms of the kinds of taxes they emphasized. All medieval monarchs relied on feudal dues, sale and leasing of the products of their lands (especially forest) and sometimes of the lands themselves, revenue in kind from crown lands, the occasional expropriation of a defeated noble's property, fines, grants of title or right, taxes on the Jews, taxes on the clergy, and loans from financiers. Revenue production possibilities changed and expanded in the thirteenth and fourteenth centuries. The collection of traditional revenues intensified. Jewish property was expropriated and Jews expelled from both France and England, creating a short-run windfall but closing a past revenue source. New tolls, market dues, and taxes on customs, trade, and property were introduced. Payments for the commutation of military services were increasingly permitted. In addition, monarchs began to sell monopolies, protective legislation, and offices to a greater and greater degree. As the revenue production systems evolved with the evolving modern states, both France and England continued to rely on dynastic marriages, direct taxes (the *taille* in France and the tenths and fifteenths in England), taxes on the church, sales of monopolies, and loans. However, by the seventeenth century, France had more regional variation in the kinds of taxes, a more troubled relationship between monarch and creditors, and less reliance on customs.

The distinctiveness of the two systems was the result of differences in the relative bargaining power of agents and constituents in relation to the ruler; the measurement, monitoring, negotiation, and agency costs of revenue extraction; and the extent of quasi-voluntary compliance by constituents.

RELATIVE BARGAINING POWER

The fact that French monarchs had relatively greater bargaining power vis-à-vis their constituents than did English monarchs helps to explain the greater range of lay taxes in France. Determinants of the relative bargaining power of rulers and lay constituents include military conflict and the economic organization of the economy. War increased fiscal pressure on rulers but also increased their power. The sources and distribution of economic wealth affected the class structure and the political, as well as economic, resources of lay constituents in relation to rulers.

Finer (1975) details the influences of the military format on state building in Britain and France. Quinlan and Fisk (1982) claim that the existence of absolutism is a function of different experiences of war. They argue that the military occupation experienced by France enabled French monarchs to wrest concessions from the nobility to build standing armies, which they then used to usurp the local authority of that same nobility.

Ames and Rapp (1977) make a somewhat different argument about the effect of war on the ruler's bargaining power and on the tax systems that the ruler can impose. They claim that war is not a sufficient justification for permanent taxation as long as the war is perceived as a one-time threat. The French, however, perceived war as interminable and, thus, "the promise of perpetual defense from a king was worth the price of 'immortal' taxation while the more peaceable birth of English taxes preserved the heritage of negotiation between crown and subject" (171). In other words, Ames and Rapp claim that constant war produces high constituent discount rates and that intermittent wars produce low constituent discount rates, with important fiscal and parliamentary consequences.

Theoretically elegant, this argument is unsatisfying empirically. The differentiation between the French and English systems had its origins in the thirteenth and fourteenth centuries, as Ames and Rapp claim. However, social disorder and nearly constant warfare were as much the English as the French condition in these centuries. Indeed, the two countries were at war with each other much of this time.[16] Where, then, is the dividing line, theoretically or empirically, between intermittent and perpetual in this instance? Both France and England experienced "perpetual" warfare, which enhanced the power of monarchs and justified taxation in both countries. The French and English experiences are consistent with the theory but not with the findings of Ames and Rapp.

What did make a difference was the greater intensity of war in France — as distinct from the regularity of its occurrence. Subsequently, French monarchs accrued greater power and taxes than English rulers. Because France itself was the battlefield for the Hundred Years' War, the French experience was more severe and possibly more costly. Although France was plagued more by war in later centuries, the crucial distinction is in the costs

---

[16] War between England and France began long before the Hundred Years' War (1337–1453). King John and Philip Augustus battled in 1214, and Edward I fought Philip IV in 1294–97.

to both constituents and rulers of waging war. Differences in military technology, in the experience of occupation, and in a long list of other factors (Tilly 1985, esp. 181–84; Kiser 1986–87) also account for variation in the bargaining position of French and English monarchs.

Elias ([1939] 1982) presents another perspective. He argues that military conflict was the path to power over territory and control of economic resources (also see Tilly 1985). For Elias "the sociogenesis of the state" lay in a "monopoly mechanism," fostered by competition among rival lords and powers within the territory. As some win and others lose, "fewer and fewer will control more and more opportunities, and more units will be eliminated from the competition, becoming directly or indirectly dependent on an ever decreasing number" (106). In Elias's view a balance of class forces accounts for strong central power.[17] Such a formulation is a conclusion, not an explanation. It may account for a general increase in royal power, but it does not account for variation in the distribution of power.

War, which occurred in both France and England, set the stage for the most important determinant of variation in power and in state building. Following Brenner (1976, 1982), I argue that differences in the economic organization and distribution of economic resources in the two countries crucially defined and delimited bargaining power. Because of the importance of trade and the establishment of agricultural capitalism in England, English landlords and capitalists were stronger than their French counterparts (Brenner 1982). Consequently, English monarchs had worse terms of trade with capitalists (some of whom were nobility) than did the monarchs of France, where trade was less dominant and traditional agricultural relations more prevalent.

These economic differences made for important political variations in the relative power of classes and in the evolution of the form of central state power. Zolberg (1980) points out that the English tendency to tax trade led to the rise of parliamentary democracy and that the French tendency to tax fiscal assets led to absolutism.[18] Bates and Lien (1985) provide a theoretical explanation for this observation. They demonstrate formally and historically that constituents with secure property rights (other than Jews or

---

[17] Elias ([1939] 1982, 171) argues:

The hour of the strong central authority within a highly differentiated society strikes when the ambivalence of interests of the most important functional groups grows so large, and power is distributed so evenly between them, that there can be neither a decisive compromise nor a decisive conflict between them.

[18] Friedman (1977) argues that the kinds of taxes collected also affect the "size and shape of nations."

Italian bankers) who controlled mobile assets had more bargaining lever-age with monarchs than those sectors of the economy that were less elastic. They note that "in both England and France it was the taxation of 'movable' property that promoted the conferral of political representation by reve-nue-seeking monarchs" (55). Since movables[19] could change hands easily, both monarchs and constituents preferred collective negotiations concern-ing taxes on similar assets. Collective negotiations reduced the transaction costs and increased the revenues for the rulers and assured the taxpayers that others were paying at the same rate (Bates and Lien 1985, 56–57).

Since the mid-fourteenth century, England had relied more heavily than did France on the taxes on movables. It also relied more heavily on indirect taxes on trade. In France, with its quite different economy, direct taxes on agricultural land and production were a better source of revenue.

In both countries direct taxes on movables led to consultation with representative institutions. However, the overwhelming importance of a single product in England (first wool and then cloth) was complemented by a central Parliament. To achieve their policies, English rulers had to make concessions to the magnates, who had forced King John and many other monarchs to heel. They also were accountable to the squires, urban repre-sentatives, and merchants (see, for example, Prestwich 1980, chap. 4; Russell 1971). Thus, North and Thomas (1973, 83) can claim, "In En-gland from the *Magna Carta* on, we observe that the English Crown was forced to trade privileges for revenue." This arrangement achieved its culmination in mercantilism.[20] The medieval concessions of English mon-archs, motivated by the search for revenue, led to the development of a Parliament that only further increased constituent bargaining power. By the reign of Elizabeth I, "there was a perceptible weakening of the royal grasp on parliamentary business" (MacCaffrey 1981, 464). In particular, Com-mons was coming into its own, although it had not yet, of course, become a modern legislative body. Well into the seventeenth century, it was still

---

[19] According to Willard (1934, 3):

A new kind of taxation came into existence in England during the later Middle Ages, the taxation of personal property, known to contemporaries as the taxation of movable goods. Movable goods were cows, oxen, grain, household goods, and other posses-sions — property that could be transferred from place to place.

Rents were also subject to taxation, but a person's house and land were exempt. Also exempt were a knight's arms, horses, and clothing; the clergy's vestments, church furniture, clothing, horses, and books; and the jewels of both clergy and laity (see Dowell 1888, 61). The French also introduced a tax on movables, but it was one of many taxes they levied, and its use — and the exemptions it incorporated, varied from locality to locality.

[20] Ekelund and Tollison (1981) provide an account of mercantilism consistent with the approach offered here. Olson (1982, 121–30) offers some additional insights.

relatively unproductive of legislation and more concerned with correcting abuses than with molding policy (Hirst 1986, 33–42). Nonetheless, it was to Parliament, and especially the Commons, that monarchs had to come to authorize new taxes.

There was no such development in France.[21] Even in the Middle Ages, French monarchs negotiated with numerous local assemblies, but these tended to diminish in significance over time (Guenée 1981, Book 3, chap. 2). French reliance on a greater diversity of taxes is crucial to the explanation. Another critical factor is the difference in the size of the two countries. In an important article, Fawtier (1953, esp. 277–78) discusses the implications of France's size for the development of medieval representative institutions. He argues that the journey to Paris was long, dangerous, and expensive for most delegates to the central assembly, the *Etats généraux*. Moreover, they perceived their task as, ultimately, to confirm the decisions of the monarch and the Royal Council. Thus, they preferred negotiations with royal agents: "N'était-il pas plus simple de se faire dire par l'agent royal le plus proche, le montant de la somme à payer et d'économiser ainsi sa peine, son argent et son temps?" (278). The result was that French monarchs did not experience challenges to their power in the form the English did. Moreover, royal agents continued to function as intermediaries between the provincial notables and the monarch until the Revolution (see, for example, Beik 1985, chap. 5; Root 1987). It is these facts that have led many observers to conclude that French royal power was more absolute.

The decline of centralized consultative assemblies in France is an indicator of the greater relative bargaining power of French monarchs vis-à-vis their resource-rich constituents than that of the monarchs of England. This comparative lack of bargaining power closed off certain options in England that were available in France and compelled English monarchs to make concessions not expected of French monarchs.

TRANSACTION COSTS

The factors that account for the difference in bargaining power of French and English monarchs, as well as that very difference itself, created variation in transaction costs. The nature of the primary revenue sources, the

---

[21] My account in this section and later relies heavily on the detailed accounts provided by Strayer and Taylor (1939), Bisson (1972), and Brown (1981) of how monarchs achieved consent in France from 1295 to 1319, often in pointed contrast to the English. Also see Villers (1984) and Fawtier (1953). For 1322–56 see Henneman (1971). Wolfe (1972) takes up the story from the fifteenth century. Beik (1985) makes important new contributions to understanding the developments of the seventeenth.

relative sizes of the two countries, and the institutions of representation made for greater regional variation in taxation and tax collection, higher agency costs, and higher costs of negotiation in France than in England.

The English reliance on revenue from taxes and licensing of a single major export precipitated the growth of Parliament but also reduced the transaction costs of tax collection. These were relatively easy revenues to monitor. The French, on the other hand, relied on revenue from a myriad of extremely diverse sources, some of which were extremely costly to monitor.

Among the easiest taxes to measure and monitor are customs dues. Large ships need harbors, can usually be discovered if they try to avoid official ports, and can be observed during the process of loading and unloading. To explain the differences in French and English fiscal policies, one must take into account the importance of the wool trade (Prestwich 1980, *passim*) and later the cloth trade in England and the absence of an equally important single export in France (Miller in Postan, Rich, and Miller, 1971, 291). The wool and cloth trades provided a major source of revenue for the English crown. By the end of the fifteenth century, they yielded 30,000 pounds a year (North and Thomas 1973, 83). Stone (1947, 104) argues:

> The economy of England during the first half of the sixteenth century was concentrated to an increasing degree upon a single produce handled through a single port and directed along a single trade route. When Edward VI ascended the throne, the prosperity and indeed the very existence of England depended to a very large extent on the export of cloth through London to the great international mart of Antwerp, where was obtained those import goods and manufactures demanded by the English consumer.

The cloth trade was not only lucrative but also easy to monitor — although it was, of course, also a source of considerable bargaining strength by those who controlled it. France had nothing comparable on which to rely. Thus, English transaction costs of tax collection were relatively low compared to the French costs; and from 1334 on, when the tax on movables was established, England's revenue was somewhat more stable and predictable.

Both English and French monarchs relied heavily on loans, but French monetary crises were more common — not only because of maladministration and the difficulties of extracting taxes but also because of war. France had been a battleground for over a hundred years, which significantly raised the cost of government and the pressure for funds. War also raised the discount rates of French monarchs. The result was dependence on creditors and financiers, who ultimately extorted privileges as well as money from the monarchs in return for the loans (see, esp., Bonney 1981; Dessert 1974; Dent 1973). Monarchs who put their creditors in jail or otherwise ignored their obligations, as Louis XIV did, only provoked creditor distrust and increased both the price of borrowing and the costs of negotiating a loan. English monarchs seem to have been more restrained in their borrowing.

Differences in the size of the two countries also affected their transaction costs. France was burdened by its size, especially in a time when communication and transport were extremely expensive and difficult. England was small in contrast. To ensure any semblance of communication between Paris and the provinces required more agents and greater bureaucratic centralization than England needed. Bureaucracy need not lead to waste, but there is no evidence of economies of scale and there is considerable evidence of corruption (see, esp., Bonney 1981; Dent 1973; Wolfe 1972; Strayer 1971, 49).

Plagued by uncertainty and by the complexity and number of the taxes they had negotiated, pre-Revolutionary French monarchs rediscovered tax farming as a way to ensure funds while buying compliance. Tax farming was consistent with the Coase theorem. It was a solution to the high costs of communication and information in France. Instead of trying to monitor agent behavior, which was too expensive, the rulers sold off rights to collect taxes to informed buyers.[22] Not surprisingly, rulers had little control over the tax farmers, whose behavior, particularly in the last days of the *ancien régime*, won the system the reputation for extortion that it bears today. ·

During the reign of Louis XIV, the authority of the state, through supervision of village finances by its provincial administrators, was extended to the village level. However, Root (1987) argues that the "Ludovician reforms" were ad hoc, made in response to immediate needs and circumstances. The end result, however, was to reconstitute village communities as bases for monarchical rather than seigniorial power.[23]

Another development in France was venality of office, that is, the selling of offices. Although venality developed more as a source of revenue than of agency, it created the kind of property in officeholding that concerned Weber. The monarch sold offices and often sold the same offices over and over. Charges accompanied each sale. In 1604 the crown established the extremely lucrative *Paulette,* a form of annual dues on officeholding (Mousnier 1984, 36–52).

---

[22] Philip Hoffman pointed out the relevance of the Coase theorem here.
[23] These points are drawn from Root (1987). Also see Lodge (1931).

Despite various attempts to raise revenue from those who were collecting revenue on behalf of the central state, there is evidence that a relatively small proportion actually reached the monarch. For example, Beik (1984, 1286–87ff.) estimates that in Languedoc only 47.9 percent of the revenues from the 1677 *taille* actually reached the coffers of Louis XIV; agents of various kinds received at least a third. Moreover, the percentage accruing to agents represented an increase from 1647, raising questions about the nature of Louis XIV's "absolutism" (Beik 1984, 1291ff.).

Very early on, England succeeded in developing an efficient administration based on local officials but with a hierarchy of officers and a system of checks and double-checks.[24] There was, perhaps, some deterioration of administrative effectiveness and some loss of royal control between the fourteenth and sixteenth centuries (Williams 1979, chap. 3). Certainly, by the seventeenth century the costs of administration included a hefty expenditure on patronage (Hirst 1986, 30–33). However, the English bureaucracy never earned the reputation for corruption that its French counterpart possessed (although corruption there certainly was), nor did it arouse the resentment of the populace as in France. Moreover, it stayed relatively small in comparison. Under Elizabeth there was approximately one royal officer for every four thousand inhabitants; the contemporaneous French population suffered one officer for approximately four hundred inhabitants (Williams 1979, 107). For several reasons, then, the English crown seems to have been better able to measure taxable material and monitor its agents. Shirking and slippage certainly occurred, but they never reached the dimensions that they did in France.

The difficulties that French rulers had in maintaining a cheap and stable system of agency indicate that their bargaining power in relation to important segments of the population was not as great as the label of absolutism implies. What commenced in the Middle Ages continued into the Renaissance: constant negotiations and renegotiations with an array of individuals, towns, and cities over the kinds of taxes and their collection (Wolfe 1972, 7, 21; Henneman 1971, 16).

This situation was partially caused by and certainly exacerbated by the differences between England and France in incorporating conquered territories. Internal colonialism in England was characterized by imposition of English law and customs (Hechter 1975). France permitted the

---

[24] Particularly useful and detailed accounts of the assessment and collection of lay taxes before the Tudors appear in Dowell (1888), Dietz (1921), Willard (1934), Morris and Strayer (1947), and Mitchell (1951, esp. chap. 1). The Tudor period is covered in Dietz (1932), Elton (1982, esp. chap. 4), and Schofield (1963).

provinces to preserve their customs and institutions. Consequently, "England failed in its attempt to annex Scotland, made only slight headway in Ireland, and spent several centuries in gaining full control of a small piece of Wales. France, on the other hand, attached firmly to the Crown territories as diverse as Normandy, Languedoc, Dauphine, and Brittany" (Strayer 1971, 49).

The ultimate costs were high to France, however. Not only did this system require an additional layer of bureaucracy, in the form of agents of the central administration, to enforce and monitor agreements with the ruler; it also led to the establishment of two very disparate kinds of administrative units, the *pays d'états* (Burgundy, Languedoc, Brittany, Province, and Dauphine), which retained the medieval right of assembly, and the *pays d'élections,* which came under the direct jurisdiction of the central apparatus. Most of the *pays d'états* were incorporated later, thus enabling them to bargain for concessions either not considered or already given up by the *pays d'élections.*

The fact that tax collection systems were local enterprises, at least initially, made for costly negotiation, however. Local and regional autonomy created separate readings of the terms of trade, separate decisions about whether to go along. Consequently, the monarch often could not ensure the compliance of others. One solution was the more national and centralized administration that marked the sixteenth century. Another solution turned out to be parliaments. The existence of strong parliaments in England ultimately made it easier to extract revenues there than in France. I shall return to this point later.

Ceteris paribus, it seems that rulers in England had lower transaction costs than did their counterparts in France. The French state may have needed more per capita to fund its expenditures, particularly on war. Nonetheless, the deadweight costs of agency and negotiation in France still appear to be considerably higher than they were in England.

QUASI-VOLUNTARY COMPLIANCE

In principle monarchs in both countries established that taxation represented an exchange for valued goods and services. Each change or extension of taxation was a new contract whose consistency with the general taxation policy had to be examined. Noncompliance or even resistance was likely to increase where the examination failed to reveal an adequate justification for the new contract. Compliance was more likely when taxpayers were sanguine that the contract gave them what they expected in return for their contributions.

The initial establishment of a parliament may represent a concession to powerful constituents who demand a say in government; however, one of its effects is to create some of the factors necessary for quasi-voluntary compliance or legitimacy. The ruler can use this forum to make clear the terms and benefits of the contract; the members of parliament need not accept it until they are satisfied that they—and perhaps their constituents in the modern democracies—will indeed benefit from its establishment. Parliamentary procedures also tend to reveal both the ruler's and the constituents' preferences and to provide a location for continued and repeated interaction. Moreover, rulers are accountable to parliaments. If they have not kept past contracts, it will be difficult for them to make new ones. If they have failed to enforce the contributions of some parties to the contract, this too will be known. Finally, parliament helps rulers assert social pressure on constituents to keep their side of the bargain. It is hardly surprising to claim that parliamentary consent enshrouds a ruler's policies in legitimacy,[25] but this analysis provides some reasons why this is so.

England and France differed in their reliance on parliaments. No ruler could collect taxes without consulting the people to be taxed. Feudal practice, the reemergence of Roman law, and the power of the taxed partially account for this requirement, but equally, perhaps principally, important was the fact that medieval governments had so little information about the numbers and wealth of their subjects that they had to bring them into the taxing process simply to get the necessary information (Strayer in Strayer and Taylor 1939, 22). These assemblies were "instruments through which the king could get in touch with public opinion in preparation for carrying out difficult national policies" (Taylor in Strayer and Taylor 1939, 168).

English monarchs used Parliament to gather information and mold public opinion and to bring local representatives together into one central institution. They also used it for consultation, legislation (over time), and the forming of "definite commitments on more than principle" (Taylor in Strayer and Taylor 1939, 170).

---

[25] It should be noted, however, that the existence of a parliament can have exactly the opposite effect. By bringing nobles together, it facilitates collective action. By enabling these nobles to assess and monitor the acts of the ruler, it can clarify targets of rebellion. In other words, parliaments are both bulwarks of legitimacy and hotbeds of rebellion. This may at first seem impossible. However, rebellion is most likely when the rebel believes himself stronger than the target of rebellion. Participation in parliament permits nobles to calculate their comparative advantage. Brustein and Levi (1987) develop this argument further.

French monarchs used assemblies less for achieving consent and action than as a forum for assessing potential problems, and they negotiated with a multitude of individuals and local governments. In France the emphasis was on local assemblies. Moreover, there was considerable regional disparity in the power of local assemblies (see, for example, Dunkley 1981; Beik 1985).

I have already discussed the relative importance of taxes on movables and the differences in the sizes of the countries as crucial factors in accounting for the emergence of a central Parliament in England and local assemblies in France. However, another factor is French provincialism, as much on the part of the nobles as the general population (see, for example, Henneman 1971, 320–29); but provincialism was a result, not a cause (at least initially), of the economic and political structure. It can be argued that the more localized markets of France and the stronger hold of feudal privileges made it harder for the population as a whole to recognize a common interest, let alone organize around it.

The institutional mechanisms devised for achieving consent in the fourteenth century predominated throughout the Renaissance. English royal power enabled the monarch to be an entrepreneur in the use and calling of Parliament. Initially, French monarchs could not convince the populace that there was a mutual benefit in ongoing general assemblies. Indeed, most French perceived that individual and collective bads were more likely than collective goods to emanate from a uniform system of taxation. The only good that monarchs could provide through coordination was private, the reduction of their own transaction costs.

Subsequently, French rulers evolved a very different fiscal system from the English. By the seventeenth century, a general assembly would have upset this system and threatened royal power. Moreover, in the absence of a well-established general assembly, French rulers could impose a variety of taxes and mechanisms of tax collection not available to English monarchs. They had a greater capacity to discriminate among different sectors. More commercialized regions paid sales taxes, and less commercialized regions paid direct property taxes; some individuals and groups were exempt; and administrative strategies varied with locale as well as tax (Henneman 1971, *passim;* Wolfe 1972, esp. 25–40 and 304–29). Considerable statistical evidence on the level of the *taille* during the seventeenth century confirms the considerable regional variation (Collins 1979; Beik 1984, 1985).

English rulers had to go to Parliament for approval of taxes early on, while in France the *Etats généraux* met erratically and then in the fifteenth century finally gave power of taxation over to the monarch (see, esp., Wolfe

1972, 25–66). The result was that the monarchs of France had greater absolute power, but their costs of achieving compliance were much higher than those of their counterparts in England. Without a forum in which to engage explicitly in repeat transactions and renegotiations, they were more subject to tax resistance in the form of both noncompliance and actual rebellion.

CONCLUSION

France and England both established national tax systems during the thirteenth and fourteenth centuries. This institutional change in the nature of the revenue production system was unquestionably a consequence of the expanded relative bargaining power of the ruler in relation to powerful constituents. New resources of royal power and increased dependence on the monarch by subjects facilitated extensions of taxation. In particular, the development of new military technology raised the costs of conflict and enhanced the monarch's bargaining power. War justified taxation. It was defined as a collective good that the ruler provided with funds furnished by the polity. War was the initial basis for a social contract theory of the state, in which rulers collected taxes to enable them to act on behalf of the common good.

By the sixteenth century, the two national tax systems were quite dissimilar. Differences in constraints on English and French monarchs led them to implement distinct policies. Transaction costs were a significant factor. The variation in the size, economic base, and representative institutions of France and England created variations in sources of revenue, forms of agency, and costs of negotiation. Bargaining power also accounts for some of the variation. French monarchs had greater resources of power relative to powerful constituents than did English monarchs. They were better able to act like discriminating monopolists in regard to what taxes they imposed upon whom. On the other hand, the English had lower costs of compliance.

The central paradox of this chapter is that English monarchs, relatively weak in relation to their resource-rich constituents, were able to govern more effectively and efficiently than French monarchs, whose absolute power was greater in terms of their ability to make pronouncements than in their ability to act—at least when it came to lay taxes. In France the economic structure inhibited collective action and collective interests. Dominant economic classes formed alliances when necessary to contest extensions of royal power but did not maintain a general assembly. In

England, on the other hand, the magnates, emerging capitalists, and urban burghers supported a central representative institution that could control royal power and, ultimately, legislate economic policy.

Since the existence of a central parliament ultimately reduces the costs of creating compliance, one wonders why the French rulers failed to recognize its advantages. Why did they not copy the English example? There is some evidence that Philip the Fair did experiment with parliaments as a means to reduce the costs of negotiation and information. However, parliaments are risky; they coordinate resistance as well as compliance. Moreover, French monarchs who glanced across the channel saw that the English rulers were having difficulties in imposing taxes. They were less able than the French to act like discriminating monopolists.

The argument offered here is distinct from the traditional claim. The importance of fiscal pressures in creating the basis for the extension of royal power is acknowledged, but I argue that rulers will try to extend their revenue base even in the absence of such pressures. What stops them is oppositional power and high transaction costs that make the return hardly worth the outlay. However, the fact that revenue production policies impose a contractual obligation on the ruler as well as on the revenue payer and revenue collector may help explain why rulers, particularly those of France during the *ancien régime,* found it hard to make a profit and often faced actual bankruptcy. The commitment to revenue maximization does not imply the capacity to exploit all potential revenue sources to their fullest. The ultimate test of this model is not the amount of revenue rulers actually collect. The ultimate test is the accuracy of the explanation of rulers' policy choices, of why they make the choices they do.

CHAPTER VI

Introduction of the Income Tax in Eighteenth-Century Britain

The revenue of the state is the state. In effect all depends upon it, whether for support or for reformation. . . . Through the revenue alone the body politic can act in its true genius and character, and therefore it will display just as much of its collective virtue, and as much of that virtue which may characterize those who move it, and are, as it were, its life and guiding principle, as it is possessed of a just revenue.

Edmund Burke
Reflections on the Revolution in France

Capitation taxes, if it is attempted to proportion them to the fortune or revenue of each contributor, become altogether arbitrary. The state of a man's fortune varies from day to day and, without an inquisition more intolerable than any tax renewed at least once every year, can only be guessed at. His assessment, therefore, must, in most cases, depend upon the good or bad humor of his assessors and must, therefore, be altogether arbitrary and uncertain.

Adam Smith
The Wealth of Nations

The introduction of the direct income tax in 1799 marked an important turning point in British fiscal history. The income tax reflected a major transformation in prevailing economic thought and fundamentally altered the individual's relationship to the central state. It provided the state with both an enormous new source of revenue and access to information regarding individual wealth and lifestyle that had never before been available. Over time, increased revenues permitted the state to extend its provision of collective goods, ranging from social insurance and welfare programs to the roads and communication systems that are the infrastructure of modern business. Consequently, the power of the central state was enhanced as citizens became more dependent on it. Every level of British society, from the upper class to the working class, from center to periphery, felt the impact of this fiscal revolution.

This chapter[1] demonstrates that the imposition of the income tax rested on the creation of quasi-voluntary compliance, that is, the extraction of tax payments without constant resort to direct coercion. An income tax is too expensive to administer in the absence of citizen acquiescence. Quasi-voluntary compliance requires the evolution of institutions providing assurances that the tax will be "fair," equitably assessed and administered, and used to promote the common good. The case of the 1799 income tax also demonstrates that even rulers reluctant to maximize revenue are compelled to choose policies that increase returns to the state. William Pitt the Younger instituted the income tax as a last resort. All the evidence points to his distaste for the tax and his preference for alternatives.

In what follows I take up several propositions deduced from the theory of predatory rule:

Once the specialization and division of labor evolve to create large-scale markets and relatively widespread wealth, all rulers will, ceteris paribus, seek to institute that most lucrative of all taxes, the income tax. Only insufficient bargaining power and high transaction costs would constrain rulers from implementing this policy.

Given that the relative universality and invasiveness of the income tax creates significant opposition, the imposition of the tax will correlate with (1) increasing state expenditures on collective goods that citizens seek or, at least, accept as government responsibility; and (2) the evolution of institutions of rule that give rulers significant fiscal policymaking power.

Given that an income tax is unthinkable until the transaction costs of measuring and monitoring income are sufficiently low, its imposition will correlate with the evolution of an efficient administrative apparatus.

Given the political difficulties of imposition and the high costs of monitoring the income tax, its introduction will correlate with the establishment of institutions that create quasi-voluntary compliance.

The Roman Republic had a form of progressive head tax administered by the gens. The Medici experimented with the *scala* in fifteenth-century Florence. The idea of an income tax was hardly new, but an income tax is

---

[1] Written in collaboration with Stephanie Todd.

exceedingly expensive to administer. The transaction costs of estimating income and monitoring payments are extremely high, even in cash economies. The opportunities for agent corruption and abuse are very great, especially in societies without an elaborated bureaucracy. Finally, the income tax requires detailed examination of individual financial records, a practice that citizens continue to resent and initially resisted.

Widespread commercialization and increasing industrialization made the income tax viable. An income tax requires an economy in which income can be easily assessed and monitored. However, it was not actually instituted until political circumstances were conducive. William Pitt the Younger introduced the first income tax in 1799 during the Napoleonic Wars. Its justification was the failure of alternative forms of revenue production to cover the expenses of war and an ever-rising national debt.

Ministers revised tax policy within a context of emerging parliamentary government. The representative branch of government increasingly controlled fiscal decisions. Its relative bargaining power in relation to the rule of the monarch through the offices of the crown had grown significantly over the course of the eighteenth century. Indeed, this is an important period in the transition from crown to ministerial rule. Ultimately, and paradoxically, the executive was more constitutionally constrained but more administratively free. An English monarch could not have imposed an income tax. A chief minister, accountable to Parliament, could.

Between the Glorious Revolution and the end of the Napoleonic Wars, incremental changes in taxation revealed the need for a fundamental revision of tax policy in the form of an income tax. At the same time, incremental changes in tax administration made the government capable of administering such a tax. Changes in the economy were accompanied by a virtual revolution in administrative practice. An income tax cannot succeed without a well-ordered bureaucracy in which venality plays a small role. Otherwise, the costs of measuring and monitoring taxable property, the costs of administering and enforcing payment, and the costs of monitoring the collectors are likely to outweigh the returns from the tax. Major administrative reforms in the seventeenth and eighteenth centuries paralleled the evolution of parliamentary fiscal control.

Accompanying these important transformations in government structure and policy was the creation of quasi-voluntary compliance. War, administrative reform, and evolution of ministerial and parliamentary government all were elements in its construction.

Most of this chapter discusses the governmental factors that led to the introduction of the 1799 income tax. The first is the changing balance of power between crown and Parliament and between the monarchs and ministers. The second is the reform of tax administration and policy, which reduced the transaction costs of revenue production and made an income tax possible. The third is the link between representative government, efficient and equitable tax administration, and quasi-voluntary compliance. All occurred within the context of a changing economy, war, and growing demands on government coffers. It is with these contextual factors that I begin.

JUSTIFICATIONS FOR INCREASED TAXATION

For Britain the eighteenth century was a period of economic growth and change and of increased central state power. Indeed, historians generally argue that between 1750 and 1830 "sustained economic growth . . . radically altered the manner and standard of living of Western men and women" (North 1981, 158). Population growth, the development of the industrial and service sectors relative to the agricultural sector, urbanization, and continuous technological and organizational change characterized this period throughout the Western world (North 1981, 158–59).

Brewer (1985, chap. 2) documents the experience of Britain throughout the eighteenth century. He notes the expansion of markets, the reduced costs of communication and travel due to more newspapers and better roads, the growth of both international and domestic trade, and the development of complex credit markets. The qualitative changes in the British economy of the eighteenth century "meant that changes in state policy — the imposition of a new tax, an alteration in the rate of interest or the annexation of a new possession — not only affected those directly involved, but also had important consequences for other economic actors who had commercial, industrial and credit connections with those who were the immediate subjects of state policy" (12–13).

Britain had already, by Brewer's account, developed a "fiscal-military state" by the end of the seventeenth century. The eighteenth century witnessed a further growth in central state power. By the end of the century, "Unlike the unwieldy empires of Russia and Austria, and in contrast with new, aspiring but uncertain nations like post-Revolutionary France and America, the British state was highly compact and immensely strong" (Colley 1986, 106). One indicator of the relative strength of the British state was that the burden of taxation it imposed was considerably higher than in France throughout the eighteenth century (Mathias and O'Brien 1976).

The policymaking rulers of the British state faced significant political constraints, however. Although the landed classes were hardest hit by war and taxes at the beginning of the century, they used Parliament to restrict the land tax to 10 percent in peacetime and twice that in war (Mathias and O'Brien 1976, 614). The burden of taxation shifted to merchants, traders, and, most of all, consumers (Mathias and O'Brien 1976, esp. 616–24). Perhaps the major beneficiaries of state policy were a new class of financiers (Brewer 1985, chap. 2). Both the gentry and the financial interests used state policy to achieve their ends and to further transform the British economy.

Throughout the eighteenth century, costly foreign conflicts put increasing stress on British revenue production. Both Mann (1980) and Brewer (1985, chap. 1) present impressive documentation of the growing costs of war and the mammoth increases in government expenditure during the Nine Years' War (1688–97), the War of Spanish Succession (1702–14), the War of Austrian Succession (1739–48), the Seven Years' War (1756–63), and the American War (1775–84). One consequence was that annual state expenditure increased fifteenfold over the century (Brewer 1985, chap. 1, p. 37). This calculation does not include the largest expenditure of them all, the Napoleonic Wars.

British war funding depended heavily "upon the ability of governments to raise loans through the accumulation of a permanent National Debt" (Mathias and O'Brien 1976, 623). In the eighteenth century, 75 to 85 percent of British government expenditures went to pay for the military or to service debts incurred during earlier wars (Brewer 1985, chap. 1, p. 36). Interest charges represented a major component in the rising national debt. Between 1695 and 1795, annual expenditure on debt repayment rose (in constant pounds) from .6 million pounds to 6.8 million pounds (Mann 1980, 193). The interest charges in 1816 were three times those of 1790 (Silberling 1924a, 216). The necessities of debt repayment largely account for the fact that postwar taxation and spending seldom reverted to lower prewar levels (Mann 1980).

There is another crucial link between the national debt and taxation policy. Successful reliance on credit requires lender confidence that the borrower will repay loans and interest. The tax system provided this confidence. Particular taxes were often linked to debt repayment (Ehrman 1969, 269). Moreover, and more important, the repeal of taxes, once in place, threatened the security of credit. They could be eliminated only if replaced by other taxes (Brewer 1985, chap. 1, p. 75; 1988, 3).

War and the national debt intensified the strains on the economy and the government. The first French War in 1793 was accompanied by a commercial crisis that continued until the end of the wars. The Bank of England was particularly hard hit by the combination of heavy commercial loans, specie depletion, and government demands for advances (Silberling 1924b, 398). The already overburdened fiscal system relied on a mixture of land, customs, and excise taxes and borrowing. The eighteenth century is marked by ministerial efforts to revise this system. Ultimately, this required a transformation in the relationships of governmental power.

PARLIAMENT, CROWN, AND MINISTERS: CHANGES IN RELATIVE BARGAINING POWER

The Glorious Revolution began a process that continued throughout the eighteenth century. The year 1688 is often considered the watershed year, "the landmark between the period of autocratic Monarchy and that of constitutional Monarchy" (Einzig 1959, 117).[2] By 1799 Parliament, especially the Commons, had significantly increased its control over tax policy (Reitan 1966). Parliament had also significantly reduced the "influence of the Crown"—that is, the ability of the office of the monarch, including his ministers, to control Parliament by filling it with placemen, those who held their positions through crown patronage (Foord 1947). At the same time, within the executive, the balance of power between sovereign and ministers was shifting to the ministers.

Cooperation between monarch and Parliament had long marked British government (see chapter 5), but after 1688 cooperation was ensured. Brewer (1985, chap. 1, p. 89) argues that the key was the price Commons set for its cooperation with William III:

> The price the Commons exacted was two-fold: a guarantee of royal dependence on the lower house for its finances and greater scrutiny of the financial workings of the executive by the legislature. . . . After 1688 the Commons deliberately refused to provide the monarch with an adequate "ordinary" income. They worked to ensure that the head of state would have to depend on the lower house and would have to return to it frequently to fund the day-to-day running of government. Regular parliaments were no accident, brought about by the financial exigencies of war, but an act of policy on the part of parliamentarians who had learned the hard lesson of the previous two reigns about the dangers of a financially independent king.

---

[2] See Hirst (1986) for a quite different evaluation of the seventeenth century from that held by many historians.

One key to Parliament's control of the monarch's income was the Civil List, initially instituted by the Civil List Act of 1698.[3] The Civil List covered the costs of civil government and the royal household (Reitan 1966, 319). These costs included the salaries of ministers, judges, ambassadors, consuls, and numerous other public officers and officeholders as well as a variety of pensions, fees, and allowances. Disbursements of the Civil List were also used to maintain royal buildings and parks, support the "dignity of the Crown," endow charitable organizations, and finance the Secret Service. Revenues to cover Civil List expenditures were drawn from the Duchy of Cornwall, the 4½ percent duties from the West Indies, customs and excise, and various hereditary revenues.[4] Parliament granted these revenues to the reigning monarch for life but appropriated any surplus, should there be one. It also reassigned the Civil List with each succession to the throne.

A second key to growing parliamentary control of finances was its increasingly aggressive role in determining taxes. Parliament no longer simply constrained the monarchs in their fiscal policy. It actively made tax policy. Moreover, it chose taxes, such as the land tax imposed after 1688, that "maximized parliamentary control of government spending" (Brewer 1988).

Despite limitations on the monarch, the crown (in contradistinction to the monarch) was able to retain considerable power relative to Parliament.[5] Ehrman (1969, 40) writes, "Throughout the second half of the century, the followers of the crown formed the largest and most stable voting element in the House." Accusations of venality abounded, based on instances of crown payment—with revenue and jobs—to the aristocracy and other private persons for the right to appoint nominees. There is no evidence of direct crown bribery of voters, but the crown did influence the outcome of elections by providing free beer and food, special events, and patronage. The crown was also known to use peerages as patronage.

However, such behaviors seem to have been less prevalent and the crown's direct control of seats less complete than is generally presumed. For

---

[3] The most complete and interesting discussion of the Civil List is contained in Reitan (1966). Also see Einzig (1959).

[4] Foord (1947, 489–91), Einzig (1959, 132), and Reitan (1966, 319) itemize the Civil List. Reitan cites the *Report on Public Income and Expenditure,* H.C. 1868–69 (366), XXXV, part 2, pp. 585ff., as the summary source.

[5] Ehrman (1969, 39–43) offers a useful discussion of the crown's influence. Foord (1947) discusses this "influence" and its "waning." Reitan (1966, 322–23) notes that the crown patronage provided a *cursus honorarium* to young men of good families, opportunities for intelligent young men of middle-class families, and virtually the only jobs and income for high-born ladies.

example, in the election of 1780, Ehrman calculates (1969, 42) that "Government returned twenty-four members to Parliament, and . . . another 221 seats lay more or less at the disposal of 119 private persons." The crown maintained its parliamentary following primarily through the manipulation of selective incentives in the form of job opportunities. Placemen represented a proportion of parliamentary seats, but the largest contingent of "King's Friends" came from seats in which the crown had used its patronage to bargain for electoral favors.

David Hume, writing in 1741 (cited in Foord 1947, 484), was relatively sanguine about the effects of crown influence:

> The Crown has so many offices at its disposal, that when assisted by the honest and disinterested part of the House, it will always command the resolutions of the whole so far, at least, as to preserve the ancient constitution from danger. We may, therefore, give to this influence what name we please, we may call it by the invidious appellations of *corruption* and *dependence;* but some degree and some kind of it are inseparable from the very nature of the constitution, and necessary to the preservation of our "mixed government." (his emphasis)

Others, however, were convinced that crown patronage undermined rather than maintained the constitutional balance of the "King in Parliament." They perceived the influence of the crown as corrupting to Parliament. The Place Acts, which were enacted from 1693 to 1742, were designed to bar officeholders from sitting in Commons. Only partially successful, they did nonetheless "reduce the political value of many government offices" and "prevent administrators from meddling too much in parliamentary politics" (Brewer 1985, chap. 1, p. 49).[6]

The Civil List was the primary source of crown patronage. The fact that the crown did not have to itemize expenditures to Parliament or to disclose state financial records for which it was responsible fed parliamentary and popular distrust of the crown's use and possible misuse of the Civil List. In 1760, at the occasion of George III's accession, Parliament transferred the Civil List revenues to itself and granted the king a fixed annuity of £800,000 per year to cover Civil List expenses. Thereafter the Civil List was constantly in arrears, so that the crown had regularly to turn to Parliament for additional revenues, thus providing the occasion for new concessions by the crown and new impositions by the Parliament.

---

[6] Patronage continued well into the nineteenth century. In 1810 George Rose documented many of these complaints. By 1834 Commons had appointed a select committee to investigate the persistence of the patronage system. The committee's report was stinging, particularly in its attack on sinecures (Foord 1947, 499–500).

The denouement was the Economical Reform Act of 1782, originally proposed by Edmund Burke in 1780. In support, John Dunning argued:[7]

> 1. That it is the opinion of this committee, that it is necessary to declare, that the influence of the Crown has increased, is increasing, and ought to be diminished.
>
> 2. That it is competent to this House, to examine into and to correct, abuses in the expenditure of the Civil List revenues, as well as in every other branch of the public revenue whenever it shall appear expedient to the wisdom of this House to do so.

The thrust of the reforms was to redefine as public property what had previously been defined as the private property of the crown. First, Parliament classified the crown's hereditary dues as public monies under parliamentary supervision. Second, it established clear-cut spending guidelines and demanded full accountability for any and all expenditures made from the Civil List. Third, the Irish and Scottish pension funds, the revenues accruing from the Post Office, and the scattered landholdings of the crown all came under public scrutiny.

The crown's influence did not crumble overnight as a result of Parliament's efforts to control the disbursement of funds. However, English historians generally acknowledge that these reforms, initiated in the late eighteenth century and continuing until about 1830, did diminish the crown's ability to dominate the fiscal machinery of the state. Burke's purpose was to prevent abuses and mismanagement. His unintended effect was to alter the constitutional basis of the Civil List.[8] Reitan (1966, 337) notes that "Burke's act completed the long struggle between crown and Parliament for the control of finance; it was the final step in the separation of the crown from the finance of government."

Reduction of crown power vis-à-vis Parliament was complemented by a change in the balance of power between monarchs and their ministers. There was, as yet, no prime minister in the Victorian sense, nor had the cabinet system evolved. In the late eighteenth century, the monarch was still the chief executive of a series of relatively independent departments. Governments were formed from shifting alliances with the help of a chief or first minister, who usually was the First Lord of the Treasury and Chancellor of the Exchequer, the posts that William Pitt the Younger held.

I argued in chapter 5 that war can enhance the ruler's power by increas-

---

[7] The debate in the Commons can be found in *Hansard's Parliamentary History* 1780–81, 221:340–53.

[8] This is Reitan's conclusion (1966, 328–36). Also see Foord (1947, 491–93) and Ehrman (1969, 60–61).

ing constituent dependence on a centralized military and fiscal establishment. It raises the discount rates of constituents and makes them more willing to accept new and increased taxes.

War certainly did enhance the ruler's power in this case, but it also contributed to the changeover in rule from monarch to ministers, who used the foreign conflicts to augment their power. Britain's international problems were of intense interest to a Parliament eager to see Britain victorious in war. Parliament blamed Britain's military setback in America on the monarch's economic inefficiency and fiscal mismanagement. The outcome of the American war was further impetus to parliamentary mobilization. The aim was to redress the balance of fiscal responsibility between crown and Parliament and to change from monarchical to ministerial leadership.

Britain had only recently lost the American colonies when France declared war. Those in Parliament shared the popular consensus that French aggression posed a particularly severe risk. They feared that the French would strip Britain of her commercial advantages and that French radical ideologies would incite an already restless British populace to rebellion. Landed interests sensed a threat to their own social and material well-being and were generally willing to cooperate to repel the enemy. It was widely believed, though never proven, that French agitators had played a covert role in creating the violent unrest of the Gordon riots of June 1780.[9]

The intensity of anti-French sentiment is obvious in a speech by Lord Auckland in defense of Pitt's income tax bill in 1799. He described the French as "a credulous, subjugated, irreligious, immoral and cruel people; blind instruments of the corruptions, caprices and crimes of a few desperate regicides."[10] Indeed, even middle-class and working-class dissidents, who sympathized with French radical ideologies, found themselves committed to defending England against France.

Pitt was chief minister during most of these crucial years. He was in power after the loss of America and throughout much of the war with France. He began his career with a healthy distrust for the king or, more generally, monarchical power (Ehrman 1969, 65). He ended his career with that distrust intact. In the interim he helped build a government organization less susceptible to sovereign interference and more under the control of the ministers than when he started.

By the early nineteenth century, Pitt had succeeded in enlarging the role

---

[9] Thomas Holcroft was an eyewitness to the riots, and he has provided the principal documentation of events in his *A Plain and Succinct Narrative of the Gordon Riots* ([1780] 1944). In the last part of this tract, he alludes to possible French interference.

[10] Quoted from *Hansard's Parliamentary History* 1798–1800, 34:203.

of chief minister to the point where prime minister seems an appropriate designation. His power relative to George III was partially a consequence of the king's illness, but it was primarily a consequence of Pitt's extraordinary abilities and his longevity in office. Except for a three-year hiatus from 1801 to 1804, he served from 1783 until his death in 1806. His own confidence in the stability of his rule lowered his discount rate so that he could contemplate—and, more important, implement—a fundamental reorganization of government.

In such a context, the representative institution of Parliament both enhanced and constrained executive power. It legitimated policies by clothing them in the cloak of public debate and approval by those elected to speak on behalf of the people. It undermined monarchical power and, in the process, increased ministerial power. However, the ministers had seats in Parliament. They could be removed from their ministries, and they could fail in achieving their legislative aims. Policies were a consequence of cooperation and exchange, of conditional cooperation between ministers and members.

The result of the changing balance of power between crown and Parliament, monarch and ministers, was effective and stable rule under a changing set of ministers with policies bearing the stamp of parliamentary approval. The foundation was being laid for quasi-voluntary compliance with the income tax.

TRANSACTION COSTS OF TAX ADMINISTRATION AND TAX POLICY

Taxation in Britain evolved with changes in the return from certain taxes and in the cost of measuring, monitoring, and enforcing compliance. As the costs went down and the return went up for a particular tax, it became more important in the revenue extraction system. Transformations in the economy were the major influence on potential return. Administrative reform reduced the costs of measurement and monitoring and enhanced the possibility of quasi-voluntary compliance, which further lowered enforcement costs. This section takes up the two distinct but related issues of administrative reform and economic return. The next section addresses the factors promoting quasi-voluntary compliance.

Brewer (1985, chap. 1, p. 38) claims that the key to Britain's international success in the eighteenth century was the dual development of "the emergence of a relatively efficient bureaucracy staffed by competent administrators, and the growth of what was undoubtedly the most sophisticated financial system in Europe."[11] These developments were also factors in making the income tax both administratively viable and politically acceptable. They significantly reduced the transaction costs of a universal income tax.

Britain suffered from its share of administrative corruption. Well into the eighteenth century, it was not an uncommon practice for revenue officers to charge heavily for the "expenses" of collection and to earn interest on funds they collected before surrendering them to the Exchequer (Einzig 1959, 125). "Public money had a way of sticking to the fingers of the many officials through whose hands it passed" (Brewer 1985, chap. 1, p. 42). The length of time it took for taxes to reach the Exchequer promoted opportunism. Yet the British fiscal structure never suffered from the burden of spoils and sinecures that the French and other European systems bore (Brewer 1985, chap. 1, p. 48). Its relative administrative efficiency had a long tradition, dating back to the early days of national taxation. The Place Acts and reforms of Civil List expenditures further pared down redundant positions.

Pitt inherited a fiscal structure that was already "reformed" and efficient in comparison to its European counterparts. In 1660–80 the government exerted greater control of tax collection through the Treasury. By 1683 tax farming had ended, and after 1713 the majority of all taxes were collected by government employees.

In 1780, when the campaign for reform was at its height, Commons received from the Taxes' Office a flood of papers on arrears, the rate of payment, receivers' balances, and fees and organization. In the next twenty years, Commons called for a raft of papers on accounts of arrears and on many other administrative details in England and Scotland.

Within the context of this recognized need for administrative reform, Pitt set about to make the fiscal machinery more efficient (see, esp., Ehrman 1969, chap. 11). In 1785 he reorganized tax administration in two offices, one for customs and one for all other taxes. He reformed the administration of the revenues of crown lands and the Post Office. He reorganized the receipt system so as to create a central fund into which all revenues were to be deposited. He introduced a well-organized audit. He abolished some sinecures and allowed others to lapse through attrition. By one account he reduced revenue places by 441 between December 1783 and February 1793 (Ehrman 1969, 318).

However, Pitt was an extremely restrained reformer. Most of the admin-

---

[11] I am drawing heavily here and throughout on work by Brewer (1988).

istrative change was piecemeal and incremental. In relation to administration, he left certain realms — most notably, land tax administration — alone (Ehrman 1969, 283–85). He feared political opposition from those with vested rights that would be affected by alterations in administration or policy. He also sought economies that would not require immediate expenditures (or losses) even if the likelihood was long-term gain.

Over the course of the eighteenth century, British fiscal machinery evolved into a relatively efficient administrative apparatus under the control of Parliament and the ministers. Nonetheless, it was proving incapable of producing adequate revenue to meet the exigencies of war or debt repayment. Parliament emphasized first one form of taxation and then another as the combination of economic return and administrative viability altered the attractiveness of the options.

In the aftermath of the Glorious Revolution, Parliament initially preferred the land tax. Parliament controlled its incidence, and a local gentry, rather than a crown department, controlled its collection. However, the tax became increasingly unpopular among the landed classes. From the middle of the eighteenth century, the emphasis was on the excise tax. The thriving industry and commerce of England, based on "a reasonably well-consolidated and efficient set of industries — brewing, maltstering, candles and paper-making — and a sustained demand for their products" (Brewer 1988), ensured a high return from the excise. From 1713 until the introduction of the income tax in 1799, the excise dominated other sources of tax revenue.

The excise service was rigorously organized and supervised (Brewer 1988). Its employees engaged in difficult and sometimes dangerous work, involving constant monitoring of the industries on which the excise was imposed. It was also very large. Of the 4,780 full-time employees in the fiscal bureaucracy in 1708, excise accounted for 2,247 and customs for 1,839. By 1782–83, 4,908 full-time employees were in excise and 2,205 in customs out of a total 7,222 (Brewer table).

In the 1780s the excise service was held up as a model of administration by Treasury and by various investigatory commissions. Brewer (1988) argues that its efficiency and effectiveness derived from its professional internal organization, its expeditious process of remittance from collector to cashier, its efficient central office, and the powerful administrative law that backed its jurisdiction. It provided rewards on the basis of both seniority and skill. Political patronage might lead to appointment, but it could not ensure promotion. Indeed, the pattern of promotions created an expert top management. The fact that officers were salaried contributed to both the professionalism of the excise service and its ability to resist political influence. Moreover, elaborate mechanisms of surveillance assured near-certain detection and punishment of idle excisemen. The excisemen had to keep several sets of records, which they could not alter, and another set of records was kept by their supervisor.

The excise was also extremely efficient in its collection of revenues and intrusive in its regulations (Brewer 1988). This well-organized bureaucracy was geared to daily inspections—or even, in the case of the London brewers, inspections every six hours. Traders who breached excise regulations were subject to draconian justice.

The excise, despite its notable efficiency, had several major drawbacks for revenue production. First, by 1800 the excise and other indirect taxes had reached the limits to which they could be imposed without considerably reducing demand. Second, the excise was regressive. Its burden fell mainly on consumers, with relatively little taxation of landed wealth or business.[12] It is not clear that eighteenth-century (let alone contemporary) observers perceived indirect taxes in this way. Nonetheless, there is evidence of a growing concern for equity in taxation (see Dietz 1983, *passim*). This concern was enhanced by a third factor, the influence of Adam Smith's *Wealth of Nations* ([1776] 1937) on Pitt and other policymakers (Ehrman 1969, 248–49). Smith argued that indirect taxes interfered with commerce. Although Smith opposed the income tax, he favored direct taxes that were geared to a person's ability to pay and that fell on easily visible wealth, such as houses and land.[13] Fourth, and hardly least important, there was "rising pressure from manufacturers, beginning to test their strength, against any imposition likely to raise their prices" (Ehrman 1969, 252).

Since 1747 government had been experimenting with direct, assessed taxes on luxuries, such as carriages, silver plate, hair powder, clocks and watches, and menservants.[14] These taxes represented a first step toward progressive taxation and certainly a first step in some form of required income reporting. However, they were easy to evade and were never good revenue raisers. In 1747 they represented .83 percent of total revenue; by

---

[12] Mathias and O'Brien (1976, 1978) make this point, which Mathias (1983, 37–38; 1979, 123–29) then elaborates. McCloskey (1978) raises some questions about their calculations concerning the incidence of taxation.

[13] The extent of Smith's influence on the policymakers of this era is controversial. It is interesting to note that Smith was not always consistent, as the twelve years (1778–90) he spent as a commissioner of Scottish customs attest (Anderson, Shughart, and Tollison 1985).

[14] This account of assessed taxation draws heavily on Dietz (1983).

1776, 1.10 percent; and by 1798, the year of the "triple assessment," 8.4 percent (Dietz 1983, 118). Moreover, despite the government's claim that these taxes were progressive and did not dissuade commerce, their effect — with the exception of the carriage tax — was just the opposite.

Pitt was able to improve the revenue-generating volume of the state by gradually fine-tuning the tax rates, central machinery, and collection mechanisms. His tax policies in the 1780s and 1790s were heterogeneous rather than simple and comprehensive (Ehrman 1969, chap. 10, esp. p. 256). He emphasized existing taxes. He built on existing administrative practice. His aim was to improve return by cutting down on evasion and fraud and by increasing efficiency in collection and administration. Besides the reforms discussed above, he also undertook a major campaign against the smuggling that permitted evasion of excises on tea, tobacco, and other such consumer items (Ehrman 1969, 240–47).

By the late 1790s, financial crisis extended beyond the point at which tinkering with the fiscal machinery would result in large enough revenue increases to cover the costs of the war and debt repayment. The eighteenth-century tax system reflected the British government's "failure to tax wealth and rising incomes effectively" (Mathias and O'Brien 1976, 614).

As early as 1792, Pitt was aware that British productive power was a revenue source to be tapped. In a speech to Commons, he discussed Britain's economy and alluded to the role of revenue generation in protecting the Constitution:[15]

> Having gone thus far, having slated the increase of revenue, and shown that it has been accompanied by a proportionate increase of the national wealth, commerce and manufactures, I feel that it is natural to ask, what have been the peculiar circumstances to which these effects are to be ascribed? . . . to that constant accumulation of capital, that continual tendency to increase, the operation of which is universally seen in a greater or lesser proportion, whenever it is not obstructed by some public calamity, or by some mistaken and mischievous policy, but which must be conspicuous and rapid indeed in any country which has once arrived at an advanced state of commercial prosperity. Let us remember, that the love of the Constitution, though it acts as a sort of natural instinct in the hearts of Englishmen, is strengthened by reason and reflection, and every day confirmed by experience; that it is a constitution which we do not merely admire from traditional reverence but which we cherish and value because we know that it practically secures the tranquility and welfare of individuals and of the public. . . . Let me express my earnest wish, my anxious and fervent prayer, that now in this period of our success, for

[15] See William Pitt's "Speech on the State of Public Finances," 17 Feb. 1792 (reprinted in Wiener 1974, 598).

the sake of the present age and posterity, there may be no intermission in that vigilant attention of Parliament to every object connected with the revenue, the resources, and the credit of the state.

Pitt's speech establishes the fact that he was aware of Britain's rapid economic growth and that as early as 1792 he tried to establish the legitimacy of the state's claim on some of those gains. To realize those gains, he was willing to undertake the costs of initiating a politically risky tax scheme with a very high start-up investment.

He first attempted to generate additional revenue with the Aid and Contribution Act of 1798, the "triple assessment" as it was informally called. Pitt hoped to avoid a direct tax on income or increased intrusions into individual financial records. Previous assessments were multiplied two to five times in order to arrive at the individual's tax obligation. In the process Pitt managed both to preserve traditional assessments and to make them more progressive. The triple assessment's great achievement was to bring "assessment, although calculated according to expenditure, into relation with income" (Dietz 1983, 38–39).

Financially, it was not so successful, however. Dowell (1888, 2:157) labels the result "a fiscal fiasco unequaled in the history of our taxation." Hope-Jones (1939, 14) calls it "a failure; Pitt had hoped for £4,500,000; only £2,000,000 was collected." Evasion appears to have been a significant problem.

It was in the wake of the triple assessment's failure that Pitt proposed and justified his plan for a direct income tax replete with a large and carefully conceived enforcement mechanism. His income tax plan was necessary, he argued (cited in Seligman 1911, 72):

> to prevent those frauds which an imperfect criterion and a loose facility of modification have introduced to repress those evasions so disgraceful to the country, so injurious to those who honorably discharge their equal contribution, and above all, so detrimental to the great object of national advantage which it is intended to promote.

CONVINCING THE POPULACE: CREATING QUASI-VOLUNTARY COMPLIANCE

The introduction of the first income tax in Britain in 1799 was possible because, first, government successfully convinced the citizenry that the income tax was necessary to finance a popular, if costly, war. Second, government could provide assurances that it would come through with its side of the bargain—that is, use the funds to support the military and, ultimately, wage a successful campaign in the Napoleonic Wars. Third, it could provide assurances that other citizens would pay their shares and that government agents would be relatively honest, that no one (or virtually no one) would be a sucker. Assurances of progressivity, protections of privacy, and public confidence that there would be little administrative waste, corruption, or mismanagement were the prerequisites, the conditions for quasi-voluntary compliance.

This is not to deny that coercion underlay quasi-voluntary compliance. However, its significance lay not in its direct use but in the calculation each taxpayer made that the others would certainly pay or be punished. Government coordinated punishment. Its power of coercion provided the promise that others would indeed comply. To ensure compliance with taxes, the government had to be able to monitor and enforce taxpaying.

By the mid-eighteenth century, centralization of the British state, efficient tax administration, and "the great legitimacy accorded parliamentary statute" made it difficult to overtly resist taxes within England (Brewer 1985, chap. 2, p. 7). Britain was a highly taxed country in the eighteenth century. Mathias and O'Brien (1976, 610–11) claim that:

> on a per capita basis, in Britain taxes were more than double the level attained in France at the beginning of the century (1715–1730), remained at twice the level of those in France for most of the rest of the period up to the Revolution, and during the years thereafter reached almost three times the level imposed on the French population.

This is a highly contested estimate (see, for example, McCloskey 1978), but it does provide some sense of the difference in the central government figures between the two countries. Whatever the actual incidence of taxation relative to France, it was certainly higher in Britain than it had been in the past.

Nonetheless, there were some serious limitations on what the populace would accept. "The free-born Englishman" (Thompson 1963, chap. 4) and the *homo economicus* of Adam Smith were highly individualist and highly opposed to arbitrary central state power. They possessed few positive rights, but they did possess the right to be left alone. (It is not clear that the Englishwoman possessed even this right.) Direct taxes were deemed an unwarranted intrusion on privacy, and direct income taxes were considered both an intrusion and likely to be unfair. Many parliamentarians shared this perspective. Moreover, this was a period of intense political expression, in which patriotism and nationalism often were invoked to protect particularist and traditional interests (see, esp., Colley

1986; also see Dinwiddy 1985). Even so, most[16] taxpayers came to accept, if briefly, the first income tax.

Only the failure of all other alternatives overcame hostility to the income tax enough to permit its passage. Tax collection was not keeping pace with expenditures, and the income tax was the solution to this fiscal crisis. Even so, Pitt and other members of Parliament faced obstacles, including their own reluctance, to its introduction. It was an expensive tax to administer even if generally accepted, and it was far from being popular. A growing and vocal electorate had to be convinced of the benefits of an income tax if it was to be implemented without expensive coercion. Both the land tax and the excise had been modified in response to political pressure even before Pitt came on the scene. Pitt, as much as his predecessors, was wary of stirring up too many political waters — as is evidenced by his incremental reforms (Ehrman 1969, chaps. 10–11).

The Napoleonic Wars provided the justification for the tax. Administrative safeguards provided assurances of general compliance. The government had already demonstrated its effectiveness in detecting and sanctioning evaders with the administrative structure developed for expenditure taxes, first in the excise service and then refitted for assessments. This "comparatively sophisticated mechanism" was taken over for the income tax (Sabine 1966, 25).

The administration of the income tax was designed to circumvent venality on the part of agents as well as evasion by citizens. In 1785 Pitt had created two revenue departments, the Customs and the Commissioners for the Affairs of Taxes, which managed the land tax, the assessed taxes, and after 1799 the income tax. Despite a recent scandal over the quality of the land tax commissioners, in 1798 Pitt argued for using carefully selected and qualified commissioners, drawn from the local gentry, as the principal agents of the income tax (Sabine 1966, 27–28). He felt that the income tax would evoke more confidence if administered by "persons of a respectable situation in life: as far as possible removed from any suspicion of partiality or any kind of undue influence: men of integrity and independence" (quoted in Sabine 1966, 27).

Checks and double checks were built into a hierarchical system in which each agent was directly accountable for collections at the level below. Records were carefully maintained, and the accounts of collectors and commissioners at all levels were monitored by a thorough and regular

---

[16] A mob physically attacked one local official a short time after the income tax was implemented. Hope-Jones (1939, 68–69) documents several instances of violent attacks on tax officials.

system of audits. Civil servants were expected to live on their salaries without dipping into the returns. While the crown still maintained some of its capacity to sell governmental offices in exchange for votes, this practice became less and less common. Moreover, with the reduction of the opportunities for venality, bureaucratic appointment became less attractive to those who sought to profit by it. One analyst (Hope-Jones 1939, 41) notes that:

> The ordinary routine work performed by the central organization controlling the Income Tax was sweeping in scope and effective in result. . . . The detection of errors and frauds in accountancy, the establishment of uniform standards of book-keeping and the securing of settlements at the specified date were the chief concerns of the auditors.

Equally important to the establishment of quasi-voluntary compliance was the evolution of representative institutions and greater popular control of government. The increasing reliance on volunteers for the army increased the bargaining power and "democratic impulse" by nonvoters as well as electors (Colley 1986, 113–15). Parliament and ministers depended on popular support. If elected officials did not deliver on basic promises, they could be embarrassed by popular protest and ousted from office at the next election.

The income tax represented a major new intrusion of government into privacy and private rights. The populace would never have permitted a strong monarch that kind of power. Citizens allowed the income tax only when they believed there was no alternative, only with reasonable assurances that government would provide what it promised (more or less) and that the distribution of taxpaying would be relatively equitable, and only when they felt some confidence that their political influence was adequate to limit its application. With the convergence of all three of these conditions, quasi-voluntary compliance became an option.

The decision to comply was more negative than positive in form. Citizens did not seek to pay the income tax; they chose not to resist it in the face of politically acceptable, even popular, government expenditures—namely, for the Napoleonic Wars. When the wars ended, so did the income tax. It was not until the 1840s that ministers could again convince the Parliament or the populace of its necessity.

THE SHORT-LIVED INCOME TAX

Income tax by placing men's interests in regular and
systematic opposition to their conscience holds out a
direct premium of fraud and perjury.
        Reverend G. Glover
        Thoughts on the Character of the Property Tax

The initial income tax, known as the "war income tax," lasted until 1816 with a brief period of repeal in 1802. The forebearer of the contemporary income tax was not instituted until 1842. The initial income tax represented a bargain between the ministers and Parliament and between Parliament and citizens. The terms included an understanding that, first, the income tax was a war levy and, second, it would be fairly administered.

The first repeal of the tax was in 1802 as a direct result of the Treaty of Amiens. Henry Addington, who briefly (one year) replaced William Pitt as chief minister, revoked the income tax in his first budget. This decision "was forced on the new Prime Minister by its unpopularity and the promise that it was a war tax exclusively" (Sabine 1966, 34). It is highly unlikely that Addington would have been able to muster support in Parliament. He was a weak prime minister without even the rudimentary "party" that Pitt's friends represented (Webb 1968).

With the recurrence of war with Napoleon, Addington reintroduced the income tax in his 1803 war budget. He called it a property tax, but this ploy fooled no one. Since it included two major innovations, Sabine (1966, 35–37) argues that the new tax was not a simple revival of Pitt's tax. The first innovation—to which Pitt strongly objected—was the allowance of deductions at source on interest, dividends, rent, and income from the funds and emoluments of crown servants. The second was the introduction of the five schedules, which in modified form persist to the current day.

There was debate over the tax, but the priority of the Commons was repelling the French. To that end the government needed the additional resources the income tax provided. Although the income tax remained "a comparatively unimportant tax instrument" for the government (Hope-Jones 1939, 17), it did provide significant additional funds. The 1800 income tax, which yielded approximately £6 million, was well below Pitt's £10 million estimate (Sabine 1966, 33). Nonetheless, this was more than three times the revenue from the triple assessment. In 1800 there were only 321,000 returns, well below the expected million (O'Brien 1959, 255)—out of a population that by 1801 reached 10.943 million in Great Britain, excluding Ireland (Hope-Jones 1939, 124).

However, in 1813 the "war income tax" achieved its highest yield of £15,795,691. During the life of the income tax, administrative practice improved significantly. Hope-Jones (1939, chaps. 3–4) praises the competence and integrity of the income tax staff. He credits the system with a well-articulated system of agency checks and balances. Certainly, for its time the administration of the British income tax was a model of efficiency.

Nonetheless, it remained a small and understaffed bureaucracy (Sabine

1966, 34). Although the income tax administration was relatively adept at monitoring taxpayers — and got even better over time — there was still considerable slippage. Public awareness of evasion added to a general sense that the income tax was not only a heavy burden, unnecessary except during war, but also likely to be unfair and inequitable.

With the end of the Napoleonic Wars in 1815, pressure for repeal of the tax once again overwhelmed the arguments on its behalf. Robert Banks Jenkinson, Lord Liverpool, was the prime minister in 1816, and he had no intention of voluntarily withdrawing the income tax even though the war had ended (see discussion in Brock 1967). The national debt stood at £9 million, and annual interest payments had creeped up to £32 million, over one-third of all government expenditure. Liverpool's aim was to use the income tax to service the debt, although he planned to lower the rate from 10 percent to 5 percent.

Liverpool failed in his policy because of a massive campaign for the repeal of the tax. The Whigs, under Henry Brougham, led the attack (Gash 1984 documents their efforts). Indeed, the issue did much to improve Whig cohesion. So universally unpopular was the income tax that moderates and radicals alike joined hands in protest. Even die-hard Tories in Parliament joined the opposition to fellow-Tory Liverpool and the income tax. There was not yet a party system in Britain, and elections did not yet decide who constituted the government. Nonetheless, during the campaign for repeal of the income tax, "the opposition Whigs behaved like a party in the modern sense" (Cookson 1975, 61).

Citizen petitions against the tax accumulated in Parliament in 1816 (Sabine 1966, 43–44). Even the unfranchised working poor could express their political views through petitions, and many did. The agitation for repeal was both deep and broad.

The opposition believed that the government's attempt to continue the tax was devious and deliberately deceptive.[17] The drive for continuation of the tax in peacetime was perceived as rank opportunism, breaking faith with the terms of citizen agreement to the tax. Opponents argued that the government was greedy for revenue and power. They claimed that the government was unwilling to give up the means by which to pry into personal financial records. They also pointed out that the government might use the proceeds of the tax to police and oppress the citizenry.

The campaign was successful. The income tax was repealed. Moreover,

[17] See the parliamentary debates in *Hansard's Parliamentary History* 1782–83, vol. 22, esp. pp. 437, 877, 974.

Parliament passed a measure calling for the physical destruction of all individual income tax returns. A public burning of the records took place. What the public did not know was that the Tax Office had duplicates, which were hidden until 1932.

CONCLUSION

The story of Pitt and the origin of the income tax represents an interesting case for the model of predatory rule. Pitt's personal aims were neither to build a bigger state nor to extract all the revenue that could in principle be extracted. He believed in a limited state that carried out its limited responsibilities efficiently. After all, he was a self-professed follower of Adam Smith.

The British state of the eighteenth century was a fiscal and war-making state. It was not yet deeply involved in education or social programs; it invested little in developing national consciousness or mobilization (Colley 1986, 104–106). Indeed, Pitt felt strongly that it was impolitic to rouse nationalist fervor and addressed his early appeals for volunteers to those with wealth and property (Colley 1986, 109).

War compelled Pitt to become a revenue maximizer. He sought the income tax because it was the most lucrative available means for producing revenue. However, he came to this policy reluctantly. The logic of institutional change — the necessary evolution of the state to meet new demands within a changed economy — required that, whatever his personal goals, he, as chief executive, maximize revenue to the state. Addington learned the same lesson. Liverpool, benefiting from his predecessors' experiences, actively sought the maintenance of the income tax. He justified his proposal on the basis of growing government expenditures.

This chapter also illustrates the close interconnection of bargaining power and transaction costs. Political opposition to the income tax made this otherwise economically efficient form of revenue production very costly. British rulers found themselves making a trade-off between the constraints imposed by their relative bargaining power and the possibility of achieving greater revenue with reduced transaction costs. The income tax was not even possible until Parliament and ministers held the balance of fiscal power relative to the crown. A Parliament concerned with constraining the crown would never have permitted to the monarch such a lucrative resource. In eighteenth-century and early-nineteenth-century Britain, the dependence of chief ministers on Parliament constrained even them, except during war, from imposing the income tax.

The most important finding of this case study is the relationship between quasi-voluntary compliance and the income tax. A highly commercialized economy, ruler power, and a well-developed fiscal bureaucracy are necessary but insufficient prerequisites. In the absence of widespread quasi-voluntary compliance, the transaction costs of administering the tax would have been too high. However, the taxpayers had some confidence in the evenhandedness and uprightness of the collection agencies and therefore also had some confidence that all who were subjected to taxation would pay and that what was collected would actually reach the public coffers.

The evolution of representative institutions was essential to the passage of the income tax. Increased parliamentary control of expenditures and public discussion of tax policy provided some assurance that taxation was in the collective good. Improved communications throughout the countryside meant that the decisions of Parliament were comparatively public. Thus, the populace could develop a sense of whether a policy was "fair" and whether past contracts were being kept. The existence of the institution of Parliament helped promote the quasi-voluntary compliance that was necessary to make the income tax cost-effective.

However, this was an era of widespread dissemination of information on parliamentary action by an ever-growing media. Because publicly debated legislation lay at the heart of fiscal policy, rulers — that is, prime ministers — had both to negotiate with legislators and to convince a populace ready and ever more able to mobilize against policies they disliked. The institutionalization of quasi-voluntary compliance had its costs for rulers. It transformed the constraints on their bargaining power.

CHAPTER VII

Compliance with the Commonwealth Income Tax in Australia

The rights of self-government of the States have been fondly
supposed to be safeguarded by the Constitution. It has left
them legally free, but financially bound to the Chariot wheels
of the Commonwealth.

Alfred Deakin, quoted in Robert Menzies
Central Power in the Australian Commonwealth

This chapter focuses on two very different kinds of compliance: (1) state
government compliance with the Australian Commonwealth government's
imposition of a uniform income tax in 1942; (2) Australian citizens' quasi-
voluntary compliance with the payment of that tax. The first resulted from
increased relative bargaining power of the central government vis-à-vis the
states. The second declined in the 1970s and 1980s with increased citizen
perception that the tax contract violated existing norms of fairness. By
investigating these events, the chapter also deals with the relationship
between the bargaining power of contemporary — and democratically
elected — rulers and major tax changes.

The theory of predatory rule implies that prime ministers will institute
reforms and changes in tax arrangements that enhance net revenue to the
central government. However, the content of their revenue-maximizing
policies and their ability to implement them will vary with the constraints
on their relative bargaining power in relation to constituents. Within a
federal system, prime ministers and presidents will face constraints imposed by other levels of government as well as by individuals, interest
groups, and classes. The existence of such constraints suggests the following proposition:

> *Given a federal system, Australian prime ministers will attempt to build Common-
> wealth government power relative to that of state and local governments. Increases*

in bargaining power will correlate with (1) their manipulation of the central position in the bargaining network among the federal and state governments and (2) their provision of collective goods, including the management of war.

The second part of the case study explores another aspect of the theory, the conditions that promote or undermine quasi-voluntary compliance. The theory implies that quasi-voluntary compliance will decline when citizens become aware that compliance is no longer general and when they believe that the tax contract violates existing norms of fairness. Thus, one should observe in Australia of the 1960s and 1970s that:

The decline in quasi-voluntary compliance will correlate with publicity about (1) tax evasion and avoidance and (2) government failure to deliver promised collective goods.

Throughout, this chapter takes up the issue of tax reform, an issue on the agenda of most contemporary advanced capitalist countries. The theory suggests that prime ministers will undertake only those tax reforms that powerful constituents permit. Party label—indeed, party faction label—is shorthand for describing which constituents constrain government policymaking. Thus, one should observe that:

Reform proposals will vary significantly with the political party in power.

From 1900 until 1910, the Commonwealth government of Australia was permitted to keep only one-quarter of the net revenues it collected from excise and customs duties, one of its principal revenue sources. The rest went to the states. In 1941 the six states of Australia imposed eleven separate income taxes on their citizens, and the Commonwealth government imposed yet another.[1] The rates varied widely. So, therefore, did citizen payments (Butlin and Schevdin 1977, 331). By 1942 there was a single and uniform income tax. To understand how the Commonwealth government attained sufficient power to impose the uniform tax requires more than a descriptive history. At issue is the process of central state building. The answer must include a theory of how central governments can wrest power from other entities, whether they be individual actors, colonies, regions, or, as in this case, states.

I suggest that the answer is not straightforwardly Hobbesian, although

---

[1] Maddock (1982, 356) quotes an important contemporary observer: "At the height of the confusion in 1935, some taxpayers were paying as many as fourteen different taxes, and receiving as many as a dozen rebates in the following year. . . . It was thus possible for the same income to be taxed by two or more States on an aggregate greater than the total income."

the problem is one of collective action. The Federation, proclaimed on New Year's Day 1901, represented a compact between the six previous colonies and the new Commonwealth government. The Commonwealth government was but one actor among seven. It had little coercive power over the states. Although it had more by 1942, its increase in power was hardly the result of a Hobbesian social contract, in which central government is given sufficient legal coercive power to impose its policies without question or restraint. Consent to legal coercion, once given, was not given once and for all. In Australia citizens and states did not self-consciously cede the predominance of power to the federal government. What happened in Australia was the incremental creation of power through legislative enactments, favorable High Court interpretations of centralizing policies, and cooptation of states by means of fiscal inducements.

The second issue this chapter takes up is the maintenance of quasi-voluntary compliance. With the uniform tax in effect, the Commonwealth government faced a new array of bargaining and transaction cost problems. Tax evasion and tax avoidance seem to have undergone major fluctuations in post–World War II Australia, with a significant rise in the 1970s (Mathews 1980; Norman 1985). As has been argued in chapter 3, obtaining compliance with taxes is costly for governments if they must rely solely on enforcement procedures. An alternative is to establish mechanisms that make taxpayers calculate that it is in their self-interest to pay up. When these mechanisms break down, noncompliance should increase.

Finally, my Australian research sheds light on the relationship between political party and policymaking in representative governments. Major parties varied in their visions of reform and in their abilities to implement it. Nonetheless, all advocated tax reform in the 1940s and again in the 1970s and 1980s. Even the most conservative prime ministers — rhetorically committed to individualism, states' rights, and the reduction of big government — sought to maximize revenue and their control of the distribution of revenue.

As in the previous chapter, I am designating as rulers the prime ministers in Australia's parliamentary system. In the case of the 1799 income tax in Britain, the prime minister was confirming his power relative to both the crown and the Parliament. In this case prime ministers — and the Commonwealth government — are establishing their dominance relative to the states and to the electorate.

Australia is a good site for researching the power of rulers who are elected heads of state. Its history of intergovernmental relations is shorter and less complex than that of Britain or France. Its Constitution is not even one hundred years old and involves, still, only six states — in contrast to a United States Constitution two hundred years old and involving first thirteen and now fifty states. Australia's relative simplicity permits a sharper focus on federalism, the decline in quasi-voluntary compliance, and the process of tax reform than is possible in more complex polities. At the same time, the Australian case provides a basis for comparison with other advanced industrial countries that have democratic governments.

THE UNIFORM INCOME TAX

On New Year's Day 1901, the Commonwealth of Australia became a federated and independent government within the British Empire. The population was 3,750,000, of whom two-thirds lived in New South Wales and Victoria alone (Crowley 1974, 261). Australia was constituted from six former colonies — New South Wales, Victoria, South Australia, Western Australia, Queensland, and Tasmania — each of which had a distinct history and a strong individual identity.

The role of the new federal government was still far from clear. One major underlying issue was how to provide adequate income to the six state governments, which had experienced a loss of income when the Constitution was adopted. They initially retained autonomous management of their lands, roads, schools, railways, and most industrial matters (Crowley 1974, 260).[2] But they gave up their right to collect excise and custom duties and to impose import tariffs.

The new federal government was faced with the task of compensating the states for lost income while at the same time taking fiscal responsibility for national defense; foreign affairs; immigration; interstate trade and commerce; customs; postal, telegraphic, and telephonic communications; currency and banking; copyrights and trademarks; and a variety of pension and insurance programs. Although the states relied heavily on borrowing, the pre-1968 Commonwealth did not, except during periods of war (Barnard 1985, 16–18). Tariffs were important sources of revenue for the federal government. Because customs and excise accounted for 76 percent of Australian taxation in 1899–1900 (Groenewegen 1983, 173–74), the drafters of the Constitution believed that funds from customs and excise would be more than enough to finance national functions. This belief led them to write Section 87, the "Braddon clause," which restricted the

---

[2] By 1985 the federal government was deeply involved in all these areas, but the story of its acquisition of power in these domains would require another chapter.

Commonwealth during its first ten years to one-quarter of the net revenue, with the balance going to the state governments. As Sir Robert Menzies (1967, 75) noted, "Section 87 was based upon what was soon discovered to be a starry-eyed expectation the new Commonwealth Parliament and Government would be cheap."

Even more influential on federal-state relations over time was Section 96 of the Commonwealth Constitution. It reads:

> During a period of ten years after the establishment of the Commonwealth and thereafter until the Parliament otherwise provides, the *Parliament may grant financial assistance to any State on such terms and conditions as the Parliament thinks fit.* (emphasis mine)

This section was the key to the building of federal power. It did not provide the Commonwealth government with coercive power vis-à-vis the states. However, it did provide the Commonwealth government with an important source of relative bargaining power — namely, a means to control state policies. Over time, national governments parlayed this power into effective central dominance over the states.

The Premiers' Conferences of 1909 anticipated the expiration of the Braddon clause and proposed temporary financial provisions. The resulting Surplus Revenue Act of 1910 committed the Commonwealth government for at least ten years to pay $2.50[3] per capita to the states. To compensate the needier states, the Commonwealth government could give out additional special grants. Tasmania and Western Australia were the immediate beneficiaries. South Australia was an eventual recipient.

The Act also provided for a return of a share of surplus revenue to the states on a per capita basis. No legal surplus ever existed or, indeed, could exist. Legislation, upheld by the High Court, permitted the federal treasurer to appropriate without dispersing monies by transferring any surplus to trust funds (Mills [1928] 1980, 64; Else-Mitchell 1977a, 37–38; Prest and Mathews 1980, 4). During World War I, there was in fact no surplus. To cover increased costs created by war, a growing national sector, and the per capita payments to the states, the federal government imposed a series of new direct taxes, including the federal income tax in 1916 (Giblin [1926] 1980, 56; Groenewegen 1983, 174–75).

At first glance, the Commonwealth government did not seem to have taken advantage of the enhancements of relative bargaining power provided by the negotiations over the Surplus Revenue Act and then by World War I. Mathews (1976, 11) claims, "The financial independence of the states was

---

[3] All dollars are, of course, Australian dollars.

not even threatened by the cessation of the surplus revenue payments
(1908) and of the arrangements for sharing customs and excise revenues in
1910. . . . The states became more dependent on revenue sources under
their own control." Barnard (1985, 26) argues that the reduction of Commonwealth collections from the 1922 level of $18 million to the 1924 level
of $11 million can only be considered a "retreat" from the exploitation of
the wider taxing powers of World War I. Total state collections, in contrast,
rose from $6.6 million in 1920 to $15.6 million in 1929. He goes on to
argue that the commitment of the Commonwealth government to increased
expenditures correlated with increased taxation (26). The implication is
that prime ministers were concerned less with maximizing revenues than
with acquiring enough revenue to cover increased costs.

From my perspective Commonwealth tax policy represented revenue
maximization within the existing political constraints even during the
1920s. The fact that the states won something back is an indicator of
the role that changes in relative bargaining power play.[4] War enhanced the
relative bargaining power of the prime ministers significantly during wartime. Because the costs of war to citizens were high, their discount rates
were significantly raised; consequently, they became more willing than in
peacetime to pay higher taxes and more willing to cede greater power to the
central government in order to see the war end. As in the establishment of
the national tax systems in medieval and Renaissance France and England,
war provided a justification for the demand by rulers for increased taxation, but only to cover the expenses of the war. With the end of World War I,
political resistance, especially from the states, to Commonwealth taxing
power revived. The Commonwealth had to revert to something approx-
imating its prewar position — although with one significant difference: its
income tax was now in existence.

The income tax was crucial as a resource for building future central
government power. However, the central government still lacked the relative
bargaining power vis-à-vis the states to retain many of the wartime taxes or
tax levels. Nonetheless, it was able to use the war to bolster its bargaining
power over time. With World War II, prime ministers could build on this
power to establish institutions that would permit them to control that most
lucrative source of revenue, the income tax.

My reading of the evidence is that the "rulers" of Australia taxed to the
limits of their relative bargaining power in relation to the states. Given the

---

[4] Australian economic historian Alan Barnard made this point to me in correspondence
(14 Oct. 1986).

constraints on their power, they chose the best available revenue-producing policy. Their subsequent actions—that is, their continuing to build that power and then using it to increase the Commonwealth's power to tax and its share of taxation—lend further support to my view.

The Financial Agreement of 1927, which was confirmed by constitutional amendment in 1928 (Mathews 1976, 10–29; also see Martin 1982, 37–38), was the next step in the building of central power. Mathews labels this the period of "cooperative federalism" (as opposed to the coordinate system of the early years). The mark of cooperation was the establishment of the Loan Council to coordinate public borrowing by the state governments and the Commonwealth. Over time, it is argued, the Loan Council became an important institution in "coercive federalism" (Gilbert 1973; Menzies 1967, 99; Mathews 1976, 22; Else-Mitchell 1977b; Groenewegen 1983, 175). The Commonwealth dominated the states within the Loan Council. Its two votes, including the casting vote, enabled it to decide any issue with the votes of but two states. Other developments virtually assured the Commonwealth the votes it required. The initiation of specific-purpose grants in the 1920s and the establishment of the Commonwealth Grants Commission in 1933 both gave the federal government considerable discretion and power over additional monies to be allotted to the states. The Commonwealth government then used these monies as carrots for compliance by the states with the Loan Council's recommendations.

The imposition of the uniform income tax in 1942 was but a next step in a process that had been going on for years. But there are those who would disagree. Laffer ([1942] 1980) and Bailey ([1944] 1980), for example, argue that tax reform was a consequence of war. Maddock, in his interesting analysis (1982), denies that war was the cause of reform but also concludes (366) that tax reform was not a natural outcome of the long struggle between Commonwealth and states. He claims that reform came about only because a Labor government, under John Curtin, came into office.

In contradistinction, I argue that Australian Labor Party (ALP) power was the intermediate, not the ultimate, cause of policy change. I agree that only the ALP could have implemented the income tax at that juncture, but I disagree that the United Australia Party–Country Party coalition's failure was a failure of will. Rather, it was a failure of power. Both major parties were centralizing in regard to the purse strings. Alternatively, I argue that war, combined with a history of high administrative costs and inequitable tax arrangements, increased the relative bargaining power of the national government vis-à-vis the states. National defense, as I have argued in earlier chapters, is a collective good that makes it possible for rulers to be granted the necessary coercive power to promote their policies. It also, in the form of war, raises the discount rates of citizens. The result was sufficient bargaining power to impose the uniform income tax.

By 1941 there was a general public and governmental outcry for tax reform. Specifically, the states and private citizens wanted a more equitable tax system, and the government needed to finance the war and reduce transaction costs by simplifying a complex and burdensome tax system.

Since the institution of the Commonwealth income tax in 1916, administrative arrangements and equity considerations had been on the agenda of Premiers' Conferences and the subject of government inquiries (Laffer [1942] 1980). L. F. Giblin and R. C. Mills, two important Australian economists, evaluated the income tax a decade after its introduction and noted certain advantages. Mills ([1928] 1980) argued that covering payments to the state with the income tax was more equitable than covering them with the customs revenue and that even greater equity would be achieved if the Commonwealth had sole income tax power. Giblin ([1926] 1980) argued that the combination of the income tax and the $2.50 per capita payment would make for an efficient and equitable system in which adjustments were automatic. Mills and Giblin were assuming that the income tax was uniform and uniformly administered, which it was not. The 1942 "Report to the Treasurer on Uniform Taxation" (Committee on Uniform Taxation 1942) described the situation:

> The varying rates and conflicting principles of taxation applied throughout the States create anomalies that operate to the detriment of Commonwealth revenue and to the confusion of taxpayers. . . . A striking example is that under the present system rates of taxation could rise above 20s in the Pound.

Section 51(ii) of the Constitution enabled the Commonwealth to impose any rate it wanted as long as there was no discrimination among states; its tax had to be uniform. Given the lack of uniformity among state rates, the Commonwealth felt restricted to a rate that entailed a serious loss of revenue in some states while overtaxing individuals in others (Bailey [1944] 1980, 310–12; Greenwood 1976, 249–50). According to Menzies (1967, 79), it was conceivable that some higher-income taxpayers in Queensland could be asked to pay "more than 100 cents in the dollar." The fact that each state had its own administrative machinery further increased the costs of government.

Administrative costs and inequities did not suddenly intensify with the onslaught of World War II. However, two contemporary observers (Laffer

[1942] 1980, 301; and Bailey [1944] 1980, *passim*) argued that the requirements of war finance made unnecessary administrative costs a luxury no longer to be afforded. Laffer ([1942] 1980, 303) estimated that uniform taxation would save approximately 250,000 pounds in salary through the release of 1,000 agents.

Maddock (1982) claims that war could not have caused the implementation of uniform taxation. First, he argues, the policy was not even put into effect until after the major crises—and costs—of the war were over. However, it is not clear from his account whether the government was aware of the imminent end of the war. Certainly the public was not. Second, he demonstrates that the legislation was not implemented until long after its passage. He concludes that "the immediate effect of the legislation was to lighten the tax load of a majority of taxpayers—those at the lower end of the distribution" (366). This proves, he argues, that the government's aim was more social than military.[5]

Unquestionably, a Labor government was more likely than a non-Labor government to support uniform taxation. Labor governments were more committed to highly progressive taxation. They openly advocated centralization. The United Australia Party (UAP), which later became the Liberal Party, and the Nationalist and Country parties, which merged, were more likely to favor states' rights and aid to business interests. Nonetheless, they also were committed to increased centralization of revenue. The differences in the constituencies of the two kinds of government meant that each had to strike a somewhat different set of bargains to achieve that end.

The Fadden government (UAP–Country Party coalition) did try to introduce uniform taxation (see, esp., Bailey [1944] 1980, 309–10; Butlin 1955, 380–90). It tried to win allies among party members by offering preferred treatment to business interests at the likely expense of new impositions on lower-income groups (Butlin 1955, 380–96). At the same time, Fadden appealed to the needs of war finance to win support from his powerful constituents. The fact that he did not push even harder for reform—"bite the bullet," as Maddock (1982, 357ff.) puts it—does not detract from his centralizing aims. It was at least as much an indication of the clout of the groups with which the government had to bargain. As

[5] Barnard (correspondence 14 Oct. 1986) disagrees with Maddock that "the immediate effect was to lighten the load on the bottom end of income recipients and that therefore the aim was more social than military. My impression is that in the first years, it brought income tax to all low wage earners, even those who had escaped it in one state or another. . . . And when the Social Service Contributions were begun just a little later it both increased effective rates on that group and dropped the income threshold lower."

usual, the Country and UAP leadership deferred to the states and corporations, who tended to oppose the policy—despite the appeal to the war.

The oncoming election had the effect of raising Fadden's discount rate. He was not going "to bite the bullet," despite its long-term advantages, if it meant losing the election. Under these circumstances his willingness to concede to powerful constituents increased. The war did not affect the prime minister's discount rate, but the election certainly did.

The proposal for a uniform income tax was more viable for a Labor than a non-Labor government because more of the ALP's voters recognized its advantages to them. Uniform taxation was in the interest of the Australian working people, who formed the base of the ALP. Commonwealth control of taxation could ensure that there was a single rate based on principles of progressive taxation. Both Fadden and Curtin used the war to promote policies their parties sought anyway, but Curtin got away with it.

Strong constituent support made Curtin more tenacious than Fadden in pursuit of tax reform. When the states rejected the uniform income tax plan at the Premiers' Conference of 1942, Curtin bypassed them by going to Parliament.

South Australia, Victoria, Queensland, and Western Australia, four out of six states, continued in opposition.[6] They took the matter to the High Court. The major issues were, first, the power of the Commonwealth to impose a uniform tax without consideration of state taxes and, second, the requirement that the Commonwealth tax be paid first. The Court upheld Parliament. Still the states balked. Several wanted to continue to impose their own taxes in addition to the centrally imposed tax.

The national government now had the power to coerce the states into acquiescence to the uniform tax but not to prevent them from imposing their own taxes. It tried the carrot instead of the stick. The solution was one of the classic solutions to free-rider problems. The Commonwealth would return a portion of the uniform income tax only to those states that complied. Menzies (1967, 80) labels this tactic "veiled coercion,"[7] failing to mention similar tactics on his part in reference to Commonwealth subsidies of state roads.

There is considerable evidence that prime ministers generally desired to

---

[6] Butlin and Schevdin (1977, 334) explain that "Tasmanian governments had never been unwilling to allow the Commonwealth to find their revenue, while in New South Wales the government beat a hasty retreat when it became clear that its own supporters were, in this matter, on the side of their party in the Commonwealth Parliament."

[7] However, he does admit (1967, 80), "In the Parliament, rather boldly *but, as it turned out, wrongly* [my emphasis], I said that the substance of the legislation was to compel the States to forgo their right to levy income taxation."

implement and extend the income tax with the greater revenues it made viable. The innovation of the income tax and, later, of withholding taxes existed in principle long before prime ministers had the power to make them fact. My argument is that what stopped the prime ministers was not the transaction costs of measurement and monitoring but inadequate bargaining power.

By the end of World War II, the Commonwealth government succeeded in achieving sufficient bargaining power that it could attain acquiescence. Its tools were a combination of financial inducements and legal sanctions. However, the crucial point is not that it had to resort to these tools but that it had acquired these tools. The selective incentives proffered by the Commonwealth government in 1942 did not even exist in 1900, when the Constitution was first implemented. The increasing bargaining power of the federal government, developed by governments of all parties, created these selective incentives. The result was state compliance in a policy area that lies at the heart of state rights: the power to tax.

An interesting and illuminating footnote to this discussion was the disingenuous offer (Martin 1982, 40) by Sir Robert Menzies to return the income tax to the states, resulting in a Special Conference in 1953. Western Australia and Tasmania objected to the return of taxing powers. New South Wales wanted the taxing power returned, accompanied by an unacceptable reduction in Commonwealth income and expenditures (Menzies 1967, 90–91).

The states could only lose if they once again took over the income tax. The administrative costs would revert to the states. Political costs would also be significant. Dissatisfied taxpayers would hold the states responsible for high rates but would not credit the states with federally provided services. Paradoxically, even states that initially fought increased national power and even states that still gave lip service to states' rights actually preferred — and chose — central over state management of the income tax. Sawer (1977a, 17) notes, "The result could reasonably be called a consensual system."

Menzies claims (1967, 89) that his motivation for calling the Special Conference was his belief, as a federalist, "in the sound political principle that governments exercising independent power should, if possible, have the responsibility for raising the revenues needed for such exercise." It seems more likely that he was currying political favor and consolidating political power. He knew the proposal would never be accepted. Tellingly, he concludes (1967, 91), "The practical effect of all this, of course, has been that in the revenue field, the Commonwealth has established an overlordship."

Indeed, the historical record shows that non-Labor governments often undertake centralizing policies (Else-Mitchell 1977b, 114–15; Troy, 1978; Martin 1982, 40; Groenewegen 1983, 188–89). One example is the construction and maintenance of roads.[8] The Constitution gave the Commonwealth no general road-making powers except within its territories or for defense. Parliament passed the Federal Aid Roads Act of 1926, under a Nationalist prime minister. This grant of financial assistance by the central government was given in return for its approval of state plans (Menzies 1967, 76–78). In 1931, under a Labor prime minister, a hypothecated tax on petrol was introduced. The revenues were to be used for road building and maintenance. The understanding was that the states would receive back amounts relatively equal to the contributions of their citizen consumers. However, this initial program was based on a perception of little demand for roads. In 1959 Menzies' Liberal government removed the hypothecated tax. Commonwealth taxes on petrol remained, but they could be used according to the discretion of the collecting authority. The Commonwealth government continued to subsidize road maintenance and construction through special grants but developed a formula for the proportion of subsidy for each kind of road, thus ensuring virtual control of road construction in Australia. State autonomy was retained only at high costs, by a reduction in federal monies should state and federal priorities differ. Sir Robert Menzies captained much of this centralization, although he had fought against the original 1926 Act for its backhanded grant of power to the Commonwealth. Malcolm Fraser, another Liberal, confirmed the practice but increased his and the federal government's power with the reintroduction of a hypothecated tax for a national highway system over and above the other taxes on petrol. The greater beneficiaries were the rural constituents composing the National Party (the reorganized Country Party), who in coalition with Fraser's Liberal Party kept Fraser in power.

Fraser was also responsible for a second Liberal government attempt to empower the states to collect income taxes.[9] His "New Federalism" was a direct response to major reforms by the ALP under Gough Whitlam, a prime minister who represented the left wing of his party. Whitlam's government was committed to fundamental social reform and greater

    [8] Patrick N. Troy brought this example to my attention. See his short discussion (1969, 12–13).
    [9] This discussion relies heavily on Else-Mitchell (1977a), Prest (1977), Scotton (Scotton and Ferber 1980, chap. 1) and Groenewegen (1979, 1983).

grass-roots participation in policy. It significantly increased Common-wealth revenue from personal income taxation from an annual increase of 11.6 percent between 1967–68 and 1971–72 to an annual increase of 31.1 percent between 1972–73 and 1975–76. In the same years, it significantly increased annual Commonwealth expenditures on health (13.8 percent to 55.1 percent), education (15.2 percent to 61.0 percent), and urban and regional development (17.5 percent to 102 percent).[10] The Whitlam government was promoting increased Commonwealth administration of these and other policies traditionally managed by state governments. It was also encouraging greater participation at the local level. It used taxation and specific-purpose grants to achieve its social ends and to bypass the states.

Even before the dismissal of the Whitlam Labor government, the Liberal Party was developing its "new federalism." When Fraser took office in late 1975, he was prepared to introduce his revenue-sharing proposal, in which states and local governments received a fixed proportion of the income tax. He was also eager to permit and encourage states to raise supplementary income taxes through a percentage surcharge on the income taxes of its residents but collected by the Commonwealth. The claimed motivation was ideological: reduction of big government, better government management of the economy through reduced public expenditures, and increased states' rights and individual freedom.

The words clothed a very different reality. First, the revenue-sharing scheme gave the impression of greater state access to income tax revenue, but any increase in revenue "was almost immediately reduced by the income tax indexation introduced for 1976–77, and by the restructuring of the tax scales introduced in the 1977–78 Budget" (Groenewegen 1979, 64). Second, the states never passed the enabling legislation for the surcharge. The specter of nonuniform tax rates once again emerged. Third, as one commentator (Scotton in Scotton and Ferber 1978, 2) notes:

> In practice, the Fraser government has been willing neither to hand over unconditionally the very substantial revenues involved nor to relinquish completely its control over expenditures. In the two largest specific grant programs—education and public hospital funding—the Commonwealth has tightened the detail of its control.

The Liberal Party–National Party coalition under Fraser reversed the experience of the Country Party–UAP coalition under Fadden. Fraser proposed reforms that his constituents sought, but he implemented a restructured centralism. Fadden advocated changes that his constituents resisted,

---

[10] These figures are provided by Groenewegen (1979, 56–58).

and he failed. However, the experience of both Fadden and Fraser—let alone that of Menzies—indicates that rulers, whatever their rhetoric, tend to maximize central government revenues and control of the purse strings. Fraser demonstrated that prime ministers can overcome constraints imposed by their powerful constituents through strategic manipulation of media and legislation and by strategic concessions to key supporters. Unless they ultimately appease powerful constituents, they will not be able to maintain electoral support.

The fact that proclaimed federalists Menzies and Fraser were centralizers does not negate the very great differences between their programs and Whitlam's. Party constituents made a difference in whose interests the increased Commonwealth power served and in many of the specifics of policy.

TAX AVOIDANCE AND TAX REFORM

During the 1970s and early 1980s, tax avoidance and evasion were major political issues in Australia. Evasion refers to illegal actions such as understatement of income, nondeclaration of fringe benefits, and over-claiming of expenses. Tax avoidance refers "to all of the tax minimization practices which the law allows" (Draft White Paper 1985, 36). A total of 4,054 Australian Taxation Office investigations in 1982–83 resulted in an increased revenue of $136.7 million in recovered tax and penalties (see table 1). In 1984–85 the Taxation Office estimated that income tax evasion could amount to $3 billion of revenue loss per year and tax avoidance to a loss of several billion dollars more (Draft White Paper 1985, 36–37).

Evasion and avoidance are transaction cost problems. Enforcement is costly. Thus, tax managers try to structure the tax system and write tax laws so as to make noncompliance unattractive and to promote quasi-voluntary compliance. Changes in the economy and in the polity often require revisions of the tax system and its laws so as to include deterrents and incentives more appropriate to the new situation. Moreover, governments vary in their desire to prevent evasion and avoidance. The evaluation by elected officials of who benefits from tax policy and who those beneficiaries support politically also affects the amount invested in compliance enforcement.

I argue that three factors contributed to the increases in evasion and avoidance in Australia. The first was a straightforward change in costs and benefits. High Court decisions legitimated a variety of avoidance schemes and opened up new loopholes. The growth of a "black economy" promoted

TABLE ONE   SPECIAL EXAMINATIONS OF INCOME TAXPAYERS

Financial Year	Special Examinations	Change from Previous Year	Increase in Tax and Penalty (in millions)	Change from Previous Year (in millions)
1966–67	7,594	NA	$ 18.5	NA
1967–68	9,360	1,766	15.9	$ − 2.6
1968–69	8,414	− 946	19.5	3.6
1969–70	6,908	− 1,506	25.3	5.8
1970–71	5,900	− 1,008	26.5	1.2
1971–72	5,672	− 228	34.7	8.2
1972–73	5,604	− 68	43.3	8.6
1973–74	5,827	223	53.5	10.2
1974–75	6,121	294	63.0	9.6
1975–76	7,173	1,052	58.6	− 4.4
1976–77	8,640	1,467	73.8	15.2
1977–78	7,747	− 893	69.4	− 4.5
1978–79	7,540	− 207	95.3	26.0
1979–80	7,037	− 503	88.0	20.4
1980–81	6,752	− 285	76.7	− 11.3
1981–82	5,395	− 1,357	92.1	15.4
1982–83	4,054	− 1,341	136.7	44.6
1983–84	1,899	− 2,155	182.9	46.2
1984–85	1,952	53	252.2	69.3

SOURCE: Commissioner of Taxation, Annual Reports, 1966–67 to 1984–85.

evasion. The Australian Taxation Office added further to a general sense of the benefits of evasion and avoidance. It seemed to be committed more to keeping its administrative costs down than to reducing noncompliance.

Second, a decline of citizen satisfaction with government promoted the perception that the tax contract was changing unfairly. Many citizens felt that their marginal tax rates were too high and their gains from trade too low. As inflation pushed people into higher tax brackets, many perceived that the tax contract had changed to their detriment. They compared their situation not only to that of others but also to their own situation in previous years. Many felt that they were paying more for less. Others complained of not receiving sufficient government services or of deteriorating services. Those who felt this way lacked the prerequisites of quasi-voluntary compliance—namely, gains from trade. In their view the bargain they had made was not being kept. Their norms of fairness were being violated.

Third, publicity indicating widespread evasion and avoidance further undermined quasi-voluntary compliance. It became evident that government either was not effective in its application of sanctions or was practicing favoritism toward special interests and actors. The more widespread the knowledge that others were not paying their share, the more non-compliance increased. Again, the motivation was a violation of the norms of fairness. However, the immediate precipitant was in the breakdown of the mechanisms that raised expectations of widespread compliance.

In what follows I focus more on avoidance than evasion. Although both represent serious problems of compliance, it is easier to document the incidence and forms of avoidance. Evasion is visible only when those engaging in it are caught.[11] Moreover, the opportunities for evasion derive from the general state of the economy. The opportunities for avoidance tend to result more directly from factors under the control of tax managers—namely, the wording of the law, the existing disincentives to tax minimization, and the zealousness with which compliance is enforced. The Australian case makes clear the extent to which the government in power can affect the amount of avoidance.

One major impetus to avoidance was a set of decisions by the High Court over which Sir Garfield Barwick, Q.C. (Queen's Counsel), presided. Barwick came to the bench after serving the Liberal Party as both attorney general and as minister for external affairs.[12] His government service was preceded by an illustrious career at the bar, usually representing the rich and powerful who could pay his high fees. Barwick liked a fight, held

---

[11] There is an interesting source of data for estimating the nature of participation in and extent of evasion. At the back of each of the commissioner of taxation's Annual Reports is a complete listing of those individuals who have engaged in breaches and evasions. It includes their names and addresses, business or occupation, financial year or years involved, the understatement of taxable income, the increase in tax assessed, and any additional tax charged. Individuals appear in the financial year in which the reassessment and charge are made. There are usually pages and pages of these names. Norman (1985) has developed a technique for using this material, but his effort is still limited and, so far, the only such effort I have encountered.

[12] Prime Minister Menzies, who appointed Barwick as chief justice, was certainly aware of Barwick's stance toward tax avoidance. Menzies may even have been pleased to have tax avoidance made easier; the beneficiaries tended to be his supporters. However, Barwick's appointment to the High Court had more to do with the politics of the Cabinet than with tax policy. Barwick had just embarrassed himself and Menzies with his unsuccessful campaign for restrictive trade legislation and some of his foreign policy statements. Whether it was Barwick who demanded the new post or Menzies who insisted on kicking Barwick upstairs (Marr 1980), Barwick left the government under a cloud.

strong opinions, hated to lose, and treated lost cases as "unfinished business" (Marr 1980, *passim*). His unofficial biographer, David Marr (1980, 250), has characterized the political stance of the chief justice: "He was first a laissez-faire man, an 'old Spencerian liberal'; he was second an unrepentant centralist; but, fundamentally, he was a Tory."

As a barrister, he liked to take on the Income Tax Assessment Act, particularly Section 260. In two famous cases, *Kerighery Pty Ltd* v. *Federal Commissioner of Trade (F.C.T.)* (1957) and *Newton* v. *F.C.T.* (1958), he argued that the law was written to encourage tax minimization through creative tax schemes, not to block them.[13] He won *Kerighery* in the High Court. This case established the "choice" principle: that the taxpayer has the right to choose his best tax strategy. He lost *Newton* in the Privy Council — to his chagrin and his clients' great financial disadvantage. The effect was to maintain most avoidance schemes as illegal.

When Sir Garfield became chief justice in 1964, he proceeded to change tax law by approving and incorporating his earlier arguments into a series of crucial judgments.[14] The result was to eviscerate Section 260 and to encourage tax avoidance. Barwick claimed to be engaging in legal literalism. However, his purposes seem more political than legal. Lehmann (1983), in his jurimetric analysis of income tax decisions by the High Court from 1950 to 1980, finds that Barwick was more apt to find for the taxpayer than most justices and that his judgments tended to be contentious (149–53). Barwick's "new legalism," Lehmann concludes, was a cover for a strong policy orientation. Lehmann (154–55) contrasts Barwick with his primary opponent and critic on the Bench, Justice Lionel Murphy, an outspoken Labor supporter:

> The claim of Murphy J. that strict literalism is responsible for the decay of our tax laws is not correct. Strict literalism should take into account all the precedents and achieve a balanced outcome. Barwick C.J. did not do this and was primarily policy-oriented. . . . The primary difference between Murphy J. and Barwick C.J. has been that with Murphy J. the policy inherent in a judgment is usually articulated. By articulating his policy (in cases where policy determines the outcome) a judge exposes his policy to public scrutiny and criticism. By presenting policy as literalism, which was the habit of Barwick C.J., a judge reduces his public accountability.

13 For detailed discussions of these cases see, Marr (1980, 130–31, 228–29) and Lehmann (1983). Also see Parsons (1966).
14 The cases include *F.C.T.* v. *Casuarina Pty Ltd* (1971), *Curran* v. *F.C.T.* (1974), *Mullens* v. *F.C.T.* (1976), *Patcorp Investments Ltd* v. *F.C.T.* (1976); *Slutzkin* v. *F.C.T.* (1977), and *Westraders* v. *F.C.T.* (1980). For detailed evaluation of Barwick's tax decisions, see Lehmann (1983). Grbich (1977) analyzes *Mullens, Patcorp,* and *Slutzkin.* The commissioner of taxation's reactions are found in the section of the Annual Reports entitled "Appeals to the Courts."

The Barwick Court's decisions encouraged the further development of a tax avoidance industry that had begun in the 1960s.[15] The most scandalous results were the "bottom of the harbour" schemes, in which company profits were "stripped" before they could be taxed and the records conveniently lost. The term "bottom of the harbour" comes from the excuse that the necessary papers blew off a ferry somewhere in Sydney harbour beneath the famous Harbour Bridge. These incidents drew a great deal of publicity in the early 1980s. Newspaper attention to tax avoidance increased significantly in the late 1970s, but it intensified in 1982 following the Victoria government's publication of the McCabe-Lafranchi Report.[16] This report named 923 companies that had violated the Companies Act. It was followed by the Costigan Royal Commission's revelation of links between the Painters and Dockers Union and "bottom of the harbour" schemes. Tax avoidance scandal touched government ministers, elected representatives, and other important officials. It also generally tainted the reputation of tax professionals. The accountants responded with a strong antiavoidance "Statement of Taxation Standards" (Australian Society of Accountants 1982).

In 1982 the Fraser government appointed Roger Gyles, Q.C., to serve as the first special prosecutor with reference to "bottom of the harbour" schemes. By 1984 he had identified over 6,000 companies and 150 persons as "high targets" (Special Prosecutor 1984, 27). He found that four groups of promoters were responsible for 50 percent of the companies "stripped" (Special Prosecutor 1984, 3).

The Liberal government began to introduce antiavoidance legislation in 1977. By 1978, to combat a number of other avoidance schemes, Liberal Treasurer John Howard proposed recoupment and retrospective legislation. Howard also sought means to combat evasion through better taxation at the source and other devices to tap revenue otherwise lost to the cash economy.[17] These proposals formed the prelude to the later emphasis on indirect taxes by both Liberal and Labor governments. However, there is reason to believe that the Liberal "Government response to tax avoidance in Australia was sluggish and badly targeted" (Grbich 1983, 416) until public

[15] One indicator of the tax avoidance industry is the number of registered tax agents, which more than doubled between 1964 and 1983. See table 5.

[16] The list of newspaper articles in the bibliography of this book (pp. 244–46) represents a relatively complete search of the Parliamentary Library clippings on tax avoidance in the 1970s and 1980s. The most relevant newspaper accounts are Chadwick and others (27 May 1982); Chubb and Guilliat (28 May 1982); Mannix (29 Oct. 1982); Hickie and Bacon (22–28 July 1983); and Ramsey (2–8 Sept. 1983). For a useful review of the important events, see Wilkins (1982).

[17] See his press releases. Also see Day (1982).

pressure following the McCabe-Lafranchi Report embarrassed it into stronger action (Grbich 1983, 417–18).

Labor Minister of Finance John Dawkins stepped up antiavoidance legislation (see, for example, his press releases) until responsibility for tax avoidance passed from Finance to Treasury. However, the Labor government failed to win Senate approval of retrospectivity legislation in several key areas (Draft White Paper 1985, 37).

The Commonwealth Taxation Office seems to have been just as slow to get into the fray, although its commissioners were not unaware of compliance problems. In his 1970 Annual Report, Commissioner E. T. Cain noted the growing volume of work for his office due to increases in the complexity of tax law and in tax avoidance:

> Over the years, some taxpayers have become more prone to conduct their income-producing activities through companies, trusts, partnerships, etc. The necessary elaboration of the taxation laws designed to curb tax avoidance or to provide economic incentives inevitably produces new problems of law and practice. . . . Over and above all this, there is the general problem of maintaining a level of compliance with the taxation laws which will satisfy the great majority of taxpayers that they are not bearing an excessive share of the burden of taxation — a task which becomes more onerous as some taxpayers become more ready to resort to complex arrangements to minimize their taxation burdens.
>
> (Commissioner of Taxation 1970, 2)

This was the first time that a real concern with compliance problems appeared in the Annual Reports. By 1972 the reports included a new section on "Appeals to the Court." In 1975 Commissioner Cain announced that 300 personnel had been added to the enforcement staff (Commissioner of Taxation, 1975, 7) and that the auditing techniques used in Canada and the United States were being considered for use by the Taxation Office (8–9). By 1978 Commissioner William O'Reilly, who took over in 1977, won approval for a Compliance Division. In 1979 it became operational. Since 1980 a large section of the report has been devoted to "Compliance Activities."

With the widespread introduction of computer technology in the late 1960s, monitoring of deductions became easier. Until that time the Taxation Office had to eyeball each return. Computers quickly located deductions and could even check some aspects of their appropriateness. By 1970 computers were in use in every Taxation Office in Australia. At the very time that avoidance should have become harder, it seems to have become more widespread. As the earlier evidence indicates, this was not simply an artifact of improved detection procedures. However, the fact that it became easier to document cases of avoidance did contribute to public knowledge of the extent of avoidance.

The Taxation Office also relied on departmental investigation officers. In 1970 the Annual Report noted that each officer annually produced an average of $100,000 in extra tax and penalties (Commissioner of Taxation 1970, 2). By 1976 the figure was $200,000 (Commissioner of Taxation 1976, 5). Between 1966–67 and 1982–83, the number of departmental investigations dropped from 7,594 to 4,054; but the increase in tax and penalty went from $18.5 million to $136.7 billion. There had been a steady increase in the amount collected since 1966–67, with a relatively big jump in 1971–72. (See table 1.)

Both Cain and O'Reilly emphasized the goal of keeping net costs of collecting all taxes at 1 percent of the total revenue collected. They constantly reminded their readers of the trade-off between administrative costs and increased compliance enforcement. In fact, the net costs of collection for the income tax as well as all taxes stayed relatively constant throughout this period, wavering around 1 percent for all taxes and slightly over 1 percent for the income tax. It seems the commissioners never made the trade-off. Rather, the bureaucratic goal took precedence over the campaign against avoidance.

The 1982 McCabe-Lafranchi Report criticized the Commonwealth Taxation Office for delay and inaction. Special Prosecutor Gyles found the Taxation Office uncooperative and obstructionist in his criminal prosecutions.[18] Nonetheless, there is evidence that new legislation, government pressure, and public criticism made the Taxation Office more zealous than previously. By 1984 tax accountants and tax lawyers were complaining that the Australian Taxation Office investigations invaded the rights and privacy of their clients.[19]

Whatever the enthusiasm with which the Taxation Office carried out its avoidance investigations, there is no doubt that it had few weapons to deter potential tax avoiders. Gyles claims (1984, 567) that the "avalanche" of avoidance was caused at least as much by the lack of adequate deterrents in the form of criminal penalties as by High Court opinions. Commissioner O'Reilly notes, "One of the great advantages seen in tax avoidance schemes is that, win or lose, the participant is able to defer payment of all or part of

[18] See his correspondence with the Australian Taxation Office in his Annual Report (Special Prosecutor 1984, 18–30).

[19] See, esp., Hamilton (1984). A review of *The Australian Accountant* since the early 1980s reveals that these complaints emerged for the first time in 1984.

the tax. This means the participants are naturally disposed to use all possible means to delay ultimate resolution of their cases" (Commissioner of Taxation 1980, 8). Consequently, the taxpayer, even if he or she loses on appeal, "has effectively had the use of the tax payable for the period of the appeal process (in some instances not inconsiderable) at a relatively low rate of interest" (Legislative Research Service 1982, 3–4).

The legalization of tax shelters and deductions and the failure to enforce existing legislation made avoidance attractive to those who could afford to take advantage of it. The elimination of the Barwick-facilitated shelters required new legislation and a new chief justice. Mobilizing the tax commissioner required significant pressure and probably a new government.

The publicity surrounding the Barwick Court's decisions and, even more crucially, the increase in tax avoidance undermined quasi-voluntary compliance. The fact that segments of the population were not paying their share of taxes evidently made compliant individuals rethink their compliance and try to find their own tax shelters and deductions. However, the ability to use the more lucrative tax shelters requires some discretionary income to shelter. Those with such income tend to be business or professional people. Wage and salary workers usually lack capital to invest in "schemes." They do not run businesses with expenses to deduct. They are subject to withholding taxes or, as it is called in Australia, the PAYE (pay as you earn) system. They have full-time jobs that make it difficult for them also to work in the cash economy. Their opportunities for avoidance or evasion are almost nil.

Other factors exacerbated PAYE taxpayer dissatisfaction. Whatever the distribution of the burden of taxation, personal income taxation had certainly escalated. Between 1948–49 and 1982–83, the share of Australian government revenue from personal income tax rose from 41.9 percent to 55.8 percent, while the share from the company income tax dropped from 15.5 percent to 12.0 percent and the share from customs dropped even more, from 13.5 percent to 5.4 percent (Morgan 1983, table 1, p. 72). Norman (1985, table I.1, p. 15) estimates that the percentage of personal income tax to total tax went from 35.5 percent in 1959–60 to 56.1 percent in 1983–84. This increase was accompanied by rising unemployment and what was perceived as severe inflation.

Inflation moved many PAYE taxpayers into higher brackets. Increasingly, they were carrying a disproportionate share of the tax burden for the population (Draft White Paper 1985, 3–4). Between 1965–66 and 1978–79, the proportion of tax paid by wage and salary earners shifted from about two-thirds to four-fifths (Mathews 1980, 28–30; also see his table 4 on p. 29). In another estimate the percentage of personal income tax to wages, salaries, and supplements went from 12.7 percent in 1959–60 to 25.3 percent in 1983–84 (Norman 1985, table I.2, p. 16).

The unions and the general populace believed that the combination of inflation and widespread tax avoidance by the rich nullified the progressivity of the income tax. This was not an unfounded prejudice, for there was considerable evidence to that effect. The Asprey Report (Taxation Review Committee 1975) raised the alarm, which was repeated by, among others, Russell Mathews (see, for example, 1980, 1982, 1983), one of the most eminent of Australia's tax analysts and the author of the report on taxation and inflation (Committee on Taxation and Inflation 1975).[20]

If taxes are indeed a form of contract, an exchange of benefits to citizens in return for payments to government, widespread tax avoidance should produce dissatisfaction with a tax system that violates established norms of fairness. However, the compliance of PAYE employees with taxation was straightforwardly coerced; they had little choice but to pay their taxes. Nonetheless, the notion of quasi-voluntary compliance still applies. PAYE employees were quasi-voluntarily compliant in the sense that they went along with the taxation system and with government policy generally until the terms of their tax contracts deteriorated and until compliance so markedly differed among groups.

An increase in avoidance and evasion was only one sign of a significant decline in quasi-voluntary compliance with the taxation system and with government. The easiest route for dissatisfied taxpayers is individualized resistance. However, refusal to pay carries heavy consequences. On the other hand, if a taxpayer objects to his or her assessment but pays, the taxpayer engages in a relatively cheap guerrilla action against the bureaucracy. Interestingly, objections to assessments rose more than 300 percent between 1964–65 and 1980–81 (see table 2 and figure 1). Moreover, most of these objections were from taxpayers who were not identified as tax avoiders, as the figures in table 3 make clear. Most were by individuals (see table 4), but it appears (from tables 3 and 4) that only a small percentage of these individuals were identified as tax avoiders. The increase in tax agents (see table 5) probably accounts for some of the increase in objections, but I

---

[20] See Head (1977) for a discussion of the Asprey and Mathews reports. Kakwani (1983) finds that, despite the distortions caused by avoidance and evasion, Australia does possess a progressive tax structure — at least as long as government transfers are maintained. In her discussion and review of the literature, Harding (1983) reaches a somewhat similar conclusion. She argues that the personal income tax in itself has become more regressive toward the lower ends, a trend that government expenditure can but does not always combat.

Financial Year	No. of Objections	Increase or Decrease	Total Assessments	Objections as % of Total Assessments
1964–65	19,864		4,484,140	.44
1965–66	19,681	– 183	4,669,202	.42
1966–67	22,106	+ 2,425	4,796,374	.46
1967–68	25,292	+ 3,186	4,969,708	.51
1968–69	26,936	+ 1,644	5,050,385	.53
1969–70	37,169	+ 10,233	5,258,690	.71
1970–71	36,623	– 546	5,431,954	.67
1971–72	48,381	+ 11,758	5,626,152	.86
1972–73	58,793	+ 10,412	5,748,566	1.02
1973–74	54,401	– 4,392	5,374,216	1.01
1974–75	70,065	+ 15,664	5,722,596	1.22
1975–76	73,997	+ 3,932	5,874,227	1.26
1976–77	91,264	+ 17,267	5,472,385	1.67
	(91,466)[c]	(+ 17,469)[c]		(1.67)[a]
1977–78	132,681	+ 41,215	5,723,581	2.32
1978–79	183,101	+ 50,420	5,686,013	3.22
1979–80	188,768	+ 5,667	5,597,103	3.37
1980–81	201,376	+ 12,608	5,766,000	3.49
	(206,164)[c]	(+ 17,396)[c]		(3.58)[a]
1981–82	189,311	– 12,608	6,048,449	3.13
		(– 16,853)[c]		
1982–83	187,006	– 2,305	6,273,886	2.98
1983–84	236,127[b]	49,121	6,180,906	3.82
1984–85	254,824	18,697	6,310,594	4.04

SOURCE: Commissioner of Taxation, Annual Reports, 1964–65 to 1984–85 (except for calculation of percentages).

[a] My revisions.

[b] "Includes cases which in prior years would not have been classified as objections. This follows from a change in classification rules to ensure taxpayers receive the benefits of the interest on overpayments arrangements" (Commissioner of Taxation, Annual Report, 1983–84, 53).

[c] Figures revised by the Commissioner of Taxation during the following year.

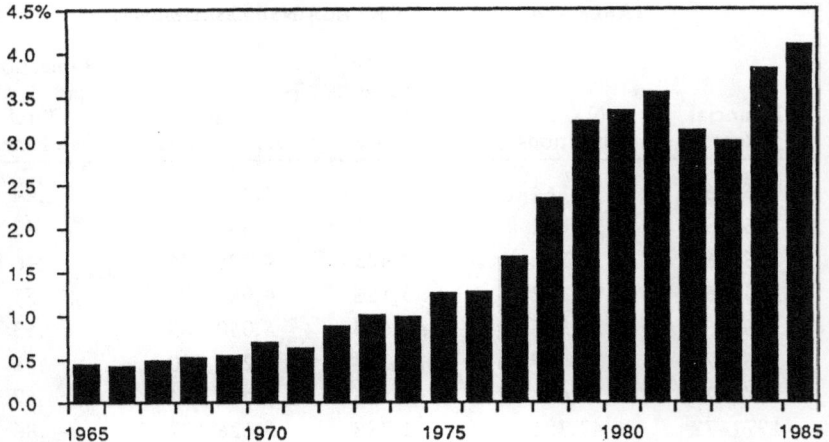

1. Rate of Objections Against Assessments
SOURCE: Commissioner of Taxation, Annual Reports, 1964–65 to 1984–85.

suspect that many of the objections were lodged by individuals acting without agents.[21]

An alternative to both avoidance and individualized resistance is organized resistance and campaigns for reform. Macintyre (1985) has recently documented the development of government-provided social justice throughout the history of Australia. He argues that those whose expectations are disappointed often put pressure on government to change its policies in line with their notions of what is just and fair. I argue that taxpayer revolts are an example of such pressure. Some taxpayer revolts did begin to develop,[22] but they never achieved the success of the Proposition 13 campaign in the United States. The lack of a referendum procedure intensified collective action problems of such a strategy.

Probably the strongest indicator of the breakdown of quasi-voluntary

[21] After I had spent over a year writing letters and making telephone calls trying to extract more detailed statistics on objections, the Australian Taxation Office claimed that, with the exception of the statistics from which I have composed table 4, its only relevant statistics were those published in the Annual Reports. I have used these to construct tables 2 and 3 and figure 1. In correspondence dated 7 March 1985, Assistant Commissioner J. McHugh wrote that the Taxation Office had no statistics that break down objections lodged on behalf of individuals, companies, and trusts prior to 1981. I constructed table 4 out of the statistics he subsequently provided for 1981–82 through 1982–83. He also wrote that statistics breaking down the objections by male-female or by kind of tax avoidance scheme did not exist. He claimed that the Taxation Office would send me further information on a number of other questions I posed. However, some material was incomplete, and some never arrived.

[22] See, for example, Head (1983).

TABLE THREE   OBJECTIONS BY TAXPAYERS IDENTIFIED AS
               TAX AVOIDERS

Financial Year	No. of Objections	Total Tax in Dispute (in millions)
1974–75	76	$ 2.3
1975–76	910	26.6
1976–77	3,326	83.5
1977–78	11,648	334.8
1978–79	10,092	280.8
1979–80	11,658	316.8
1980–81	8,296	211.7
1981–82	2,885	42.1
Total by: Individuals	38,699	663.9
Companies	6,553	484.6
Trusts	3,639	150.0
Total	48,891	1,298.5[a]

SOURCE: Commissioner of Taxation, Annual Report, 1982–83, 9.
[a] The top eight figures equal $1,298.6, and the bottom three equal $1,298.5. The error is in the report.

compliance among PAYE employees and the major form of pressure to reconstitute government provision of social justice was the mobilization of the labor unions. The unions, in response to the demands of their members, pressed for a clampdown on the avoidance industry and for reform of the whole tax system.

The Fraser government sought a wage and price policy, but the high incidence of evasion and avoidance combined with the increasing burden of personal income taxation reduced the willingness of PAYE taxpayers to undertake wage restraints (Nevile 1983). Indeed, wage and price policy and tax reform became linked. It seemed that only the ALP would be likely to achieve these joint ends. This was confirmed in February 1983, a month before the federal election, when the Australian Labor Party and the Australian Council of Trade Unions (ACTU) negotiated the Accord on economic policy.[23] Its agenda included both wage and price surveillance

[23] The full text of the "Statement of the Accord by the Australian Labor Party and the Australian Council of Trade Unions Regarding Economic Policy" can be found as Appendix 2 in the report of the Advisory Committee on Prices and Incomes (1984, 120–44).

TABLE FOUR   BREAKDOWN OF OBJECTIONS AGAINST
ASSESSMENTS

	1981–82	1982–83	1983–84
Individuals			
Objections	106,707	156,395	217,096
Assessments	7,260,969	7,466,504	7,466,504
Objections as % of total assessments	1.47	2.09	2.91
Trusts and Partnerships			
Objections	3,386	5,347	7,255
Assessments	846,018	876,947	897,703
Objections as % of total assessments	.40	.61	.81
Companies			
Objections	3,927	6,361	7,484
Assessments	295,993	313,406	373,616
Objections as % of total assessments	1.33	2.03	2.0

SOURCE: Assistant Commissioner M. J. McHugh, Australian Taxation Office, in telephone interview, 8 March 1985.
NOTE: These assessment figures are different from those in the Annual Reports.

and tax reform, with an emphasis on "tough new measures to smash the tax avoidance industry" (Advisory Committee on Prices and Incomes 1984, 129).

In March 1983 the ALP won the election, and Bob Hawke, a representative of Labor's right wing, became prime minister. A month later he convened the National Economic Summit, with representation from industry as well as labor, to implement the Accord.[24]

Tax reform was the next major undertaking. The government's avowed aim was comprehensive reform rather than "further running repairs" (Draft White Paper 1985, 1). During the 1984 election campaign, Hawke aimed for the "median voter" (as opposed to more left-wing Labor voters) and promised that the government would seek to curtail taxation and government spending. This was not at the time general party policy, but the

[24] The "Communique" of the National Economic Summit Conference is reprinted as Appendix 3 in the report of the Advisory Committee on Prices and Incomes (1984, 145–53). For a discussion see pages 2–4 of the report.

TABLE FIVE   USE OF TAX AGENTS

Year	No. of Registered Tax Agents as of March 31	Claimed Deductions for Tax Agent Services	Claimed Deduction as % of Total Assessment Dollars
1964	12,799	NA	NA
1965	13,188	NA	NA
1966	13,635	NA	NA
1967	14,055	NA	NA
1968	14,630	NA	NA
1969	15,327	NA	NA
1970	16,180	NA	NA
1971	17,217	NA	NA
1972	18,048	NA	NA
1973	18,697	NA	NA
1974	19,423	NA	NA
1975	20,097	NA	NA
1976	21,133	NA	NA
1977	22,418	$1,124,376	19.6
1978	23,138	1,220,191	21.5
1979	23,610	1,270,933	22.7
1980	24,028	1,378,026	23.9
1981	25,036	1,548,178	25.6
1982	26,312	NA	NA
1983	26,325	NA	NA
1984	26,184	NA	NA
1985	26,450	NA	NA

SOURCE: Commissioner of Taxation, Annual Reports, 1964–85 (except for calculation of percentages).

Parliamentary Labor Party (as opposed to the general membership of the ALP) did subsequently endorse Hawke's promise. In the Draft White Paper (1985, 1) was the following language: "For the life of the present Parliament, outlays and taxes will not increase as a share of national product."

This was not the first discussion of major tax reform in Australia. In 1953, under Menzies, there had been a review of the tax system, but it resulted in few recommendations for significant change (see, for example, Commonwealth Committee on Taxation 1953a, 1953b, 1953c). The

Asprey Report (Taxation Review Committee 1975), under Whitlam, presented a more significant set of recommendations. ALP Treasurer Bill Hayden incorporated some into the 1975 budget, but implementation was prevented by a change in government. The emphasis then was on equity, efficiency, and simplicity. It was to that three-pronged basis of reform that the government returned in 1985, a decade later. In the interim the Fraser government had experimented with income tax indexation (Morgan 1983) and with a somewhat increased reliance on indirect taxes.

Tax reform represented a battle from the start, with every faction of the ALP,[25] let alone the community at large, pushing for its own view of reform (see, for example, Staples 1985; Stilwell 1985; Groenewegen 1985). The emphasis was on greater indirect taxation, through more general consumption taxes, and on taxes on wealth, through capital gains and death and gift duties (neither of which exists in Australia). There was also a concern, among some, about protecting the poor and the unemployed. The decrease of tax avoidance was on everyone's list.

The National Tax Summit met in July 1985 and quickly came apart. It was hardly the clear success that the National Economic Summit had been, although some (for example, Groenewegen 1985) argue that it contributed to a higher and better level of tax debate and may be an important preliminary step toward change.

Tax reform was presented as the solution to the transaction cost problems posed initially by widespread evasion and avoidance. Government sought to get the most tax at the least cost. This led to a concern with reducing the costs of enforcement by increasing deterrents to non-compliance and by resorting more to indirect taxes — that is, taxes on sales and exchanges rather than on income. However, tax reform also raised considerations of the political costs of taxation. Non-Labor governments seemed more concerned with decreasing the burden on business, even if it meant an increase in avoidance. The Whitlam and, initially, the Hawke Labor government[26] seemed more concerned with decreasing the burden on those subject to the PAYE system. Both parties sought reform, or at least alterations of the tax system, and both sought to extract as much tax as they can. Their very different strategies reflected their very different constraints.

[25] Among the recognized ALP factions are the Left, Centre Left, and Right.
[26] However, as the 1986 budget demonstrates, Hawke and his treasurer, Paul Keating, are now more concerned with stimulating business. Their commitment to the Labor Right and their wooing of big business support won the day over Cabinet representatives of other Labor constituencies.

CONCLUSION

The Australian case illuminates several aspects of the theory of predatory rule. It also demonstrates the power of the theory by offering better explanations than alternative accounts of various events in Australian history: the introduction of the uniform income tax in 1942; the apparent increase in tax avoidance and tax evasion in the 1970s and 1980s; and the various campaigns, especially the 1985 campaign, for tax reform.

The case material highlights several arguments made in or derived from the theoretical chapters. First, all governments, whatever their rhetoric or party label, maximize revenues within the existing political constraints. Australian prime ministers and their governments chose the taxation system that would produce the most revenue. The differences in their policies reflected differences in political constraints more than differences in goal. Second, rivalry for power affects the discount rates of rulers and, therefore, their policies. The more contested an election was, the more likely there would be a change in policies. Third, war enhances the relative bargaining power of prime ministers vis-à-vis both state governments and constituents. This was clearly the case in Australia. Fourth, quasi-voluntary compliance fluctuates with perceptions of the extent to which the tax contract violates or is consistent with established norms of fairness. Again, the Australian material provides evidence for this proposition.

The Australian case has produced some additional refinements to the theory of predatory rule and has provided new insights into certain aspects of Australian fiscal history. One important finding is that the substance of government policies does vary with party and, even more precisely, with party faction. The Australian state is not essentially reducible to an "administrative agency of the masses" (Encel 1960, 73). Indeed, the prime ministers and their governments are more restrained by their supporters than by their opposition. The desire to appease powerful constituents is what prevented Fadden's government from pushing for uniform taxation or Fraser's government from clamping down sooner and harder on tax avoidance.

Such a statement seems in direct contradiction to the work on voting derived from Downs's (1957) "median voter" hypothesis. Given a normal distribution of voters, Downs and his followers predicted that parties would ideologically converge and that each candidate would take for granted those farthest from the competing party and, thus, campaign among the opposition.[27] I, on the other hand, am suggesting that parties do not

---

[27] See the discussion in the appendix.

converge and that elected officials pay considerable attention to their particular electorates. Yet I am not in total disagreement with the "median voter" argument. The difference is the context. The implications of the "median voter" *may* hold during elections (and when there are only two parties). However, special interest groups, and particularly those actors on whom an elected official particularly depends for votes and financing, dominate the interelection policymaking. It is they who incrementally alter the tax contract.

This case study clearly demonstrates the importance of relative bargaining power as a constraint on policymaking, but it also demonstrates that some kinds of transaction costs are less a constraint than a dependent variable. In particular, the extent of noncompliance, as measured either by state resistance to the uniform income tax or by evasion and avoidance, is manipulable through a change in incentives and disincentives.

Reducing the transaction costs of measurement and monitoring is generally less important in determining policy than is reducing the transaction costs of creating and maintaining — and re-creating — quasi-voluntary compliance. For example, one of the arguments in favor of tax reform, including the uniform tax, is that tax administration is thereby reduced. Fewer and simpler taxes mean fewer personnel and paperwork. Gough Whitlam's specific-purpose grants, Malcolm Fraser's revenue sharing, and Robert Hawke's proposed reforms for the 1980s had efficiency as well as equity goals. But to what extent did a reduction in the transaction costs of measurement and monitoring actually influence policy outcomes? The evidence suggests that the overwhelming determinants were relative bargaining power and the minimization of the costs of enforcement through the promotion of quasi-voluntary compliance.

Transaction costs are crucial in an analysis of predatory rule. However, those that derive from the form of administration and legislation are within the power of the rulers to use for their own revenue-maximizing ends. Only those that derive from the structure of the economy — for example, whether wealth is fundamentally agricultural or industrial — are constraints. Even so, they are more likely to be the necessary than the sufficient conditions for change. New technologies of taxation often exist long before it is possible to implement them. The income tax is a case in point.

CHAPTER VIII

Conclusion

The theory of predatory rule proves to be a useful model for understanding revenue production historically and comparatively. By combining structural constraints and individual action into one model, the theory of predatory rule illuminates aspects of the story that might otherwise be overlooked. It provides a road map to guide the analyst through complex historical data. Moreover, and unlike other structural work that offers this guide service, its emphasis on decision making leads to explanations of what more standard structural analysts can only note or correlate.

The empirical payoffs from using the theory of predatory rule to analyze revenue production policies are new insights and interpretations. The first two case studies (in chapters 4 and 5) draw from a vast secondary literature and add little new material. The third and especially the fourth cases (in chapters 6 and 7) build on the work of others but also present new material. The primary empirical contribution of all the cases lies in the way they illuminate the facts.

The case study of ancient Rome builds on Ernst Badian's (1972) description of the *publicani,* but it puts his findings in theoretical perspective. Badian's concern was to debunk New Testament labels of tax farmers as "sinners" and to present them instead as businessmen, who were sometimes venal. My discussion brings out the factors that led policymakers both to choose tax farming as a form of agency and to permit tax farmers to take from taxpayers more than the contracted amount. The emphasis on those making revenue production decisions for the government reveals the importance of the transaction costs of monitoring and measuring tax payments.

More crucially, it reveals the extent to which bargaining power and discount rates affect policy decisions. Insecure control of government led policy-makers to make concessions to powerful business interests and, later, to use tax farming to provide funds for particularistic rule. This is quite different from Weber's conclusion that "political lords" are concerned with the general interest and long-term economic growth and that tax farmers consider only their immediate profit. Under conditions of intense rivalry and instability, political decision makers are concerned with what they can get fast and cheaply. Under conditions of stability and relative democratic control, tax farmers, like other businessmen, act to promote economic growth and, therefore, long-term profit.

The crucial finding in the discussion of medieval and Renaissance reve-nue production is the paradoxical role of a strong parliament. Its emergence in England reflected the power of the nobility to delimit royal power, but in the long run it permitted English monarchs to reduce signifi-cantly the transaction costs of tax collection. In both England and France, tax imposition required monarchs to bargain with potential taxpayers. The difference was that in England negotiations were centralized and their results generally binding. This was not true for France.

The English Parliament provided a forum for conditional cooperation between monarch and members of Parliament and among the members of Parliament themselves. Regular meetings of Parliament and a relatively representative composition (for the times) increased the ability of taxpayers to assess whether or not monarchs were delivering on their promises and permitted monarchs to establish reliable procedures for requesting and collecting taxes. Parliamentary approval, once given, ensured a high degree of quasi-voluntary compliance. Consequently, monarchs had considerable control over financial policy as long as they worked closely with Parliament. Monarchs who tried to sidestep Parliament found themselves in very serious trouble indeed.

In France, however, monarchical power blocked the development of a strong and centralized representative institution. Monarchs could impose almost any tax they could think of, but with little assurance of compliance in the absence of costly and numerous local negotiations. Such negotiations raised the costs both of bargaining and collection and led to a far more ad hoc and far less efficient revenue production system than in England.

The imposition of the first income tax in Britain in 1799 and its repeal in 1816 illuminate a similar paradox. Such an intrusive and unpopular form of taxation could occur only when the Parliament and not the crown controlled tax policy. The income tax was a major extension of government authority. "The free-born Englishman" and the Smithian merchant would consider such an incursion on privacy and individual rights only when there was some assurance that the government worked on behalf of its ordinary citizens. An increasingly strong House of Commons seemed far more (although hardly totally) trustworthy than the crown or the House of Lords. A monetized and commercialized economy is a significant factor in reducing the transaction costs of assessing and collecting an income tax. However, without public acquiescence the costs of achieving compliance to an income tax are formidable. War provided the justification of need and the basis for the tax contract, but it was the existence of representative institutions that ultimately promoted widespread quasi-voluntary compliance. According to this argument, the income tax is possible only where there are representative institutions. Parliaments, but not monarchs, can institute such a tax.

On the other hand, parliamentary control of fiscal policy makes taxing decisions more accessible to public scrutiny and pressure—especially when good communications networks exist to disseminate information about government debate among the polity. Such networks existed by the end of the eighteenth century. Consequently, Lord Liverpool found it very difficult to retain the income tax in peacetime. The people were all too aware that the conditions under which they had submitted to the tax had changed; its retention would represent a broken contract. Despite its obvious advantages to government, Liverpool and his ministers had to concede to the campaign for repeal.

The first aspect of the Australian case study alters traditional Australian interpretations concerning the causal force of war in the imposition of the uniform income tax and reveals the role of a governing party's supporters in constraining its policies. The finding here is that the opposition party has less restraining effect on a government's policies than that government's most powerful constituents do. Once in power, elected heads of government—that is, prime ministers and presidents—face a constituency broader than their initial supporters. The demands upon them, as well as their own concerns, will, the theory of predatory rule suggests, lead them to seek revenue-maximizing policies that many of their original constituents may resist. Policymaking by prime ministers is highly constrained by those on whom they depend for future election.

The second part of the Australian study raises the important issue of tax avoidance. There are two significant findings. First, widespread public knowledge of avoidance leads to more avoidance. Quasi-voluntary compliance cannot thrive if people think they are suckers. Second, tax avoidance is only partially and perhaps secondarily a problem of measurement and monitoring. Economists tend to emphasize the relationship between the level and kind of auditing and tax avoidance. At least equally, if not more, important is the capacity of powerful political and economic interests to influence rules that make avoidance possible. To promote political ends, rulers will often tolerate avoidance.

At a more general level, the case studies illustrate the processes that promote the evolution of state forms. The increasing specialization and division of labor within the economy lead to the development of a specialized agency, government, established to provide collective goods. Technological changes in warfare require ever more centralized and expensive militaries, armies which further enhance the relative bargaining power of rulers. As the citizenry expands to include more of the population, limited government gives way to governments concerned with welfare, education, and other social programs. The contemporary governments of advanced industrial countries are probably more powerful than historical governments or less elaborated governments, but their rulers are not necessarily more powerful. In principle they control great coercive, economic, and political resources, but most rulers are also subject to significant constraints on their relative bargaining power. The resources of power and the groups on whom rulers depend are transformed over time.

Transaction costs change as well. The development of the economy and of government has reduced some transaction costs. Factories and payment in money make it easier to monitor compliance. Improvements in communication and the development of sophisticated forms of agency make it easier to check on agents. However, the very factors that reduce transaction costs also add costs. Bureaucracy requires considerable personnel and efficient dissemination of quality information. The revolution in information provision has, at the same time, made it easier for taxpayers to learn of new means of avoidance and evasion or even of the fact that others are avoiding and evading. An increased specialization and division of labor means that there are more factions with which to bargain and that more differentiated measurement and monitoring are required. Although the creation of quasi-voluntary compliance is always an issue for rulers, it is an exceedingly complex problem in advanced industrial countries with relatively democratic institutions, because the citizens of these countries have greater economic and political resources.

The factors that affect the discount rates have also undergone a historical evolution. Instability of rule due to the rivalries of periodic elections has very different consequences from instability that derives from military conflict, in which both the ruler and all the ruler's resources may be destroyed. Certainly, elections raise the discount rates of challenged rulers. However, the response is more likely to be unkeepable campaign promises than plunder.

Revenue production evolves with these changes in relative bargaining power, transaction costs, and discount rates. Taxes become more sophisticated, more universal, and more bureaucratic. They also appear to increase.

The empirical payoffs from the applications of the theory of predatory rule are inextricably linked with the theoretical payoffs. On the one hand, the material demonstrates the superiority of the micro-macro to the purely macro or purely micro approach. On the other hand, it demonstrates the superiority of a model that is both political and economic to one that is derived solely from economics.

Understanding the linkages between one macro-state and another requires analysis at the micro level. Such analysis is grounded in a form of methodological individualism that derives fundamentally from neoclassical economics. When the micro and macro levels are integrated, the formal elegance of modern economics is exchanged for a greater realism. Although the explanations are not nearly so clean, they refer to a complex reality rather than to an oversimplified and unrecognizable world. Thus, the micro-macro approach may be less "powerful" than the purely micro, but it is far more useful.

The advantage of the micro-macro approach is its ability to offer fine-tuned explanations that provide the links between one macro-state and another. This characteristic of the micro-macro approach was discussed in chapter 1 (also see appendix), and the case studies were meant to demonstrate these linkages.

Nowhere is the superiority of the micro-macro over the purely macro approach so clear as in the treatment of the variable that macro-theorists call legitimacy. I argue that legitimacy is rooted in numerous decisions to comply. Rulers construct or use institutional arrangements to encourage citizen compliance.

In principle, agreement to a tax is not enough. Effective tax policy also requires actual compliance. Once revenue production policy is understood as a result of bargaining, the need for rulers to reduce the costs of bargaining makes parliaments attractive. Moreover, and more paradoxically, the existence of representative institutions gives rulers more effective tax power, not less. Representative institutions enhance the monitoring of both rulers and taxpayers, promote cooperative arrangements among the relevant actors, and permit the establishment of realistic and accepted sanctions for noncompliance.

Representative institutions "legitimize" tax power by creating conditional cooperation, which is one basis for quasi-voluntary compliance, and by providing a forum for precommitments, which is another. Once Parliaments are in place, rulers can count on fairly wide compliance, as the cases of Renaissance England and Republican Rome demonstrate. And rulers can impose taxes and forms of agency unthinkable under a seemingly less constrained form of rule, which is what the material on eighteenth-century Britain and contemporary Australia reveals.

The superiority of the theory of predatory rule to a purely macro or purely micro approach does not surprise me. What I did not expect, despite my disciplinary persuasion, was the importance of political relative to economic analysis and the dominance of political over economic factors in accounting for revenue production policies.

This is not to deny the importance or usefulness of economic theory. Rather, I am arguing that political-economic analysis left solely in the hands of economists tends to have an unsophisticated and narrow view of the political. For example, the case studies demonstrate considerable rent-seeking behavior. Rent seeking characterizes the tax farmers of ancient Rome; the landed nobility, merchants, and bankers in both Britain and France; and the tax avoiders of Australia. However, their actions are in response to incentives provided by government and can be controlled by government. Their behaviors are less the cause of policies than the result of policies undertaken to promote other government ends, which are sometimes economic but more often political. Moreover, the rent-seeking literature emphasizes the social waste inherent in most government policies but defines social waste solely in terms of economic efficiency. As both the Roman and Australian cases illustrate, in widely divergent eras and in societies with widely divergent kinds and levels of economic development, government policies that appear to promote rent seeking and social waste are often policies that reduce political unrest and promote (or at least are meant to promote) long-term economic growth.

Transaction cost analysis is a more appropriate tool for analysis of revenue production than rent seeking is. It does not preclude rent seeking, but it neither assumes nor is limited to such behaviors. Transaction cost analysis focuses attention on the costs of measuring, monitoring, and enforcing revenue production policies, and especially on the costs of agency. Certain policies, such as the income tax, are unthinkable until the transaction costs of tax collection are made low by the existence of an appropriate economy. However, as all the cases illustrate, the relative difficulties of measurement and monitoring are more likely to be the consequences of policies than to be the causes of changes in policy. Relative bargaining power and enforcement costs are the more important determinants.

All the cases also illustrate that the costs of measuring, monitoring, and coercion significantly constrain policy choices if they are so high that they make certain policies unthinkable. Otherwise, the costs of determining and establishing the appropriate form of agency, on the one hand, and of creating quasi-voluntary compliance, on the other, are far more analytically important. Both agency costs and quasi-voluntary compliance depend heavily on political institutions and political exchange. Transaction cost analysis highlights and analytically distinguishes these crucially important *political* factors.

Bargaining power delimits what and who can be taxed within the general parameters of the ruler's discount rate and transaction costs. The most economically "efficient" policy, even if it could be determined, takes a clear back seat to the most politically acceptable. Moreover, bargaining is not just a matter of resources; some rulers are better than others at making deals with powerful constituents and agents. The ruler's entrepreneurial skill becomes a crucial determinant of policy.

The major theoretical and empirical findings in *Of Rule and Revenue* have to do with the creation and maintenance of quasi-voluntary compliance. Agreement to a revenue policy is but a first step toward quasi-voluntary compliance. The second step is the construction of institutions that encourage compliance without resort to coercion and other costly kinds of inducement and enforcement. The form of agency is obviously a crucial variable, but the cases illuminate other equally important processes and institutions that previous analyses have overlooked.

The initial bargain in ancient Rome was between the Senate and the tax farmers, on the one hand, and the Senate and the taxpayers, on the other. To the agents the gains from trade were profits; to the taxpayers the gains from trade were protection from barbarians and provision of an infrastructure for commerce. These were collective goods and cannot in themselves account for compliance. Agent compliance, I argue, rested on conditional cooperation. Future contracts depended on present behavior. If they abused the terms the Senate laid out for tax farming, they would not get another tax collection contract. Taxpayer compliance rested on precommitment mechanisms, also contractually established. The government punished

both agents and taxpayers who did not perform according to their negotiated agreements.

Later bargains in ancient Rome between the military rulers, the tax
farmers, and the taxpayers rested on the pure might of the rulers. Quasi-
voluntary compliance was not at issue. With the return of peace and the
desire of the emperor for a stable and growing source of revenue, gains
from trade once more accrued to taxpayers and led them at least to
consider complying quasi-voluntarily—but only if there were assurances
that the agents would not overstep their bounds. In a joint effort to reduce
the power of economic interests who controlled tax farming and to achieve
a bargain with the bulk of taxpayers, Augustus replaced tax farming with a
government bureaucracy.

In medieval France and England, monarchs could establish desired
policies only after bargaining with the nobility. They agreed to taxes only in
cases of clear threat. However, they engaged in quasi-voluntary compliance
only if tax legislation precommitted the monarch to spend the money on a
particular war. By the time of the Renaissance, local gentry, urban bourgeoisie, and other new commercial groups had entered the bargaining
arena. Civil protection, economic aid, and commercial infrastructure
joined with war as gains from trade that justified taxation. Quasi-voluntary
compliance for them rested on conditional cooperation through Parliament
and other representative institutions. It also rested on the conviction that
the government would sanction the noncompliant.

In eighteenth-century Britain, the crown and the ministers bargained
with each other and then with Commons and the citizenry to establish tax
policy. Justifications for increased taxes continued to grow, but war was still
chief among them. As in the medieval period, major transformations of
revenue production policy required a precommitment by the government to
spend the funds collected on the particular end for which it had been
permitted. So, at the end of the Napoleonic Wars, which had rationalized
the imposition of the income tax, Commons eliminated the income tax
itself. The maintenance of the policy in the interim required assurances that
no one legally liable was in fact exempt. Relative faith in both Commons
and the tax bureaucracy, confirmed by public knowledge of their actions,
provided the necessary assurances.

During World War II, Australian prime ministers—after many attempts—finally succeeded in getting Parliament to pass a centralized and
uniform income tax. In this way they overcame formal state resistance, but
without state acquiescence the victory would have been Pyrrhic. Quasi-
voluntary compliance by the states was achieved initially through a series of

selective incentives on which the states crucially depended. Quasi-voluntary compliance was maintained, however, by institutions that established conditional cooperation between the states and the Commonwealth government. In the 1970s and 1980s, the federal government found itself faced with tax avoidance by powerful citizens. As long as the power of the avoiders was high relative to the government, little was done. When the balance of power changed and when the incentives to act against avoidance increased, government clamped down. Reinstitution of quasi-voluntary compliance required more than verbal promises of the closing of loopholes and tax office reforms, however. It also required evidence that the government would indeed act against those engaged in evasion and avoidance.

Without quasi-voluntary compliance reductions of transaction costs and the bargaining of policies are unlikely to produce the greatest amount of revenue at the lowest cost to the ruler. Quasi-voluntary compliance is the foundation on which policies must be built. Precommitments established by law and contract and conditional cooperation established through communal or representative institutions are two of the major sources of quasi-voluntary compliance. Both succeed because they provide assurances that rulers will keep their bargains and that others will pay their share.

Underlying precommitment, conditional cooperation, and other mechanisms for establishing quasi-voluntary compliance is law. This is hardly a new finding. I have already cited many of the classical political theorists. Let me cite one more, Bellarmine, writing in the late sixteenth century ([1576] 1928, 48):

> Many things are necessary or harmful to the common good, which, nevertheless, are neither good nor bad for any one in particular, unless they are commanded or prohibited by law. For example, tribute is necessary for a king, yet, if there be no law, it is not necessary for me to pay it, for what I pay profits the king little and it is not my business to look out for the needs of the State, and so all might say. . . . Law, therefore, is necessary which commands and prohibits to all in general what is for the common welfare.

Law makes quasi-voluntary compliance possible; but unless there is already a significant degree of quasi-voluntary compliance, law itself is not viable. As Hart (1961, 196) has noted, "If a system of rules is to be imposed by force on any, there must be a sufficient number who accept it voluntarily. Without their voluntary cooperation, thus creating authority, the coercive power of the law and government cannot be established." Part of my aim in *Of Rule and Revenue* has been to disentangle this problem. By focusing the analysis on the ruler as an entrepreneurial decision maker and by illustrating the theory of predatory rule with detailed case studies, we begin to construct a fine-tuned explanation. Rulers, in their attempts to maximize revenue, establish de facto policies within the constraints of their bargaining power, transaction costs, and discount rate. But to make that policy a reality requires the creation of quasi-voluntary compliance. Once rulers have made the precommitments, used to advantage organizations that promote conditional cooperation, and demonstrated willingness to punish the noncompliant, they have effectively developed laws, norms, and rules they then can use as additional means of enforcement and inducement.

The creation of quasi-voluntary compliance is the key to what policies a ruler can and cannot enact. When quasi-voluntary compliance cannot be created, new policies cannot emerge. When quasi-voluntary compliance breaks down, old policies can no longer be enforced. When a form of agency is considered untrustworthy or unfair by the taxpayers, a revenue-maximizing ruler may be compelled to change it—even if it is the most economically efficient for revenue production.

Thus, I conclude where I began: Rulers maximize revenue to the state, but not as they please. Nearly all are predatory, whether they want to be or not, and all operate within significant constraints. Sometimes they maximize revenues through increases in revenues, sometimes through reductions in expenditures and agency costs. Sometimes they increase taxes; sometimes they lower them. How much, from whom, and what they can collect in revenues are highly constrained and vary with time and place. Always and everywhere, the fundamental constraints are political-economic. They rest on political management of economic and political resources.

Appendix: Bringing People Back into the State

A Bibliographical Essay

The state is currently the focus of considerable scholarly attention and controversy. Contemporary Marxists emphasize the relative autonomy of the state from the dominant classes; Chicago-school economists write about the high costs the state imposes on its citizens; Weberians document the historical evolution of states into monolithic bureaucracies; and political philosophers, as well as public choice scholars, search for rules that ensure justice and equity in the decision-making process. There is a lack of consensus—even among those working within the same perspective—concerning the primary requirements and objectives of a theory of the state.

I have read the literature on the state with an eye to uncovering testable hypotheses or explanations of variation. Although my own interest is in variations in revenue production policies, I have also investigated accounts of variations in social welfare programs, repression, and state form. Some of the contributions are stimulating, some are not; but so far none has offered answers to the questions I raise.

MARXIST THEORIES OF THE STATE

Underlying all Marxism is "an analysis of the consequences of forms of property for historical processes" (Przeworski 1985b). Defined this way, Marxism has made at least two important contributions to social science that are essential to understanding variations in state policy. First, the emphasis on historical materialism, class relations, and property rights has produced a literature describing the constraints on, the capacity for, and the economic interests underlying conflict in different societies at different times. Second, Marxism has added a sociological dimension to economic theory by establishing the notion of a group, class, or institution on which people depend to such an extent that it largely determines their political and economic calculations. Although individuals do not always coalesce as a class or group, their socioeconomic position, largely determined by their property rights, nonetheless affects their behavior.

These two contributions have led to the development of a Marxist view of the state as an object manipulated by competing classes and class factions.[1] This perspective has proved useful in accounting for the transformation from one mode of production to another (particularly from feudalism to capitalism) (see, for example, Wallerstein 1974; Anderson 1974a; Dobb 1978); in illuminating possible sources of variation in governmental forms among and within modes of production (see Moore 1966; Anderson 1974a, 1974b; Poulantzas 1974); and in clarifying the relationship between the policies of modern democratic governments and capitalist interests (see Bowles and Gintis 1976; Block 1977, 1980; Therborn 1978; Bowles, Gordon, and Weisskopf 1984).

Within Marxism the state is generally treated as a dependent variable, a product of the mode of production and an instrument of the dominant economic class (see the critique by Bowles and Gintis 1982). At most the state is granted "relative autonomy" (see, for example, Miliband 1977, 66–74; Poulantzas and Miliband 1973; Hindess 1978; Holloway and Picciotto, 1978, esp. the introduction; Poulantzas 1978, esp. 25–27). However, this formulation is only a more sophisticated version of what Block (1980) characterizes as the Marxist tendency to reduce state power to class power. Unfortunately, neither Marx nor his immediate followers subjected the state to the systematic attention they gave to the economic system, that is, uncovering its most elemental components and then constructing a model of its behavior. Contemporary Marxists have tried to correct this major shortcoming. However, their reluctance to conceptualize the state as an institution composed of and pressured by individuals, who sometimes act as a class (or for a class) but at least as often do not, is a major reason for their failure to develop an adequate theory of the state.

Marxists assume a predatory state through which the dominant class

<hr />

[1] Three particularly useful reviews of the neo-Marxist literature on the "theory of the state" are Jessop (1982), Carnoy (1984), and Alford and Friedland (1985).

exercises power over the dominated class or classes. If this is the nature of the state, then how does the ruling class manipulate the state for its purposes, especially in advanced capitalist countries with democratic institutions? The answer, for most contemporary Marxists, is that the capitalist class grants the state "relative autonomy." The debate is over how relative that autonomy is, but there is general acknowledgment that the state, or at least its executive, often has to implement policies that hurt particular capitalists, that the state is sometimes the independent variable.

The necessity for relative autonomy lies in the individualism of civil society, particularly as described by Marx in *Capital*, "Capital Accumulation" ([1867] 1906, chap. 25). In this view cooperation among capitalists is at best an unstable phenomenon. One consequence is that particular capitalists will make policy demands on the state that may have beneficent effects for their individual profits but disastrous effects on the economy as a whole. Whereas competition in the marketplace may aid capitalist development, competition in the political arena may undermine economic growth. Thus, one of the most important roles of the state to many Marxists (see, esp., Mandel 1972; Poulantzas 1973; Holloway and Picciotto 1978) is to recognize and act in the common interest of the bourgeoisie. Relative autonomy presumably makes this possible.

A related argument for why the bourgeoisie need a semi-independent state is derived from Lenin's *Imperialism* (Cumings 1976; von Braunmuhl 1978; Mandel 1972; O'Connor 1973; Wallerstein 1974, 1979). All Marxian political economists, and some who are not Marxist, perceive capital as constantly seeking to expand. In this quest for expansion, it must cross international boundaries to secure raw materials, new markets, and cheaper labor. The state has historically subsidized capital's explorations through tax breaks, grants, and — if need be — colonization of the territory to be exploited. Capital eventually must confront competing capitals, first from other imperializing powers and later from the colony itself. From a Marxist perspective, such confrontation inevitably leads to war, and it is the state, not capital, that provides the army. But to be able to raise an army, the state must mobilize and draft its citizens on the basis of principles other than capitalist profits — namely, nationalism or some other appeal to the general welfare.

A further reason why the state must be "disassociated from the dominant class" is its requirement of legitimacy. Class dominance through acceptance of that dominance is less costly than coercion. The perception of the state as acting in the general interest forestalls conflict. Marxists often assume that the proletariat has not attempted to overthrow the state because, among other reasons, it recognizes the state's legitimacy. For many Marxists the concept of legitimacy seems to refer as much to the observable absence of revolution in advanced capitalism as to trust or distrust of government.

Two separate kinds of arguments are made by contemporary Marxists in accounting for the legitimacy of the state. The first has to do with the existence of an ideology that promotes belief in the benefits of democracy as it is combined with capitalism. In other words, citizens are socialized to support the status quo. But the fact that a legitimating ideology exists and benefits the bourgeoisie is not at issue. As Pashukanis ([1928] 1951, 185) notes, "While this cannot possibly be impugned, it does not explain to us why this ideology could be created and so why the dominant class can make use of it." What is problematic is its persistence in the light of material conditions that to a Marxist should have produced an oppositional class consciousness. Theoretically, the fact that the proletariat has increased its economic welfare should not reduce its organizing potential as long as its members are subject to fluctuations in wages and the threat of unemployment. The central contradiction in capitalism for a Marxist is not poverty but the combination of socialized production and the private appropriation of the surplus.

Gramsci ([1919–37] 1971) attempted to resolve this dilemma with his notion of hegemony, based on a theory of intellectuals whose function in the social division of labor is to promote acceptance of ruling-class domination (also see Karabel 1976; Laclau 1977; Anderson 1977; Mouffe 1979; Carnoy 1984, chap. 3). Gramsci's work may begin to get at the source and content of ideology, although the research of contemporary sociologists indicates other sources (see, for example, Kohn and Schooler 1983). But neither he nor contemporary Marxists, despite interminable debates, satisfactorily account for its continued hold over the proletariat. Burawoy (1979) comes closest, in large part because he illustrates his notion of the mechanisms of consent with a case study of an actual work process. Althusser (1971) and Habermas (1973), I dare to suggest, obfuscate more than they clarify.

In the second neo-Marxist argument concerning the state's legitimacy, socially ameliorative policies — such as the progressive income tax, social welfare, health insurance, and even universal suffrage — are understood as acts of legitimation. They are concessions made by the state in an attempt to mediate class struggle. Legitimation is both a cause and an effect of the continued acceptance of the state. It also accounts for the growth of welfare spending (see, for example, Altvater 1973; O'Connor 1973; Gough 1975).

However, even from a Marxist perspective, there is a problem with analyzing policies in such blatantly functionalist terms. Social disruption may precipitate the enactment of socially ameliorative policies. However, policymakers are more likely to be motivated by reelection or the reduction of problems than by legitimation. Legitimation may be the consequence of socially ameliorative policies, for resulting concessions and tangible rewards may give their beneficiaries a stake in the system. As with Lenin's labor aristocracy, members of the proletariat may glean major material advantages from capitalism. These people have appropriately calculated the costs and benefits of compliance. They are not suffering from false consciousness. Thus, Marxists are beginning to recognize what Wolfe (1977) labels the "limits of legitimacy," both as a fact and as a theory (Wolfe 1977; Przeworski 1985a, esp. chap. 4).[2]

The question of state policies—why, when, and how they are implemented—has become central to contemporary Marxists analyzing bourgeois rule in advanced capitalist countries with democratic governments. Engels and Lenin were more concerned with similarities among capitalist states than with their differences, while Marx's famous writings on France were too specific and contingent to make generalization easy. However, since Gramsci ([1919–37] 1971) and Trotsky (see Anderson 1976, esp. 96–101 and 119–21), writing in the 1920s and 1930s, Marxists have been turning to the state as an important factor affecting class consciousness.

A considerable Marxist literature on the mechanisms of capitalist rule now exists. Some authors, in the tradition of C. Wright Mills, have been labeled "instrumentalists" (for a discussion of this perspective, see Gold, Lo, and Wright 1975, 32–35, and Domhoff 1986–87; also see Sweezy 1942; Domhoff 1978; Miliband 1969; Reich and Edwards 1978; Glyn and Sutcliffe 1972). They emphasize the existence of personal ties between state managers and capitalists. These can take the form of actual relationships based on previous family, business, and social connections or on current corruption. In the more sophisticated works of the instrumentalist perspective, the personnel who manage the state are subject to pressure from the capitalists. In other words, because of the cost of nationwide elections and because of their need for business support, they develop dependent relationships with particular capitalists.

There is also a "structuralist" perspective (see discussion in Gold, Lo, and Wright 1975, 35–40, and Block 1977; also see O'Connor 1973;

[2] There is, of course, an important radical but non-Marxist literature on the causes and consequences of social policy (see, esp., Piven and Cloward 1971, 1977).

Poulantzas 1975; Offe 1975; Miliband 1977). In this view the personnel of the state operate within limited degrees of freedom, determined by the requirements of maintaining and reproducing the capitalist economic system. The nature of their links with members of the capitalist class is relatively unimportant—and for some authors almost irrelevant. The essential observation is that what state managers must do to stay in office ultimately serves the interests of the capitalist class. They must respond to economic problems, secure business confidence in the regime, and maintain stability. The result is policies and programs that ensure the conditions of capitalist production and profit, prevent or at least ameliorate the consequences of economic fluctuations on the capitalists, and contain class struggle to nonrevolutionary forms.[3]

Despite the policy emphasis of this literature, relatively few Marxists have investigated the ways in which capitalists express their demands to the state. Nor have many explored the mechanisms for executive coordination of capitalist interests and cooptation of unrest. Marxist analyses of possible mechanisms of coordination and cooptation—such as bureaucracy, universal suffrage, and the labor relations system (see, for example, Offe 1975, 1983; Block 1977; Therborn 1977; Wright 1978; Perez-Diaz 1978; Bowles, Gordon, and Weisskopf 1984)—bring them perilously close to the Weberian and neoclassical economic position that the state is an independent institution acting in its own right (Parkin 1978) or to the pluralist position that the state is but an arena for social conflict (see discussions in Skocpol 1979, 24–28; Mann 1984). The alternative is a functionalist and conspiratorial approach (see O'Connor 1973; Bowles and Gintis 1976) that is as flawed as it is stimulating. The new literature on class structure and the related corporatist literature have clear links to Marxist analysis but are not so committed to its underlying assumptions about the state. The resulting work offers more promising analytical guidance than the original neo-Marxist perspective (see, for example, Cameron 1978; Schmitter and Lehmbruch 1979; Skowronek 1982; Korpi 1983; Hicks and Swank 1984; Goldthorpe 1985; Esping-Andersen 1985).

Historical states have also come under the neo-Marxist microscope. Anderson's (1974a, 1974b) study of the transformation of modes of production in the Western world has had wide influence. Anderson proposes that politics—and the state—have more autonomous power relative to the economy and more causal significance than Marxists have traditionally

---

[3] I have chosen not to address what have been characterized as the state monopoly or capital logic "schools." See Jessop (1982) and Schott (1984, chap. 6) for relevant discussions.

credited. He makes this view consistent with Marxism by arguing that such autonomous power permits the state, most of the time, to promote the power of the dominant class. In other words, it is a "tool" of the ruling class but at one remove (Elster 1985, 422). To support his propositions, Anderson offers historical accounts of the transition from the ancient mode of production and of the development of absolutism. Unfortunately, his teleology leads him too often to rewrite history as if it were ineluctably progressing to a more advanced technological and liberating world (Bates 1987, 171, notes 29 and 33, also makes this point). Wallerstein (1974, 1979) also offers historical treatments of the emergence of the modern mode of production. However, for Wallerstein change occurs at the level of the world system. Although he provides considerable analysis of state power, his primary concern is with the relation of states to other states rather than to the domestic society. Wallerstein's major influence has been to revive sensitivity to the importance of the international system and modern imperialism (also see Frank 1978; Brewer 1980). However, he offers little explanation of state policy or internal state action. Moreover, his account of the world system tends, ultimately, to neglect political dynamics except as they are a reflection of major economic factors.

Underlying all the Marxian work on both contemporary and historical states is the hypothesis that the state arises out of class conflict. If there were no class conflict, there would be no need for a state. Pashukanis ([1928] 1951), a major Soviet legal philosopher of the 1920s, points out the problems with this proposition in his friendly critique of Engels:

> The state emerges because the classes would otherwise mutually put an end to each other in savage conflict and would thereby destroy society. Accordingly, the state emerges at a time when no single one of the conflicting classes can achieve a decisive victory. In that event, one of two things happens: either the state makes this relationship secure (and in that case it is a supra-class force, which we cannot admit), or the state is the result of the victory of some class, but if this is so, society's need of a state is gone since the decisive victory' reestablishes equilibrium and society is saved. Behind all these controversies one fundamental problem lies concealed: why does the dominance of a class not continue to be that which it is — that is to say, the subordination in fact of one part of the population to another part? Why does it take on the form of official state domination? Or, which is the same thing, why is not the mechanism of state constraint created as the private mechanism of the dominant class? Why is it disassociated from the dominant class — taking the form of an impersonal mechanism of public authority isolated from society?

This is a central question that any Marxist analysis must face. Posed another way, it is the issue of whether the state exists to benefit the dominant economic class or whether it arises and is maintained for other reasons altogether.

The contemporary analyses we have just discussed begin to get at an answer to Pashukanis's question about why the ruling class cannot dominate directly, particularly in advanced capitalist societies. First, competition among capitalists—both internally and internationally—must be moderated for the good of the capitalist class as a whole, requiring a separate institution for that specific purpose. Second, when the oppositional class, the proletariat, is also a majority class, the bourgeoisie wishes to provide an illusion of a government that acts on behalf of the whole populace. Nonetheless, as the explanations of state behavior only too clearly demonstrate, Marxists still suffer from a serious functionalist tendency. The state is understood to be acting in order to save capitalism, and no other explanation seems necessary.

No discussion of Marxism is complete without some attention to the notion of class struggle and the problem of class formation. Although Marxists have argued that legitimation policies can best be understood as a response to group disruptions, this is far from positing a class. The whole contemporary Marxian conception of the state in capitalism rests on the assumption that it could be overthrown by a class-conscious proletariat: the state acts to prevent such a contingency. Thus, the state is used to account for the fact that no advanced capitalist country has yet experienced a full-blown proletarian revolution and that in the United States, the most advanced of all capitalist countries, the proletariat is more disorganized politically than its counterparts elsewhere are (Schott 1984, *passim*).

This suggests a serious theoretical problem for Marxism. Marx and Engels claimed that class consciousness would emerge naturally out of the industrial setting ([1848] 1978, 480–83). For them there was no need for individual incentives to motivate people to action. Everyone or nearly everyone in the proletariat would spontaneously participate. Lenin was at least intuitively aware of the free rider, the individual who would benefit without contributing to the organization (Olson 1965). His analysis of the need for political leadership and education by a vanguard party results from his observation that trade unions are built upon and reinforce the economism, or narrow self-interest, of their members. Although Marx ([1865] 1935) made a similar observation (also see Blackburn 1976, 18–21), he never fully appreciated its theoretical consequences the way Lenin did. Moreover, Lenin understood cooptation. He argued that the wealth of imperialist countries "makes it economically possible to bribe the upper strata of the proletariat" ([1917] 1975, 255ff.). These factors, economism and cooptation, represent partial recognition of the free-rider dilemma and partial account for the failure of class formation.

Until Marxists have a theory of class action or, more generally, group formation, they will fail to develop a theory of state policy. Marx and Engels believed that capitalism would lead to increased immiseration and exploitation of the proletariat. The failure of capitalism to provide adequate benefits would further provoke organization. Contemporary class analysts know better. They posit obstacles to class formation, such as the segmentation of the labor market (see, esp., Gordon, Edwards, and Reich 1982), the cultural division of labor (Hechter 1975), the separation of the politics of work from the politics of community (Katznelson 1981), or the state. But without a positive theory of class-based collective action, it is as possible to make the argument that capitalism in fact, and not just in perception, serves the interests of the proletariat—in other words, that the state is merely an arena of group pressures.

Three contemporary Marxists who have directly tried to reformulate historical materialism so that it provides a more powerful theory of the relationship between production, property rights, class action, and the state are Perry Anderson (1974a, 1974b, 1976), G. A. Cohen (1978), and Robert Brenner (1976, 1977, 1982). All three are concerned with developing a more adequate Marxist theory of history than that bequeathed by Marx himself. All three have a long-range and comparative perspective on the major social, political, and economic structures they analyze. None focuses solely on capitalism.

As befits an analytical philosopher, Cohen is both more abstract and more precise than Anderson, whom I have already discussed. Cohen's is not a study of particular periods of history but a careful treatment of the concepts and constructs necessary for theory. He claims that individuals are rational in the sense that "to satisfy compelling wants they have they will be disposed to seize the means of satisfaction of these wants" (1978, 152). Given the possession of an intelligence that "enables them to improve their situation" and given conditions of scarcity (1978, 152), rational beings will try to develop technologies allowing them to reap greater benefits with less work and cost. These claims lie at the heart of the "development thesis"— that is, "that societies rarely replace a given set of productive forces with an inferior one" (1978, 153ff.). However, by Cohen's own admission, the case for the development thesis is incomplete. Nor does he fall into Anderson's teleological trap that history is the history of "progress." Indeed, Cohen argues that "progressive" development in the Marxian sense occurs clearly only with the advent of capitalism. His remarkable book provides the best and clearest account of the Marxian theory of history yet to exist. Cohen's weakness is the theory's weakness: ultimately, it is functionalist.[4]

For my purposes Brenner's work makes the most significant contribution to the development of a theory of historical change. He argues that economic actors respond strategically to limits and opportunities imposed by "specific, historically developed systems of social-property relations and given balances of class forces" (1982, 16). Social-property relations and the balance of class forces vary from society to society and, in turn, are the causes of wide variation in economic evolution in countries experiencing the same commercial and demographic trends. What makes Brenner a Marxist is his fundamental concern with property rights, class power, and surplus extraction. What sets him apart is his recognition of the relationship between individual actions and large-scale processes. However, he has yet to make explicit the micro-foundations of his perspective.

Both Brenner and Cohen imply that individuals have a role to play in history. In this respect their work is compatible with a branch of neo-Marxism that treats the problem of class formation and action as susceptible to methodological tools that most Marxists find inimical. Elster (1985, chap. 6), Przeworski (1985b, chaps. 2–5), Roemer (1982, *passim*), and, to some extent, Wright (1985) believe that rational choice can help account for the historical variation in the strength and, indeed, in the very formation of class. These authors are among the most prominent proponents of a more structural rational choice theory. This seems to me a promising approach and links directly to the kind of enterprise I advocate.

What, then, can we conclude from this discussion of Marxist work on the state? First, from the assumption of class as the central historical actor, it is possible to derive propositions that help account for variations in state form. These propositions are particularly useful for comparative modes of production in the *longe durée* and also help illuminate distinctions among states in the same mode of production. Second, Marxists offer explanations of the persistence of inequalities of wealth and power in civil society. They argue that, despite the juridical equality of modern representative governments, political and economic constraints on the oppressed class continue to inhibit action. Third, class analysis is useful in explaining variations in policy among advanced capitalist states with democratic institutions only

---

[4] See the interesting debate between Cohen (1980) and Elster (1980) and the symposium on functionalism and game theory in Marxism in *Theory and Society* (1982, 11:413ff.). Also see Elster's discussion of functionalism in Marxism (1985, esp. 27–37). Two important review essays on Cohen that focus on other issues within his approach are Levine and Wright (1980) and J. Cohen (1982).

when it is liberated from neo-Marxist assumptions about the state. The belief that the state exists only to preserve and reproduce capitalism seems to prevent a clear appraisal of the differences between and within states.

STATE-CENTERED STRUCTURALISM

Historical and comparative social science has refound its roots in Marx and Weber.[5] The result is a renaissance of important comparative historical research, especially in political science and sociology. This work is structuralist in that its emphasis is on the social relations and social institutions that affect how people behave, but the structure that gets the most attention is that of the state. The primary focus is on the ways that changes in the major political, economic, and social structures affect state structures. Research now abounds on the relationship between the state and groupings in civil society, often in reference to the "world system."

Moore (1966) led the way, but his followers are legion. Some focus on group (or class) mobilization, usually as affected by or affecting the state (see, for example, Shorter and Tilly 1974; Hechter 1975; Birnbaum 1977; Trimberger 1978; Skocpol 1979; Perry 1980). Some trace the development of the "modern" state (see Tilly 1975; Poggi 1978; Bendix 1978; Mann 1986). Others focus on the degree of "stateness" — for instance, how strong or weak the state is and the nature of its infrastructural power (Nettl 1968; Mann 1977, 1984; Krasner 1978; Nordlinger 1981; Badie and Birnbaum 1983, esp. Part 3). Others concentrate on comparing and comprehending contemporary states (see, for example, Stepan 1978; Katzenstein 1978; Goldthorpe 1985; Esping-Andersen 1985; Rueschemeyer and Evans 1985). Throughout this literature there is a general concern (although to varying extents) with the international network of states in which a particular state is embedded, but some writers focus specifically on the "world system" (following Wallerstein 1974; see, esp., Chirot 1977 and Modelski 1986).

Several attempts at synthesis already exist (Stinchcombe 1983; Tilly 1984; Alford and Friedland 1985; Evans, Rueschemeyer, and Skocpol 1985a). All emphasize the importance of comparison. All recognize conflicts within the state structure, between state institutions and societal groupings, and among states internationally. Thus, Evans, Rueschemeyer, and Skocpol (1985b, 348) advocate "analytical induction." They want to

---

[5] And, according to Mann (1984, 186), in the work of other "good" Germans, such as Hintze ([1897–1932] 1975) and Rustow (1982).

move away from "grand theory" to historically grounded comparisons — a view that Tilly (1984) most certainly shares.

The Weberianism of these works lies in their striving to be "developmental histories."[6] In this view history is full of contingencies and has no teleology. For Weber sociology has a contribution to make distinct from history's and yet "remains in some respects Clio's handmaiden" (Roth's introduction to Schluchter 1981, xxi). Weber's famous dictum concerning the role of sociology is echoed in the work of contemporary historical comparativists. He argued, it will be remembered ([1922] 1968, 19–20), that:

> sociology seeks to formulate type concepts and generalized uniformities of empirical process. This distinguishes it from history, which is oriented to the causal analysis and explanation of individual actions, structures, and personalities possessing cultural significance. The empirical material which underlies the concepts of sociology consists to a very large extent, though by no means exclusively, of the same concrete processes of action which are dealt with by historians. . . . Sociological analysis both abstracts from reality and at the same time helps us to understand it, in that it shows with what degree of approximation a concrete historical phenomenon can be subsumed under one or more of these concepts.

In 1971 Roth argued that the comparative work of Parsons, Eisenstadt, Almond, and Powell, and the others who dominated the 1960s stood in marked and inferior contrast to that of Weber. Contemporary social scientists seem to have learned this lesson and turned once again to Weber for guidance.

The influence of Weber is substantive-theoretical as well as methodological. The new state-centered structuralism relies on an essentially Weberian characterization of the state. For Weber the state is a coercive and administrative apparatus within a given territory. It has legitimacy to the extent that its coercion is practiced according to law, which can be simply what the state prescribes (Weber [1922] 1968, 56 and 666, and Part 2, chaps. 9–13). One of Weber's contributions was to give state structures importance in their own right, independent of but interacting with economic, social, and religious structures.

But modern historical comparativists have not just turned to Weber; they have also recovered Marx for mainstream social science. Nearly all of the new state-centered structuralism pays homage to Marxism. Indeed, many of its concerns are mirrored in classic Marxist texts: the role of powerful

---

6 Schluchter (1981) offers a brilliant reconstruction of the Weberian enterprise.

groups and classes; the class bias of the state; and the effect of major economic forces, domestic and international, on state actions and policies. A large proportion of these scholars consider themselves neo-Marxists or closely allied with neo-Marxism.

Where the new structuralists most clearly differ from neo-Marxists, however, is in their emphasis on "state capacities" — that is, the ability of states "to implement official goals, especially over the actual or potential opposition of powerful social groups or in the face of recalcitrant socio-economic circumstances" (Skocpol 1985, 9ff.; also see Evans, Ruesche-meyer, and Skocpol 1985b, 351–57; Nordlinger 1981, 8–28 and *passim*). While demonstrating cognizance — and even some sympathy — with the debate on "the relative autonomy of the state," they are more open to the possibility not only that the state's so-called autonomy is immensely vari-able but also that under many conditions the state is as powerful as the dominant economic classes or more so. The question for them is less who controls the state than what power the state has and what determines that power.

The strengths of the state-centered approach are many. First, it poses the question of the state's role in society in a far more useful way than the vast majority of neo-Marxists do. The new structuralists ask what is actually occurring in particular societies instead of assuming what must be going on. Second, they undertake concrete investigations of concrete situations. Following Weberian methodology, they use history to search for generaliza-tions. Third, the state has become an important actor on the historical stage. It is no longer the "arena" of the pluralists (and, to a large degree, the structural-functionalists); nor is it the pawn of dominant economic inter-ests, as the Marxists too often made it out to be. Rather, the officials of the state have interests of their own, on which they act domestically and internationally. Finally, by focusing on the state as an administrative as well as a coercive institution, the analyst can perceive conflicts among state actors as well as between state actors and other socioeconomic actors.

The approach does have some significant weaknesses, however.[7] At its worst, it is antivoluntarist. At its best, individuals become little more than the embodiment of the structures they represent. Structural explanations provide little scope for individual choice, but the evident existence of such choice leads to behavior that "will confound expectations derived from theories that only countenance aggregate-level causal variables" (Hechter 1983, 6–7). Some of the more recent state-centered work seems to recog-

---

[7] For a critique from a behavioralist perspective, see March and Olsen (1984).

nize this limitation and to attempt to correct it, either with typology (see, for example, Nordlinger 1981) or a stockpiling of concrete case studies (Evans, Rueschemeyer, and Skocpol 1985a). This is not the solution.

The state-centered structuralists must take care that they offer us either good history or the kinds of studies from which to derive useful generalizations and on which to build cumulative research. Fortunately, many of these scholars do take care, considerable care. Even so, unless their work becomes better integrated with a theory of choice, its advocates can describe only part of the story. They can offer correlations but not causes of the kind that Weber assigned to historical explanation. Without a theory of individual action, there are no mechanisms that link one structure to another. What is needed are micro-foundations for the new macro-comparative history.

PUBLIC CHOICE AND NEOCLASSICAL ECONOMICS

The third major approach to theorizing about the state is based in neoclassical economics. Since the publication of the seminal work by Arrow in 1951· and by Downs in 1957, there have been innumerable applications of the rational actor model to explanations of governmental behavior. Although most of these analyses are oriented toward the United States, they do have some general applicability to other advanced capitalist countries. Most Marxists ignore the public choice contribution (for the exceptions, see the discussion in Przeworski 1985b), but its advocates have resolved some of the questions raised by Marxists and other structuralists.

Hobbes, who lived from 1588 to 1679, is often credited with being the foundational theorist of the modern state. Certainly, he is the foundational political theorist for most neoclassical economists. Hobbes's presentation of what has come to be known as the social order problem remains the classic and dominant formulation. In *The Leviathan* ([1651] 1962) he posited a world of individuals, "the state of nature," in which each sought eminence over the others. This led to a "war of all against all," for in the absence of property rights and a mechanism to enforce property rights, each stole from the others. No contract was possible as long as the best payoff to each actor was to make a contract and then break it at the first possible opportunity. Hobbes argued that individuals prefer to live by the golden rule rather than in a state of war, because then everyone would be better off. Enforceable contracts might make it impossible to gain all that was produced, but insecurity of life, limb, and property was a negative incentive to production. Secure property rights would lead to cooperation (which could include specialization of labor, one of Adam Smith's insights) and economic growth. Hobbes's solution was an initial contract to establish a central coercive mechanism, the state, to create and enforce property rights, including compliance to the original contract.

To be sure, this formulation has its limitations. It is hard theoretically, let alone empirically, to credit the assertion that the initial social contract was the consequence of unanimity. Moreover, Hobbes neglects the existence of institutions, relationships, and norms that predate the state. Even so and despite attempts by Talcott Parsons (1937), Karl Polanyi (1957), and others to debunk the choice approach to social order, no satisfying alternative has yet been found.

Mancur Olson (1965) built on the Hobbesian dilemma to draw out an important generalization of Downs's (1957) rational voter analysis: the specification of the "free-rider" problem. Olson argues that rational individuals engage in collective action only when there are selective incentives or coercion. This formulation runs riot with the Marxist assumption that the oppressed will mobilize on the basis of their interest in change. Olson's great contribution is to explain why interests do not necessarily lead to action.

Further, Olson claims that small groups are better able to organize than large groups are. Not only is the pie divided into fewer and presumably larger pieces, but small groups are better able to exert social pressure and other sanctions. Olson's observation, if correct,[8] helps explain why governmental policies are likely to favor special interests. The literature on regulation, as articulated by both Stigler (1971) and Wilson (1980), gives further explanation of why small and already powerful groups are most likely to exert influence. A new and significant model of interest groups' power (Salisbury 1984; Laumann, Knoke, and Kim 1985) builds on Olson but emphasizes the role of institutions — corporate organizations with interests of their own, distinct from those of their membership. This model is far more compelling than Olson's own stimulating account (1982) of the relationship between interest groups and the economic health of a society.

The Downsian model of public choice is also deductive, and it also has a mathematical foundation. The Downsian public choice model characterizes people according to their political roles. All the actors are rational

[8] Hardin (1982, chap. 3) raises some serious objections to Olson's formulation of the relationship between group size and the likelihood of group success. But a considerable literature, especially in social psychology, provides some evidence for a positive relationship.

and self-interested, but their interests are expressed in different ways. There are the suppliers of governmental services, that is, elected officials, high-ranking appointees, and bureaucrats (or civil servants). Then there are the consumers of these services, the voters and interest groups. Each set of actors is utility maximizing, but their goals vary. Politicians seek votes, bureaucrats seek security, ordinary voters—to put it crudely—seek increased services and lower taxes, and interest groups seek beneficial treatment (see Bartlett 1973 for an elaboration of this version of Downs; also see Breton 1974).

Using this simple model, social scientists have derived propositions about government and citizen behavior. Downs (1957) explained why it is seldom rational to vote and, therefore, hypothesized low voter turnouts. Employing a median voter hypothesis, he further attempted to explain why two dominant and usually centrist political parties are likely to develop in democratic polities. Downs in a later work (1967), Niskanen (1971), and others offer hypotheses on both the behavior and growth of bureaucracy. These hypotheses vary widely, but all conclude that the dependence of politicians on the information and policy implementation provided by bureaucrats will lead to the growth of bureaucracy.

Drawing on Downs, public choice theorists now also address the strategic relationship between government and citizen preferences. The literature on political business cycles and other recent literature on voters' preferences about government policy, particularly economic policy, and on the government's response to these preferences raise important analytical and empirical questions, which resemble those raised by the new structuralists (see the useful reviews of this literature in Alt and Crystal 1983, chap. 7; Schott 1984, 108–11; and Mueller 1979, chaps. 3–7).

There are several problems with the Downsian model, however. First, much of it rests on the assumption that "parties formulate policies in order to win elections, rather than win elections in order to formulate policies" (Downs 1957, 28). Barry (1970, 99–101ff.) has pointed out that, among other problems, this assumption rests on the additional assumption that parties possess perfect information, which is inconsistent with Downs's arguments about "rational ignorance." Second, although the literature on political business cycles is a more sophisticated version of this argument, its findings are very inconclusive so far. There is certainly a relationship between the policies of heads of government and economic performance and a relationship between electoral popularity and economic policy, but the causal arrows remain in shadow. Alt and Crystal (1983, chap. 5) argue that the supporting evidence for any of the political business cycle hypotheses is weak. Third, this approach, despite its ability to specify the motivations of particular bureaucrats, overlooks the internal organizational logic of bureaucracies (see the telling criticisms by Joskow and Noll 1981). Fourth, because of its tendency toward mathematics and formal modeling, this literature too often sacrifices reality for elegance.

One final variant of public choice contributes to understanding government policy by raising serious questions about the possibility of ever achieving Pareto optimality in politics. This important literature is derived from Arrow's (1951) presentation of a paradox: When three or more choices are presented to a set of decision makers, there is no possible decision that is both rational and democratic. Either there will be cyclical majorities, which lead to nonrational outcomes, or dictatorial rule, which is nondemocratic. Following the normative tradition of welfare economics, Arrow, Sen (1970a, 1970b), and others in social choice use Pareto optimality as a standard for policy and find that it is a goal difficult, if not impossible, to achieve.

Social choice analysts rely heavily on mathematics for the development and proof of theorems. This enables them to illuminate normative questions and to reason systematically about them. However, the findings of social choice are often so abstract that they are not easily testable by observations of actual behaviors. Although mathematically elegant, the work of social choice tends to be empirically thin. Of course, this is not surprising given that the aim of social choice theory is to set an evaluative standard or pose a normative end, rather than to explain the "real world." The important exceptions to this rule usually are as influenced by Downs as by Arrow. Examples include recent research on committee structure and agenda setting (see Shepsle and Weingast 1984).

When one combines the Olsonian, Downsian, and Arrovian contributions, it becomes apparent that government intervention will not always produce the most economically efficient resolution of the problem it was meant to resolve. From a public choice perspective, the reason is simple: government officials respond to incentives and disincentives. They are unlikely to undertake policies that are generally unpopular or that will lose them powerful support. They make deals that keep them in power and maintain the revenue, votes, or whatever underlies their power. Since most people will not be able to organize effectively and many will not even vote, it is not surprising that government policies are particularistic. Many policies fail to serve or were never meant to serve the general welfare.

The neoclassical economic and public choice contribution to the theory of the state lies in its elucidation of the decision rules and problems of group formation that help create and maintain unequal distribution of power. The preceding review of Arrow, Downs, Olson, and their followers should make this clear.

Economics also provides a specification of the advantages of the state, thus demonstrating why and how individuals might participate in forming and maintaining a state. The advantages of the state are its provision of collective goods ranging from protection of private property rights to social welfare. For micro-economists the state is a response to the Hobbesian dilemma that it is in every individual's interest to make a contract and then, at the first advantageous opportunity, break it. The state changes the calculation of advantage by the threat of punishment for those who break contracts. More precisely, the state defines property rights, without which there would be no economic growth or production. Tullock (1974, 17), following Adam Smith ([1776] 1937), argues: "With random seizure of property it is irrational on the the part of the citizens to produce very much to be seized." With the state in place, the populace can focus more on production and less on self-defense. The state solves the free-rider problem, ensuring that the beneficiaries of its services contribute to the costs of those services. However, the neoclassical theory of the state,[9] like its counterpart theory of the firm, makes the state itself a "black box" (North 1978).

Public choice analyses of the strategic decisions of voters, policymakers, and interest groups begin to correct this deficiency.

RATIONAL CHOICE THEORISTS

If there is a single foundational theorist of the approach I am advocating, it is probably Niccolò Machiavelli ([1531, 1532] 1956). His primary concern was with the conditions that made a strategic Prince act in the general interest rather than his own personal interests. Joseph Schumpeter (esp. 1950) has also been influential. In his attempts to combine micro-theory and macro-concerns, in the substantive questions he asked about institutional tensions and change, in his rejection of teleology, and in his implied critique of neoclassical economics, he had a similar agenda to the one I am advancing here. I place myself among those scholars who practice "rational choice," although I must admit that I find the label somewhat misleading. It is true that rational choice is characterized by meth-odological individualism and the assumption of narrow or "thin" (Elster

---

[9] Auster and Silver (1979) attempted to use neoclassical economic assumptions to develop a theory of the state; but they treat the state as a corporate actor, rather than as an institution composed of actors, and they focus primarily on modern states.

1983b, chap. 1) rationality. However, rational choice theorists are both methodologically individualist (as the term implies) and structuralist (which the term does not connote). Structures[10] — that is, a collection of social relations, institutions, extant organizations, and rules of the game — are a crucial aspect of the analysis.

Like Bates (1983, 134–47) and Przeworski (1985b), I am arguing that rational choice theory stands as a challenge to both neoclassical economics and structuralism, including Marxism. It criticizes neoclassical economics and most public choice theories for being too narrow, for assuming that there is an actual equilibrium, for ignoring or misunderstanding political institutions and power, and for being too unconcerned with the big macro-questions. The transaction costs approach is a partial corrective. However, if left in the hands of economists, it will continue to suffer some of the drawbacks of economic analysis of politics: oversimplification and overformalization to the neglect of very real and pressing empirical questions.

Rational choice also poses a challenge to structural theory. It seeks to provide the micro-foundations for understanding and explaining what Tilly (1984) calls "big structures, large processes, huge comparisons." Taylor (1988; following Elster 1983a, 24, 28–29) elegantly presents the case for rational choice as I have described it:

> Good explanation should be, amongst other things, as *fine-grained* [his emphasis] as possible: causal links connecting events distant in space-time should be replaced wherever possible by chains of "shorter" causal links. This is an important reason for supplying explanations with causal links beginning and terminating at individuals. Structuralist and other holistic theories, where they take a causal form, are typically coarse-grained in this sense: they relate macro-states directly to macro-states without supplying a "mechanism" to show how the one brings about the other.

Rational choice aims at predictions and explanations that are observable and testable, as does all good social science. Not a few of its findings are self-evident or commonsensical once stated. What gives rational choice its power is that it is a deductive approach that treats people as the central actors on a historical stage replete with already existing structures and institutions. As Riker (1984, 2) elegantly stated in his 1983 Presidential Address to the American Political Science Association:

[10] Despite the wide usage of the term *structure*, it is hard to pinpoint a definition. Hechter (1983, 5) means "a particular set of social relations." North (1981, 3) means "the political and economic institutions, technology, demography, and ideology of a society." March and Olsen (1984, 740) provide the most guidance. They define structure as "a collection of institutions, rules of behavior, norms, roles, physical arrangements, buildings, and archives that are relatively invariant in the face of turnover of individuals and relatively resilient to the idiosyncratic preferences and expectations of individuals."

It allows both for regularities and for freedom of choice. Since presumably all persons with the same goals in the same circumstances rationally choose the same alternative, regularities can be observed. Inasmuch as social institutions impose similar circumstances on persons with similar goals, the role of randomness is minimized, but the role for choice is fully preserved. Thus, generalization and social science are reconciled with choice and chance.

Given the breadth of its aims, it is not surprising that the practitioners of rational choice are wide ranging in interests. Many are game theorists who investigate behaviors within given structures and rules of the game. Others are economic historians investigating the interaction between individual actions and institutions. Yet others are political economists and political sociologists trying to resolve collective action problems and/or explain government policies. Substantive questions range from long-term secular change (North 1981), development theory (Bates 1981, 1983), peasant revolution (Popkin 1979; Taylor 1988), class and exploitation (Roemer 1982), the policies of capitalist democracies (Schott 1984; Przeworski 1985a), and group solidarity and action (Hardin 1982; Taylor 1982; Hechter 1987). In addition, several important new books in world politics incorporate aspects of rational choice (Gilpin 1981; Keohane 1984). Nearly all who claim the label of rational choice explore aspects of the formation, behavior, or effects of the state.

Although some rational choice conclusions are the same as those of some Marxist findings—for example, the inordinate influence of the economically powerful or the "deadweight loss" or waste produced by government—the two approaches are easily distinguished. Rational choice is self-consciously committed to methodological individualism. Marxism (despite claims for its inherent methodological individualism; see Elster 1985, *passim*) is not. Rational choice begins at the micro level and builds to the macro. Marxism and other forms of structuralism begin at the macro level and move to the micro. However, structuralism tends to exclude micro-foundations, whereas rational choice analysis requires incorporation of institutions and other macro-level phenomena into the model itself. Thus, the rational choice model I have constructed in *Of Rule and Revenue* is consistent with at least some versions of Marxist theory (Elster 1985; Przeworski 1985b) and is certainly consistent with a large variety of structural theories.

Bibliography

The bibliography is organized into five sections. The first section (pp. 205–26) includes all the references cited in the first three chapters, the excursus to chapter 2, chapter 8, and the appendix. The subsequent sections include all the references that appear in the relevant case study (chapters 4–7)—Rome (pp. 226–29), the Middle Ages and the Renaissance (pp. 229–35), eighteenth-century Britain (pp. 235–38), and Australia (pp. 238–46).

GENERAL

Abercrombie, Nicholas, Stephen Hill, and Bryan S. Turner
    1980   *The dominant ideology thesis.* London: Allen and Unwin.
Akerlof, George
    1970   The market for "lemons": Quality, uncertainty and the market mechanism. *Quarterly Journal of Economics* 84 (Aug.): 488–500.
Alchian, Armen, and Harold M. Demsetz
    1972   Production, information costs, and economic organization. *American Economic Review* 62 (Dec.): 777–95.
Alford, Robert, and Roger Friedland
    1985   *Powers of theory: Capitalism, the state and democracy.* New York: Cambridge University Press.
Alt, James E., and Alec Crystal
    1983   *Political economics.* Berkeley: University of California Press.
Althusser, Louis
    1971   Ideology and ideological state apparatuses. In *Lenin and philosophy.* New York: Monthly Review Press.

Altvater, Elmar
    1973   Notes on some problems of state interventionism. *Kapitalistate*
                    1:96–108.
Ames, Edward, and Richard Rapp
    1977   The birth and death of taxes: a hypothesis. *Journal of Eco-
                    nomic History* 37 (Mar.): 161–78.
Anderson, Perry
    1974a   *Lineages of the absolutist state.* London: New Left Books.
    1974b   *Passages from antiquity to feudalism.* London: New Left Books.
    1976   *Considerations on Western Marxism.* London: New Left
                    Books.
    1977   The antinomies of Antonio Gramsci. *New Left Review* 100
                    (Nov.–Dec.): 5–79.
Ardant, Gabriel
    1971   *Histoire de l'impôt. Livre I: De l'antiquité au XVIIᵉ siècle.* Paris:
                    Fayard.
    1972   *Histoire de l'impôt. Livre II: Du XVIIIᵉ au XXᵉ siècle.* Paris:
                    Fayard.
Arrow, Kenneth
    1951   *Social choice and individual values.* New Haven, Conn.: Yale
                    University Press.
Auster, Richard D., and Morris Silver
    1979   *The state as a firm.* Boston: Martinus Nijhoff.
Axelrod, Robert
    1984   *The evolution of cooperation.* New York: Basic Books.
Bachrach, Peter, and Morton Baratz
    1962   The two faces of power. *American Political Science Review*
                    56:947–52.
Badian, Ernst
    1972   *Publicans and sinners: Private enterprise in the service of the
                    Roman Republic.* Ithaca, N.Y.: Cornell University Press.
Badie, Bertrand, and Pierre Birnbaum
    1983   *The sociology of the state.* Trans. Arthur Goldhammer. Chi-
                    cago: University of Chicago Press.
Balibar, Etienne
    1978   Irrationalism and Marxism. *New Left Review* 107 (Jan.–Feb.):
                    3–18.
Barnard, Chester
    1938   *The functions of the executive.* Cambridge, Mass.: Harvard
                    University Press.
Barry, Brian
    1970   *Sociologists, economists, and democracy.* Chicago: University
                    of Chicago Press.
Bartlett, Randall
    1973   *Economic foundations of political power.* New York: Free Press.
Barzel, Yoram
    1981   The firm: A coordinator of contracts. Department of Eco-
                    nomics, University of Washington, Seattle. Memorandum.

1982   Measurement cost and the organization of markets. *Journal of Law and Economics* 25 (Apr.): 27–48.

1987   The entrepreneur's reward for self-policing. *Economic Inquiry* 25 (Jan.): 103–16.

Bates, Robert H.

1981   *Markets and states in tropical Africa.* Berkeley: University of California Press.

[1983] 1987   *Essays on the political economy of rural Africa.* Berkeley: University of California Press.

Bates, Robert H., and Da-Hsiang Donald Lien

1985   A note on taxation, development, and representative government. *Politics and Society* 14 (1): 53–70.

Bates, Timothy

1976   *Economic man as politician: Neoclassical and Marxist theories of government behavior.* Morristown, N.J.: General Learning Press.

Bean, Richard

1973   War and the birth of the nation state. *Journal of Economic History* 33:203–21.

Becker, Gary S.

1968   Crime and punishment: An economic approach. *Journal of Political Economy* 76 (Mar.–Apr.): 169–217.

1985   Public policies, pressure groups, and dead weight costs. *Journal of Public Economics* 28:329–47.

Bellarmine, Robert

[1576] 1928   *De laicis, or The treatise on civil government.* Trans. Kathleen E. Murphy. New York: Fordham University Press.

Bendix, Reinhard

1978   *Kings or people.* Berkeley: University of California Press.

Birnbaum, Pierre

1977   *Les sommets de l'état.* Paris: Seuil.

Blackburn, Robin

1976   Marxism: Theory of proletarian revolution. *New Left Review* 97 (May–June): 3–35.

Block, Fred

1977   The ruling class does not rule: Notes on Marxist theory of the state. *Socialist Review* 33 (May–June): 6–28.

1980   Beyond relative autonomy: State managers as historical subjects. In *Socialist register 1980,* ed. Ralph Miliband and John Saville, 227–42. New York: Monthly Review Press.

Border, Kim C., and Joel Sobel

1985   A theory of auditing and plunder. California Institute of Technology, Pasadena. Social Science Working Paper 573.

Boudon, Raymond

1979   *The logic of social action.* Trans. David Silverman. London: Routledge and Kegan Paul.

Bowles, Samuel, and Herbert Gintis
1976   *Schooling in capitalist America.* New York: Basic Books.
1982   The crisis of capital and the crisis of liberal democracy. *Politics and Society* 11 (1): 52–93.

Bowles, Samuel, David Gordon, and Thomas Weisskopf
1984   *Beyond the wasteland.* New York: Doubleday, Anchor Press.

Brennan, Geoffrey, and James M. Buchanan
1980   *Foundations of a fiscal constitution.* New York: Cambridge University Press.
1984   Voter choice: Evaluating political alternatives. *American Behavioral Scientist* 28 (Nov./Dec.): 185–201.
1985   *The reason of rules: Constitutional political economy.* Cambridge: Cambridge University Press.

Brennan, Geoffrey, and Loren Lomasky
1985   The imperial spectator goes to Washington: Toward a Smithian theory of electoral behavior. *Economics and Philosophy* 1:189–211.

Brenner, Reuven
1983   *History— The human gamble.* Chicago: University of Chicago Press.

Brenner, Robert
1976   Agrarian class structure and economic development in pre-industrial Europe. *Past and Present* no. 70: 30–75.
1977   The origins of capitalist development: A critique of neo-Smithian Marxism. *New Left Review* 104:25–92.
1982   The agrarian roots of European capitalism. *Past and Present* no. 97: 16–113.

Breton, Albert
1974   *The economic theory of representative government.* Chicago: Aldine.

Brewer, Anthony
1980   *Marxist theories of imperialism.* London: Routledge and Kegan Paul.

Brustein, William
1981   A regional mode of production analysis of political behavior: The cases of western and Mediterranean France. *Politics and Society* 10 (4): 355–98. Revised and reprinted as French political regionalism: 1848–1978. In *The microfoundations of macrosociology,* ed. Michael Hechter, 115–57. Philadelphia: Temple University Press, 1983.
1985   Class conflict and class collaboration in regional rebellions, 1500–1700. *Theory and Society* 14 (4): 445–68.

Brustein, William, and Margaret Levi
1987   The geography of rebellion: Rulers, rebels, and regions. *Theory and Society.*

Buchanan, Allen
1979   Revolutionary motivation and rationality. *Philosophy and Public Affairs* 9 (Fall): 59–82.

Buchanan, James M.
   1980a   Reform in a rent-seeking society. In *Toward a theory of a rent-seeking society*, ed. James M. Buchanan, Robert D. Tollison, and Gordon Tullock, 359–67. College Station: Texas A & M University Press.
   1980b   Rent seeking and profit seeking. In *Toward a theory of a rent-seeking society*, ed. James M. Buchanan, Robert D. Tollison, and Gordon Tullock, 3–15. College Station: Texas A & M University Press.
Burawoy, Michael
   1979   *Manufacturing consent*. Chicago: University of Chicago Press.
Bury, J. E., S. A. Cook, and F. E. Adcock
   1969   *The Cambridge ancient history*. Vol. 6, *Macedon, 401–301 B.C.* Cambridge: Cambridge University Press.
Cameron, David R.
   1978   The expansion of the public economy: A comparative analysis. *American Political Science Review* 72:1243–61.
Carniero, Robert L.
   1970   A theory of the origins of states. *Science* 169 (Aug.): 733–38.
Carnoy, Martin
   1984   *The state and political theory*. Princeton, N.J.: Princeton University Press.
Cheung, Steven N. S.
   1978   *The myth of social cost*. London: Institute of Economic Affairs.
Chirot, Daniel
   1977   *Social change in the twentieth century*. New York: Harcourt Brace Jovanovich.
Coase, Ronald H.
   1937   The nature of the firm. *Econometrica* 4 (Nov.): 386–405.
Cohen, G. A.
   1978   *Karl Marx's theory of history: A defense*. Princeton, N.J.: Princeton University Press.
   1980   Functional explanation: Reply to Elster. *Political Studies* 33 (1): 129–35.
Cohen, Joshua
   1982   Review of G. A. Cohen's *Karl Marx's theory of history*. *Journal of Philosophy* 79 (May): 254–73.
Cohen, Ronald, and Elman R. Service, eds.
   1978   *Origins of the state*. Philadelphia: Institute for the Study of Human Issues.
Coleman, James
   forthcoming   Norm-generating structures. In *The limits of rationality*, ed. Karen Cook and Margaret Levi.
Cook, Karen S., and Richard M. Emerson
   1978   Power, equity and commitment in exchange networks. *American Sociological Review* 43 (Oct.): 721–39.

| 1984 | Exchange networks and the analysis of complex organizations. *Research in the Sociology of Organizations* 3:1–30. |

Cumings, Bruce
| 1976 | Reflections on Schurman's theory of the state. *Bulletin of Concerned Asian Scholars* 8:55–64. |

Dahl, Robert
| 1961 | *Who governs?* New Haven, Conn.: Yale University Press. |

Davis, Lance E.
| 1980 | It's a long, long road to Tipperary, or Reflections on organized violence, protection rates, and related topics: The new political history. *Journal of Economic History* 40 (Mar.): 1–16. |

Dobb, Maurice, and others
| 1978 | *Transition from feudalism to capitalism.* London: New Left Books. |

Domhoff, William
| 1978 | *The powers that be.* New York: Random House, Vintage Books. |
| 1986–87 | Corporate liberal theory and Social Security Act: A reply to Skocpol and Quadagno. *Politics and Society* 15 (3). |

Downs, Anthony
| 1957 | *An economic theory of democracy.* New York: Harper and Row. |
| 1967 | *Inside bureaucracy.* Boston: Little, Brown. |

Edwards, Richard
| 1979 | *Contested terrain.* New York: Basic Books. |

Elias, Norbert
| [1939] 1982 | *Power and civility.* Trans. Edmund Jephcoh. New York: Pantheon Books. |

Elster, Jon
1978	*Logic and society: Contradictions and possible worlds.* New York: Wiley.
1979	*Ulysses and the Sirens: Studies in rationality and irrationality.* New York: Cambridge University Press.
1980	Cohen on Marx's theory of history. *Political Studies* 33 (1): 121–28.
1983a	*Explaining technical change.* New York: Cambridge University Press.
1983b	*Sour grapes.* New York: Cambridge University Press.
1985	*Making sense of Marx.* New York: Cambridge University Press.

Emerson, Richard M.
| 1962 | Power-dependence relations. *American Sociological Review* 27:31–40. |
| 1983 | Charismatic kingship: A study of state-formation and authority in Baltistan. *Politics and Society* 12 (4): 413–44. |

Engels, Frederick
| [1884] 1973 | *The origin of the family, private property, and the state.* New York: International Publishers. |

Esping-Andersen, Gøsta
1985   *Politics against markets: The social democratic road to power.*
               Princeton: Princeton University Press.
Esping-Andersen, Gøsta, Roger Friedland, and Erik Olin Wright
1976   Modes of class struggle and the capitalist state. *Kapitalistate*
               4–5 (Summer): 186–220.
Evans, Peter B., Dietrich Rueschemeyer, and Theda Skocpol, eds.
1985a   *Bringing the state back in.* New York: Cambridge University
               Press.
1985b   On the road toward a more adequate understanding of one
               state. In *Bringing the state back in,* ed. Peter B. Evans, Dietrich
               Rueschemeyer, and Theda Skocpol, 347–66. New York:
               Cambridge University Press.
Fama, Eugene F.
1980   Agency problems and the theory of the firm. *Journal of Political
               Economy* 88 (21): 288–307.
Fama, Eugene F., and Michael C. Jensen
1983a   Agency problems and residual claims. *Journal of Law and
               Economics* 26 (June): 327–49.
1983b   Separation of ownership and control. *Journal of Law and
               Economics* 26 (June): 301–25.
Feldman, J., and J. A. Kay
1981   Tax avoidance. In *The economic approach to law,* ed. Paul
               Burrows and Cento G. Veljanovski, 320–33. London:
               Butterworths.
Ferejohn, John, Morris Fiorina, and Richard McKelvey
1984   Sophisticated voting and agenda independence in the dis-
               tributive politics setting. Hoover Institution, Stanford Univer-
               sity, Stanford, Calif. Working Papers in Political Science no.
               P-84-3.
Frank, André Gunder
1978   *Dependent accumulation and underdevelopment.* New York:
               Monthly Review Press.
Freidson, Eliot
1970   *The profession of medicine.* New York: Dodd, Mead.
Frohlich, Norman, and Joe A. Oppenheimer
1970   I get by with a little help from my friends. *World Politics* 23
               (Oct.): 104–20.
1974   The carrot and the stick: Optimal program mixes for entrepre-
               neurial political leaders. *Public Choice* 19 (Fall): 43–61.
1978   *Modern political economy.* Englewood Cliffs, N.J.: Prentice-
               Hall.
Frohlich, Norman, Joe A. Oppenheimer, and Oran R. Young
1971   *Political leadership and collective goods.* Princeton, N.J.:
               Princeton University Press.

Frohlich, Norman, and others
1975   Individual contributions for collective goods. *Journal of Con-flict Resolution* 19 (2): 310–29.

Gamson, William
1961   A theory of coalition formation. *American Sociological Review* 26:373–82.

Gilpin, Robert
1981   *War and change in world politics*. New York: Cambridge University Press.

Ginsburg, Benjamin
1984   Money and power: The new political economy of American elections. In *The political economy*, ed. Thomas Ferguson and Joel Rogers, 163–79. Armonk, N.Y.: M. E. Sharpe.

Glyn, A., and Bob Sutcliffe
1972   *British capitalists: Workers and the profit squeeze*. London: Penguin.

Goetz, Michael L.
1978   Tax avoidance, horizontal equity, and tax reform: A proposed synthesis. *Southern Economic Journal* 44 (Apr.): 198–212. Reprinted in *Toward a theory of a rent-seeking society*, ed. James M. Buchanan, Robert D. Tollison, and Gordon Tullock, 314–31. College Station: Texas A & M University Press, 1980.

Gold, David A., Clarence Y. H. Lo, and Erik Olin Wright
1975   Recent developments in Marxist theories of the capitalist state. *Monthly Review* 27 (Oct.): 29–43.

Goldthorpe, John, ed.
1985   *Order and conflict in contemporary capitalism*. New York: Oxford University Press.

Goodin, Robert
1976   *The politics of rational man*. New York: Wiley.
1982   *Political theory and public policy*. Chicago: University of Chicago Press.

Gordon, David M., Richard Edwards, and Michael Reich
1982   *Segmented work, divided workers: The historical transformation of labor in the United States*. New York: Cambridge University Press.

Gough, Ian
1975   State expenditure in advanced capitalism. *New Left Review* 92 (July–Aug.): 53–92.

Gouldner, Alvin W.
1980   *The two Marxisms*. New York: Seabury Press.

Graetz, Michael J., Jennifer F. Reinganum, and Louis L. Wilde
1984   An equilibrium model of tax compliance with a Bayesian auditor and some honest taxpayers. California Institute of Technology, Pasadena. Social Science Working Paper 506.

Gramsci, Antonio
[1919–37]   *Prison notebooks.* Ed. and trans. Quentin Hoare and Geoffrey
1971   Nowell Smith. London: New Left Books.
Groves, Theodore, and John Ledyard
1977   Optimal allocation of public goods: A solution to the free rider
problem. *Econometrica* 45 (May): 783–809.
Habermas, Jurgen
1973   *Legitimation crisis.* Boston: Beacon Press.
Hardin, Russell
1971   Collective action as an agreeable n-prisoner's dilemma. *Behavioral Science* 16 (Sept./Oct.): 472–81.
1980   The emergence of norms. *Ethics* 90 (July): 575–87.
1982   *Collective action.* Baltimore: Johns Hopkins University Press.
1985   Time and rational choice. Paper presented at the International Institute for Environment and Society of the Wissenschaftszentrum, West Berlin.
forthcoming   The social evolution of cooperation. In *The limits of rationality*, ed. Karen Cook and Margaret Levi.
Hart, H. L. A.
1961   *The concept of law.* New York: Oxford University Press.
Hechter, Michael
1975   *Internal colonialism.* Berkeley: University of California Press.
1981   Karl Polanyi's social theory: A critique. *Politics and Society* 10 (4): 399–429. Revised and reprinted in *The microfoundations of macrosociology*, ed. Michael Hechter, 16–57. Philadelphia: Temple University Press, 1983.
Hechter, Michael, ed.
1983   *The microfoundations of macrosociology.* Philadelphia: Temple University Press.
Hechter, Michael
1987   *Principles of group solidarity.* Berkeley: University of California Press.
Hechter, Michael, and William Brustein
1980   Regional modes of production and patterns of state formation in Western Europe. *American Journal of Sociology* 85 (Mar.): 1061–94.
Heimer, Carol
1985   *Reactive risk and rational action: Managing moral hazards in insurance contracts.* Berkeley: University of California Press.
Hicks, Alexander, and Duane Swank
1984   On the political economy of welfare expansion: A comparative analysis of 18 advanced capitalist countries, 1960–71. *Comparative Political Studies* 17:81–119.
Hindess, Barry
1978   Classes and politics in Marxist theory. In *Power and the state*, ed. Gary Littlejohn and others, 72–97. London: Croom Helm.

Hintze, Otto
    [1897–1932] *The historical essays of Otto Hintze.* Ed. Felix Gilbert. New
        1975   York: Oxford University Press.
Hirschman, Albert
        1970   *Exit, voice, and loyalty: Response to decline in firms, organiza-
                  tions and states.* Cambridge, Mass.: Harvard University Press.
        1982   Rival interpretations of market society: Civilizing, destructive,
                  or feeble? *Journal of Economic Literature* 20 (Dec.): 1463–84.
Hirshleifer, Jack
        1983   From weakest-link to best-shot: The voluntary provision of
                  public goods. *Public Choice* 41:371–86.
Hobbes, Thomas
    [1651] 1962   *Leviathan.* Ed. Michael Oakshott. London: Collier-
                  Macmillan.
Holloway, John, and Sol Picciotto, eds.
        1978   *State and capital: A Marxist debate.* Austin: University of Texas
                  Press.
Homans, George C.
        1964   Bringing men back in. Presidential address to the American
                  Sociological Association. *American Sociological Review* 24
                  (Dec.): 809–18.
Ilchman, Warren F., and Norman Thomas Uphoff
        1971   *The political economy of change.* Berkeley: University of Cal-
                  ifornia Press.
Jensen, M. C.
        1983   Organizational theory and methodology. *Accounting Review*
                  58 (Apr.): 319–72.
Jensen, M. C., and W. H. Meckling
        1976   Theory of the firm: Managerial behavior, agency costs, and
                  ownership structure. *Journal of Financial Economics* 3 (Oct.):
                  305–60.
Jessop, Bob
        1982   *The capitalist state.* Cambridge, England: Martin Robertson.
Joskow, Paul, and Roger Noll
        1981   Theory and practice in public regulation: A current overview.
                  In *Studies in public regulation,* ed. Gary Fromm, 1–65.
                  Cambridge, Mass.: MIT Press.
Kahneman, Daniel, and Amos Tversky
        1979   Prospect theory: An analysis of decision under risk. *Econo-
                  metrica* 47:263–91.
        1984   Choices, values, and frames. *American Psychologist* 39 (Apr.):
                  341–50.
Karabel, Jerome
        1976   Revolutionary contradictions: Antonio Gramsci and the prob-
                  lem of intellectuals. *Politics and Society* 6 (2): 123–72.

Katzenstein, Peter, ed.
1978   *Between power and plenty: Foreign economic policies of advanced industrial countries.* Madison: University of Wisconsin Press.
Katznelson, Ira
1981   *City trenches.* New York: Pantheon Books.
Kay, J. A.
1979   The economics of tax avoidance. In *British tax review,* ed. P. Lawton and J. A. Jones, 354–65. London: Sweet and Maxwell.
Keohane, Robert
1984   *After hegemony.* Princeton, N.J.: Princeton University Press.
Kindleberger, Charles P.
1984   *A financial history of Western Europe.* Boston: Allen and Unwin.
Kiser, Edgar
1986–87   The formation of state policy in Western European absolutisms: A comparison of England and France. *Politics and Society* 15 (3).
Kohn, Melvin L., and Carmi Schooler
1983   *Work and personality.* Norwood, N.J.: Ablex Publishing.
Kornmesser, Allen
1981   Regional modes of production and the emergence of the state in ancient India. Department of Political Science, University of Washington, Seattle. Unpublished paper.
Korpi, Walter
1983   *The democratic class struggle.* London: Routledge and Kegan Paul.
Krasner, Stephen D.
1978   *Defending the national interest.* Princeton, N.J.: Princeton University Press.
Laclau, Ernesto
1977   *Politics and ideology in Marxist theory.* London: New Left Books.
Laiten, David
1985   Hegemony and religious conflict: British imperial control and political cleavages in Yorubaland. In *Bringing the state back in,* ed. Peter B. Evans, Dietrich Rueschemeyer, and Theda Skocpol, 285–316. New York: Cambridge University Press.
Lane, Frederick C.
1958   Economic consequences of organized violence. *Journal of Economic History* 18 (Dec.): 401–17.
Lange, Oskar
1963   *Political economy.* Vol. 1. New York: Pergamon Press.
Larson, Magali Sarfatti
1977   *The rise of professionalism.* Berkeley: University of California Press.

Laumann, Edward O., David Knoke, and Yong-Hak Kim
    1985   An organizational approach to state policy formation: A comparative study of energy and health domains. *American Sociological Review* 50 (Feb.): 1–19.
Lenin, V. I.
    [1917] 1975   Imperialism: The highest stage of capitalism. In *The Lenin anthology,* ed. Robert Tucker, 204–74. New York: Norton.
Levi, Margaret
    1974   Poor people against the state. *Review of Radical Political Economics* 6 (Spring): 76–98.

    1977   *Bureaucratic insurgency.* Lexington, Mass.: Lexington Books.
Levi, Margaret, and Michael Hechter
    1985   A rational choice approach to the rise and decline of ethnoregional political parties. In *New nationalism of the developed West: Towards explanation,* ed. E. A. Tiryakian and Ronald Rogowski, 128–46. London and Boston: Allen and Unwin.
Levi, Margaret, and Douglass C. North
    1982   Toward a property rights theory of exploitation. *Politics and Society* 11 (3): 315–20.
Levine, Andrew, and Erik Olin Wright
    1980   Rationality and class struggle. *New Left Review* 123:47–68.
Lipsky, Michael
    1970   *Protest in city politics.* Skokie, Ill.: Rand McNally.
    1980   *Street-level bureaucracy.* New York: Russell Sage Foundation.
Lipsky, Michael, and Margaret Levi
    1972   Community organization as a political resource. In *People and politics in urban society,* ed. Harlan Hahn, 175–99. Beverly Hills, Calif.: Sage.
Locke, John
    [1690] 1968   *Two treatises of government.* Ed. Peter Laslett. Cambridge: Cambridge University Press.
Lockwood, David
    1981   The weakest link in the chain? In *Research in the sociology of work,* ed. R. L. Simpson and I. H. Simpson, 435–81. Greenwich, Conn.: JAI Press.
McCarthy, John D., and Mayer N. Zald
    1977   Resource mobilization and social movements: A partial theory. *American Journal of Sociology* 82 (6): 1212–41.
Machiavelli, Niccolò
    [1531, 1532]   *The prince and the discourses.* New York: Modern Library.
        1956
McKelvey, Richard
    1979   General conditions for global intransitivities in formal voting models. *Econometrica* 47:1085–1112.
Mandel, Ernest
    1972   *Late capitalism.* London: New Left Books.

Mann, Michael
1977   States, ancient and modern. *Archives européenes de sociologie*
            18 (2): 262–98.
1980   State and society, 1130–1816: An analysis of English state
            finances. In *Political power and social theory,* Vol. 1, ed.
            Maurice Zeitlin, 165–208. Greenwich, Conn.: JAI Press.
1984   The autonomous power of the state: Its origins, mechanisms
            and results. *Archives européenes de sociologie* 25 (2): 185–213.
1986   *The sources of social power.* Vol. 1, *A history of power in
            agrarian societies.* New York: Cambridge University Press.
forthcoming *The sources of social power.* Vol. 2, *A history of power in
            industrial societies.* New York: Cambridge University Press.
March, James G., and Johan P. Olsen
1984   The new institutionalism: Organizational factors in political
            life. *American Political Science Review* 78 (3): 734–49.
March, James G., and Herbert Simon
1958   *Organizations.* New York: Wiley.
Margolis, Howard
1985   Tax compliance and extended rationality. Paper presented to
            University of Chicago Committee on Public Policy Studies.
Marx, Karl
[1852] 1974 The eighteenth brumaire of Louis Bonaparte. In *Surveys from
            exile,* ed. David Fernbach, 143–249. New York: Random
            House, Vintage Books.
[1865] 1935 *Value, price and profit,* ed. Eleanor Marx Aveling. New York:
            International Publishers.
[1867] 1906 *Capital.* New York: Modern Library.
Marx, Karl, and Frederick Engels
[1843] 1978 The German ideology, Part I. In *The Marx-Engels reader,* ed.
            Robert Tucker, 146–200. New York: Norton.
[1848] 1978 Manifesto of the Communist Party. In *The Marx-Engels reader,*
            ed. Robert Tucker, 469–500. New York: Norton.
Michels, Robert
[1919] 1949 *Political parties.* New York: Free Press.
Miliband, Ralph
1969   *The state in capitalist society.* New York: Basic Books.
1977   *Marxism and politics.* Oxford: Oxford University Press.
Miller, Nicholas R.
1983   Pluralism and social choice. *American Political Science Review*
            17 (3): 734–47.
Mitchell, William C.
1979   The democratic state: A public choice perspective. Paper pre-
            sented at the Public Choice Society Meetings, Charleston,
            S.C.
1983   Fiscal behavior of the modern democratic state: Public choice
            perspectives and contributions. In *Political economy,* ed. Larry
            L. Wade, 69–113. Boston: Kluwer-Nijhoff.

Modelski, George
  1986   *Long cycles in world politics*. Seattle: University of Washington
                  Press.
Moe, Terry M.
  1980   *The organization of interests*. Chicago: University of Chicago
                  Press.
  1984   The new economics of organization. *American Journal of Polit-
                  ical Science* 28 (Nov.): 739–77.
Moore, Barrington, Jr.
  1966   *Social origins of dictatorship and democracy*. Boston: Beacon
                  Press.
  1978   *Injustice: The social bases of obedience and revolt*. White Plains,
                  N.Y.: M. E. Sharpe.
Mouffe, Chantal, ed.
  1979   *Gramsci and Marxist theory*. London: Routledge and Kegan
                  Paul.
Mueller, Dennis C.
  1979   *Public choice*. New York: Cambridge University Press.
Nettl, J. P.
  1968   The state as a conceptual variable. *World Politics* 20 (4):
                  559–92.
Niskanen, William A.
  1971   *Bureaucracy and representative government*. Chicago: Aldine-
                  Atherton.
Nordlinger, Eric A.
  1981   *On the autonomy of the democratic state*. Cambridge, Mass.:
                  Harvard University Press.
North, Douglass C.
  1978   Structure and performance: The task of economic history.
                  Journal of Economic Literature 16 (Sept): 963–78.
  1981   *Structure and change in economic history*. New York: Norton.
  1985   The growth of government in the United States: An economic
                  historian's perspective. *Journal of Public Economics* 28:
                  383–99.
North, Douglass C., and Robert Thomas
  1973   *The rise of the Western world*. New York: Cambridge University
                  Press.
Oberschall, Anthony
  1973   *Social conflict and social movements*. Englewood Cliffs, N.J.:
                  Prentice-Hall.
O'Connor, James
  1973   *The fiscal crisis of the state*. New York: St. Martin's Press.
Offe, Claus
  1975   The theory of the capitalist state and the problem of policy
                  formation. In *Stress and contradiction in modern capitalism*, ed.
                  Leon Lindberg and others, 125–44. Lexington, Mass.: Lex-
                  ington Books.

1983   Competitive party democracy and the Keynesian welfare state:
            Factors of stability and disorganization. *Policy Sciences* 15:
            225–46. Reprinted in *The political economy,* ed. Thomas Fer-
            guson and Joel Rogers, 349–67. Armonk, N.Y.: M. E.
            Sharpe, 1984.

Offer, Avner
1981   *Property and politics, 1870–1914: Landownership, law, ide-
            ology and urban development in England.* Cambridge:
            Cambridge University Press.

Olson, Mancur
1965   *The logic of collective action.* Cambridge, Mass.: Harvard
            University Press.
1982   *The rise and decline of nations.* New Haven, Conn.: Yale Uni-
            versity Press.

Oppenheimer, Joe A.
1980   Small steps forward for political economy. *World Politics* 33
            (Oct.): 121–51.

Orbell, John M., and L. A. Wilson
1978   Institutional solutions to the n-prisoners' dilemma. *American
            Political Science Review* 72 (June): 411–21.

Ostrom, Elinor
1985   A method of institutional analysis. In *Guidance, control, and
            performance evaluation in the public sector,* ed. F. X. Kauf-
            mann, G. Majone, and V. Ostrom, eds., 459–74. New York:
            De Gruyter.

Paige, Jeffrey
1975   *Agrarian revolution.* New York: Free Press.

Pareto, Vilfredo
1966   *Sociological writings.* Ed. S. E. Finer, trans. Derick Mirfin.
            New York: Praeger.

Parkin, Frank
1978   Social stratification. In *A history of sociological analysis,* eds.
            Tom Bottomore and Robert Nisbet, 599–632. New York:
            Basic Books, Inc.

Parsons, Talcott
1937   *The structure of social action.* New York: McGraw-Hill.

Pashukanis, E. B.
[1928] 1951 The general theory of law and Marxism. In *Soviet legal philos-
            ophy,* trans. Hugh W. Babb. Cambridge: Harvard University
            Press.

Peacock, Alan T., and Jack Wiseman
1961   *The growth of public expenditure in the United Kingdom.*
            Princeton, N.J.: Princeton University Press.

Perez-Diaz, Victor M.
1978   *State, bureaucracy and civil society: A critical discussion of the
            political theory of Karl Marx.* London: Macmillan.

Perry, Elizabeth
  1980   *Rebels and revolutionaries in North China, 1845–1945.* Stanford, Calif.: Stanford University Press.
Pincus, Jonathan J.
  1977   *Pressure groups and politics in antebellum tariffs.* New York: Columbia University Press.
Piven, Frances Fox, and Richard Cloward
  1971   *Regulating the poor.* New York: Random House, Vintage Books.
  1977   *Poor people's movements.* New York: Pantheon Books.
Plott, Charles R., and Michael E. Levine
  1978   A model of agenda influence on committee decisions. *American Economic Review* 68 (Mar.): 146–60.
Poggi, Gianfranco
  1978   *The development of the modern state.* Stanford, Calif.: Stanford University Press.
Polanyi, Karl
  1957   *The great transformation.* Boston: Beacon Press.
Popkin, Samuel
  1979   *The rational peasant.* Berkeley: University of California Press.
Posner, Richard A.
  1975   The social costs of monopoly and regulation. *Journal of Political Economy* 83 (Aug.): 807–27. Reprinted in *Toward a theory of a rent-seeking society,* ed. James M. Buchanan, Robert D. Tollison, and Gordon Tullock, 1980, 71–94. College Station: Texas A & M University Press.
  1981   *The economics of justice.* Cambridge: Harvard University Press.
Poulantzas, Nicos
  1973   *Political power and social classes.* Trans. Timothy O'Hagen. London: New Left Books.
  1974   *Fascism and dictatorship.* Trans. Judith White. London: New Left Books.
  1975   *Classes in contemporary capitalism.* Trans. David Fernbach. London: New Left Books.
  1978   *State, power and socialism.* Trans. Patrick Camiller. London: New Left Books.
Poulantzas, Nicos, and Ralph Miliband
  1973   The problem of the capitalist state. In *Ideology in social science,* ed. Robin Blackburn, 238–62. New York: Random House, Vintage Books.
Przeworski, Adam
  1980   Material interests, class compromise, and the transition to socialism. *Politics and Society* 10 (2): 125–53.
  1985a   *Capitalism and social democracy.* New York: Cambridge University Press.

1985b   Marxism and rational choice. *Politics and Society* 14 (4): 379–409.

Rasler, Karen A., and William R. Thompson
1985   War making and state making: Governmental expenditures. *American Political Science Review* 79 (2): 491–507.

Reder, Melvin
1975   The theory of employment and wages in the public sector. In *Labor in the public and nonprofit sectors,* ed. Daniel J. Hamermesh, 1–48. Princeton, N.J.: Princeton University Press.

Reich, Michael, and Richard Edwards
1978   Political parties and class conflict in the United States. *Socialist Review* 39:37–57.

Reinganum, Jennifer F., and Louis L. Wilde
1984   Sequential equilibrium detection and reporting policies in a model of tax evasion. California Institute of Technology, Pasadena. Social Science Working Paper 525.
1985   The economics of income taxation: Compliance in a principal-agent framework. *Journal of Public Economics* 26:1–18.

Riker, William
1962   *The theory of political coalitions.* New Haven, Conn.: Yale University Press.
1978   The cause of public sector growth: Resources and minority advantage. Department of Economics, University of Rochester, Rochester, N.Y. Mimeo.
1982   *Liberalism against populism: A confrontation between theory of democracy and theory of social choice.* San Francisco: W. H. Freeman.
1984   The heresthetics of constitution-making. *American Political Science Review* 78 (Mar.): 1–16.

Riker, William, and Peter C. Ordeshook
1973   *An introduction to positive political theory.* Englewood Cliffs, N.J.: Prentice-Hall.

Roemer, John
1982   *A general theory of exploitation and class.* Cambridge, Mass.: Harvard University Press.

Root, Hilton L.
1987   *Peasants and kings in Burgundy: Agrarian foundations of French absolutism.* Berkeley: University of California Press.

Ross, Stephen A.
1973   The economic theory of agency: The principal's problem. *American Economic Review* 12 (May): 134–39.

Roth, Guenther
1971   Sociological typology and historical explanation. In *Scholarship and partnership: Essays on Max Weber,* ed. Reinhard Bendix and Guenther Roth, 109–28. Berkeley: University of California Press.

Rousseau, Jean Jacques
    [1762] 1950   *The social contract.* Trans. G. D. H. Cole. New York: Dutton.
Rueschemeyer, Dietrich, and Peter B. Evans
    1985   The state and economic transformation: Towards an analysis
                   of the conditions underlying effective intervention. In *Bringing
                   the state back in,* ed. Peter B. Evans, Dietrich Rueschemeyer,
                   and Theda Skocpol, 44–77. New York: Cambridge University
                   Press.
Rustow, Alexander
    1982   *Freedom and domination: A historical critique of civilization.*
                   Trans. Dankwart Rustow. Princeton, N.J.: Princeton Univer-
                   sity Press.
Salisbury, Robert H.
    1984   Interest representation: The dominance of institutions. *Ameri-
                   can Political Science Review* 78 (Mar.): 64–76.
Schelling, Thomas C.
    1960   *The strategy of conflict.* Cambridge, Mass.: Harvard University
                   Press.
    1973   Hockey helmets, concealed weapons, and daylight savings.
                   Journal of Conflict Resolution 17 (Sept.): 381–428.
    1978   *Micromotives and macrobehavior.* New York: Norton.
Schluchter, Wolfgang
    1981   *The rise of Western rationalism: Max Weber's developmental
                   history.* Trans. Guenther Roth. Berkeley: University of Califor-
                   nia Press.
Schmitter, Philippe C., and G. Lehmbruch, eds.
    1979   *Trends towards corporatist intermediation.* London: Sage.
Schofield, Norman
    1985   Anarchy, altruism and cooperation. *Social Choice and Welfare*
                   2:207–19.
Schott, Kerry
    1984   *Policy, power and order.* New Haven, Conn.: Yale University
                   Press.
Schumpeter, Joseph
    [1918] 1954   The crisis of the tax state. In *International economic papers:
                   Translations prepared for the International Economic Associa-
                   tion,* ed. A. Peacock and others, 5–38. New York: Macmillan.
    1950   *Capitalism, socialism and democracy.* New York: Harper and
                   Row.
Scott, James C.
    1976   *The moral economy of the peasantry.* New Haven, Conn.: Yale
                   University Press.
    1985   *Weapons of the weak: Everyday forms of peasant resistance.* New
                   Haven: Yale University Press.
Sen, Amartya K.
    1967   Isolation, assurance, and the social rate of discount. *Quarterly
                   Journal of Economics* 81:112–84.

1970a   *Collective choice and social welfare.* San Francisco: Holden-
                 Day.
1970b   The impossibility of a Paretian liberal. *Journal of Political
                 Economy* 78:152–57.
Service, E. R.
1975   *Origins of the state and civilization.* New York: Norton.
Shavell, S.
1979   Risk sharing and incentives in the principal and agent rela-
                 tionship. *Bell Journal of Economics* 10 (Spring): 55–73.
Shepsle, Kenneth, and Barry Weingast
1984   When do rules of procedure matter? *Journal of Politics* 46:
                 206–21.
Shorter, Edward, and Charles Tilly
1974   *Strikes in France: 1830–1968.* New York: Cambridge Univer-
                 sity Press.
Silver, Alan
1967   The demand for order in civil society: A review of some themes
                 in the history of urban crime, police and riot. In *The police,* ed.
                 David Bordua, 1–24. New York: Wiley.
Simon, Herbert
1947   *Administrative behavior.* New York: Macmillan.
1985   Human nature in politics: The dialogue of psychology with
                 political science. *American Political Science Review* 79 (June):
                 293–304.
Skocpol, Theda
1979   *States and social revolutions.* New York: Cambridge University
                 Press.
1980   Political response to capitalist crisis: Neo-Marxist theories of
                 the state and the case of the New Deal. *Politics and Society* 10
                 (2): 155–201.
1985   Bringing the state back in: Strategies of analysis in current
                 research. In *Bringing the state back in,* ed. Peter B. Evans,
                 Dietrich Rueschemeyer, and Theda Skocpol, 3–37. New York:
                 Cambridge University Press.
Skowronek, Stephen
1982   *Building a new American state: The expansion of national ad-
                 ministrative capacities, 1877–1920.* New York: Cambridge
                 University Press.
Smith, Adam
[1776] 1937   *An inquiry into the nature and causes of the wealth of nations.*
                 Ed. Edwin Cannan. New York: Modern Library.
Spence, Michael, and Richard Zeckhauser
1971   Insurance, information and individual action. *American Eco-
                 nomic Review* 61 (May): 380–87.
Stepan, Alfred
1978   *The state and society: Peru in comparative perspective.* Prince-
                 ton, N.J.: Princeton University Press.

Stigler, George
  1970   The optimum enforcement of the laws. *Journal of Political Economy* 70 (May–June): 526–36.
  1971   The theory of economic regulation. *Bell Journal of Economics* 2:3–21.
Stinchcombe, Arthur L.
  1968   *Constructing social theories.* New York: Harcourt, Brace, and World.
  1983   *Economic sociology.* New York: Academic Press.
Sweezy, Paul M.
  1942   *The theory of capitalist development: Principles of Marxian political economy.* New York: Modern Reader Paperbacks.
Taylor, Michael
  [1976] 1987   *The possibility of cooperation.* Cambridge: Cambridge University Press. Originally published as *Anarchy and cooperation.*
  1982   *Community, anarchy and liberty.* New York: Cambridge University Press.
  1988   Rationality and revolution. In *Rationality and revolution,* ed. Michael Taylor. New York: Cambridge University Press.
Taylor, Michael, and Hugh Ward
  1982   Chickens, whales, and lumpy goods: Alternative models of public-goods provision. *Political Studies* 30 (Sept.): 350–70.
Therborn, Goran
  1977   The rule of capital and the rise of democracy. *New Left Review* no. 103 (May–June): 3–41.
  1978   *What does the ruling class do when it rules?* London: New Left Books.
Tilly, Charles
  1975   *The formation of national states in Western Europe.* Princeton, N.J.: Princeton University Press.
  1978   *From mobilization to revolution.* Reading, Mass.: Addison-Wesley.
  1984   *Big structures, large processes, huge comparisons.* New York: Russell Sage Foundation.
  1985   Warmaking and statemaking as organized crime. In *Bringing the state back in,* ed. Peter B. Evans, Dietrich Rueschemeyer, and Theda Skocpol, 169–91. New York: Cambridge University Press.
Tollison, Robert D.
  1982   Rent seeking: A survey. *Kyklos* 35:28–47.
Trimberger, Ellen Kay
  1978   *Revolution from above: Military bureaucrats and development in Japan, Turkey, Egypt, and Peru.* New Brunswick, N.J.: Transaction Books.
Tullock, Gordon
  1974   *The social dilemma.* Blacksburg, Va.: University Publications.

1975   The transitional gains trap. *Bell Journal of Economics* 6 (Autumn): 671–78. Reprinted in *Toward a theory of a rent-seeking society*, ed. James M. Buchanan, Robert D. Tollison, and Gordon Tullock, 211–21. College Station: Texas A & M University Press, 1980.

1980   Rent seeking as a negative-sum game. In *Toward a theory of a rent-seeking society*, ed. James M. Buchanan, Robert D. Tollison, and Gordon Tullock, 16–36. College Station: Texas A & M University Press.

Ullman-Margalit, Edna
1977   *The emergence of norms.* Oxford: Clarendon Press.

Umbeck, John
1981   *A theoretical and empirical investigation into the formation of property rights.* Iowa City: University of Iowa Press.

von Braunmuhl, Claudia
1978   On the analysis of the bourgeois nation state within the world market context. In *State and capital: A Marxist debate,* ed. John Holloway and Sol Picciotto, 160–77. Austin: University of Texas Press.

Walker, Jack L.
1983   The origins and maintenance of interest groups in America. *American Political Science Review* 77:390–406.

Wallerstein, Immanuel
1974   *The modern world-system.* New York: Academic Press.
1979   *The capitalist world economy.* Cambridge: Cambridge University Press.

Webber, Carolyn C., and Aaron Wildavsky
1986   *A history of taxation and expenditure in the Western world.* New York: Simon and Schuster.

Weber, Max
[1922] 1968   *Economy and society.* 2 vols. Ed. Guenther Roth and Claus Wittich. New York: Bedminster.

Williamson, Oliver E.
1975   *Markets and hierarchies.* New York: Free Press.
1979   Transaction-cost economics: The governance of contractual relations. *Journal of Law and Economics* 22 (Oct.): 233–61.
1981   The economics of organization: The transaction cost approach. *American Journal of Sociology* 87 (3): 548–77.
1983   Credible commitments: Using hostages to support exchange. *American Economic Review* 83 (Sept.): 519–40.
1985   *The economic institutions of capitalism.* New York: Free Press.

Wilson, James Q.
1973   *Political organization.* New York: Basic Books.
1980   *The politics of regulation.* New York: Basic Books.

Wittfogel, Karl
1957   *Oriental despotism: A case study of total power.* New Haven, Conn.: Yale University Press.

Wolfe, Alan
  1977   *The limits of legitimacy: Political contradictions of contemporary
                 capitalism.* New York: Free Press.
Wright, Erik Olin
  1978   *Class, crisis and the state.* London: New Left Books.
  1985   *Classes.* London: New Left Books.
Wright, H. T.
  1977   Recent research on the origin of the state. *Annual Review of
                 Anthropology* 6:379–97.
Zolberg, Aristide
  1972   Moments of madness. *Politics and Society* 2 (2): 183–207.

ROME (Chapter 4)

Anderson, Perry
  1974   *Passages from antiquity to feudalism.* London: New Left Books.
Ardant, Gabriel
  1971   *Histoire de l'impôt. Livre I: De l'antiquité au XVIIᵉ siècle.* Paris:
                 Fayard.
Badian, Ernst
  1967   *Roman imperialism in the late republic.* Pretoria: Communica-
                 tions of the University of South Africa.
  1972   *Publicans and sinners: Private enterprise in the service of the
                 Roman Republic.* Ithaca, N.Y.: Cornell University Press.
Barrow, R. H.
  1949   *The Romans.* New York: Penguin.
Broughton, T. R. S.
  1938   Roman Asia Minor. In *An economic survey of ancient Rome*,
                 vol. 4, ed. Tenney Frank, 499–918. Baltimore: Johns Hopkins
                 University Press.
Brunt, P. A.
  1962   The equites in the late Republic. *International Conference of
                 Economic History* 2. 1:118–49.
  1971   *Social conflicts in the Roman Republic.* London: Chatto and
                 Windus.
  1980   Free labour and public works at Rome. *Journal of Roman
                 Studies* 70:81–100.
  1981   The revenues of Rome. *Journal of Roman Studies* 71:161–72.
Cascio, E. Lo
  1981   State and coinage in the late Republic and early Empire.
                 Journal of Roman Studies 71:76–86.
Davison, William I., and James E. Harper
  1972   *The ancient world.* Vol. 6, *European economic history.* New
                 York: Meredith Corporation.
De Creco, Marcello
  1985   Monetary theory and Roman history. *Journal of Economic
                 History* 45 (4): 809–22.

Eisenstadt, S. N.
1963   *The political systems of empires.* New York: Free Press.
Engels, Frederick
[1884] 1973   *The origin of the family, private property, and the state.* New
                York: International Publishers.
Fowler, W. Ward
1916   *Social life at Rome at the age of Cicero.* London: Macmillan.
Frank, Tenney
1927   *An economic history of Rome.* London: Jonathan Cape.
1933   *Rome and Italy of the Republic: An economic survey of ancient
                Rome.* Vol. 1. Baltimore: Johns Hopkins University Press.
1940   *Rome and Italy of the Empire: An economic survey of ancient
                Rome.* Vol. 5. Baltimore: Johns Hopkins University Press.
Gage, Jean
1964   *Les classes sociales dans l'Empire Roman.* Paris: Payot.
Gibbon, Edward
[1776–88]   *The history of the decline and fall of the Roman Empire.* 5 vols.
1862   London: John Murray.
Gruen, Erich S.
1968   *Roman politics and the criminal courts, 149–78 B.C.*
                Cambridge, Mass.: Harvard University Press.
1974   *The lost generation of the Roman Republicans.* Berkeley: Uni-
                versity of California Press.
Haywood, R. M.
1938   Roman Africa. In *An economic survey of ancient Rome,* vol. 4,
                ed. Tenney Frank, 121–257. Baltimore: Johns Hopkins Uni-
                versity Press.
Hechelheim, F. M.
1938   Roman Syria. In *An economic survey of ancient Rome,* vol. 4,
                ed. Tenney Frank, 121–257. Baltimore: Johns Hopkins Uni-
                versity Press.
Hill, H.
1952   *The Roman middle class in the Republican period.* Oxford:
                Blackwell.
Hopkins, Keith
1978   *Conquerors and slaves.* London: Cambridge University Press.
1980   Taxes and trade in the Roman Empire (200 B.C.–A.D. 400).
                Journal of Roman Studies 70:101–25.
Johnson, Allen Chester
1936   Roman Egypt. In *An economic survey of ancient Rome,* vol. 2,
                ed. Tenney Frank. Baltimore: Johns Hopkins University Press.
Jones, A. H. M.
1970   *Augustus.* London: Chatto and Windus.
1974   *The Roman economy.* Ed. P. A. Brunt. Oxford: Blackwell.
Loewenstein, Karl
1973   *The governance of Rome.* The Hague: Martinus Nijhoff.

Marx, Karl, and Frederick Engels
    [1848] 1978   Manifesto of the Communist Party. In *The Marx-Engels reader,*
                   ed. Robert Tucker, 469–500. New York: Norton.
Montesquieu
    [1734] 1965   *Considerations on the causes of the greatness of the Romans and
                   their decline.* Trans. David Lowenthal. Ithaca, N.Y.: Cornell
                   University Press.
Nicolet, Claude
    1966   *L'ordre équestre à l'époque républicaine.* Paris: De Boccard.
    1976   *Tributum: Recherches sur la fiscalité direct sous la Republique
                   Romaine.* Bonn: Rudolf Habelt Verlag GmbH.
    1980   *The world of the citizen in Republican Rome.* Trans. P. S. Falla.
                   London: Batsford Academic and Educational Ltd.
Richardson, J. S.
    1976   The Spanish mines and the development of provincial taxation
                   in the second century B.C. *Journal of Roman Studies* 66:
                   139–52.
Rostovtzeff, M.
    1960   *Rome.* Trans. Elias J. Bickerman. London: Oxford University
                   Press.
Ste. Croix, G. E. M. de.
    1981   *The class struggle in the ancient Greek world.* London:
                   Duckworth.
Saller, R. P.
    1980   Promotion and patronage in equestrian careers. *Journal of
                   Roman Studies* 70:44–63.
Scramuza, V. M.
    1937   Roman Sicily. In *An economic survey of ancient Rome,* vol. 3,
                   ed. Tenney Frank, 225–337. Baltimore: Johns Hopkins Uni-
                   versity Press.
Scullard, H. H.
    1976   *From the Gracchi to Nero.* London: Methuen.
Shatzman, Israel
    1975   *Senatorial wealth and politics.* Collection Latomus 142.
Sherwin-White, A. N.
    1973   *The Roman citizenship.* Oxford: Oxford University Press.
Stevenson, G. H.
    1932   The provinces and their government. In *Cambridge ancient
                   history,* vol. 9, ed. S. A. Cook and others, 437–74. Cam-
                   bridge: Cambridge University Press.
Syme, Ronald
    1939   *The Roman revolution.* Oxford: Oxford University Press.
Taylor, Lily Ross
    1966   *Roman voting assemblies: From the Hannibalic war to the dic-
                   tatorship of Caesar.* Ann Arbor: University of Michigan Press.
Toutain, Jules
    1930   *The economic life of the ancient world.* London: Kegan Paul,
                   Trench, Trubner.

Van Nostrand, J. J.
1937   Roman Spain. In *An economic survey of ancient Rome*, vol. 3,
               ed. Tenney Frank, 119–224. Baltimore: Johns Hopkins Uni-
               versity Press.
Veyne, Paul
1976   *Le pain et le cirque*. Paris: Sevil.
Wallace, Sherman LeRoy
[1938] 1969   *Taxation in Egypt from Augustus to Diocletian*. New York:
               Greenwood Press.
Weber, Max
[1922] 1968   *Economy and society*. Vol. 2. Ed. Guenther Roth and Claus
               Wittich. New York: Bedminster.
[1924] 1976   *The agrarian sociology of ancient civilizations*. Trans. R. I.
               Frank. London: New Left Books.

THE MIDDLE AGES AND THE
RENAISSANCE (Chapter 5)

Ames, Edward, and Richard Rapp
1977   The birth and death of taxes: A hypothesis. *Journal of Eco-
                nomic History* 37 (Mar.): 161–78.
Anderson, Perry
1974   *Lineages of the absolute state*. London: New Left Books.
Ardant, Gabriel
1971   *Histoire de l'impôt. Livre I: De l'antiquité au XVIIe siècle*. Paris:
                Fayard.
Aston, A. H., and C. H. E. Philpin, eds.
1985   *The Brenner debate: Agrarian class structure and economic de-
                velopment in pre-industrial Europe*. New York: Cambridge Uni-
                versity Press.
Bates, Robert H., and Da-Hsiang Donald Lien
1985   A note on taxation, development, and representative govern-
                ment. *Politics and Society* 14 (1): 53–270.
Bean, Richard
1973   War and the birth of the nation state. *Journal of Economic
                History* 33:203–21.
Beik, William
1984   État et société en France au XVIIe siècle: La taille en Langue-
                doc et la question de la redistribution sociale. *Annales: Econo-
                mies, sociétés, civilisations* 39 (6): 1270–98.
1985   *Absolutism and society in seventeenth century France*. New
                York: Cambridge University Press.
Biddick, Kathleen
1985   Medieval English peasants and market involvement. *Journal of
                Economic History* 45 (Dec.): 823–31.

Bisson, Thomas N.
1972   The general assemblies of Philip the Fair: Their character reconsidered. *Studia Gratiana* 15:537–64.

Bonney, Richard
1981   *The king's debts: Finance and politics in France, 1589–1661.* Oxford: Clarendon Press.

Braudel, Fernand
1972   *The Mediterranean and the Mediterranean world in the age of Philip II.* 2d rev. ed. Trans. Sian Reynolds. New York: Harper and Row.

Braun, Rudolf
1975   Taxation, sociopolitical structure, and state-building: Great Britain and Brandenburg Prussia. In *The formation of national states in Western Europe,* ed. Charles Tilly, 243–327. Princeton, N.J.: Princeton University Press.

Brenner, Robert
1976   Agrarian class structure and economic development in pre-industrial Europe. *Past and Present* no. 70: 30–75.
1982   The agrarian roots of European capitalism. *Past and Present* no. 97: 16–113.

Brown, Elizabeth A. R.
1971   Subsidy and reform in 1321: The accounts of Najac and the politics of Philip V. *Traditio* 27:399–432.
1972   Cessente causa and the taxes of the late Capetions: The political application of a philosophical maxim. *Studia Gratiana* 15:565–87.
1974   The tyranny of a construct: Feudalism and historians of medieval Europe. *American Historical Review* 79 (4): 1063–88.
1981   Reform and resistance to royal authority in fourteenth century France: The leagues of 1314–1315. *Parliaments, Estates and Representation* 1 (Dec.): 109–37.
n.d.   Customary aids and royal finances in Capetian France: The marriage aid of Philip de Fair. Unpublished manuscript.

Brustein, William, and Margaret Levi
1987   The geography of rebellion: Ruler, rebels, and regions. *Theory and Society.*

Cipolla, Carlo M.
1980   *Before the Industrial Revolution.* 2d ed. New York: Norton.

Collins, James B.
1979   Sur l'histoire fiscale du XVII siècle: Les impôts directs en Champagne entre 1595 et 1635. *Annales: Economies, sociétés, civilisations* 34 (2): 325–47.

Dent, Julian
1973   *Crisis in finance: Crown, financiers and society in seventeenth century France.* Newton Abbot, Devon: David and Charles.

Dessert, Daniel
1974   Finances et société XVII siècle: A propos de la Chambre de
               Justice de 1661. *Annales: Economies, sociétés, civilisations* 29
               (4): 847–82.
Dietz, Frederick C.
1921   *English government finance, 1485–1558.* Urbana: University of
               Illinois Press.
1932   *English public finance, 1558–1641.* New York: Century.
Dowell, Stephen
1888   *A history of taxes and taxation in England.* Vol. 1. London:
               Longmans, Green.
Dunkley, Kenneth M.
1981   Patronage and power in seventeenth century France: Riche-
               lieu's clients and the estates of Brittany. *Parliaments, Estates and
               Representation* 1 (June): 1–12.
Ekelund, Robert B., Jr., and Robert D. Tollison
1981   *Mercantilism as a rent-seeking society.* College Station: Texas
               A & M University Press.
Elias, Norbert
[1939] 1982   *Power and civility.* Trans. Edmund Jephcoh. New York: Pan-
               theon Books.
Elton, G. R.
1975   Taxation for war and peace in early-Tudor England. In *War
               and economic development: Essays in memory of David Joslin,*
               ed. J. M. Winter, 33–48. Cambridge: Cambridge University
               Press.
1982   *The Tudor constitution.* 2d ed. Cambridge: Cambridge Univer-
               sity Press.
Fawtier, M. Robert
1953   Parlement d'Angleterre et états généraux de France au Moyen-
               Age. In *Compte rendus,* 275–84. Paris: Académie des Inscrip-
               tions et Belles-Lettres.
Finer, Samuel E.
1975   State and nation-building in Europe: The role of the military.
               In *The formation of national states in Western Europe,* ed.
               Charles Tilly, 84–163. Princeton, N.J.: Princeton University
               Press.
Friedman, David
1977   A theory of the size and shape of nations. *Journal of Political
               Economy* 85 (Feb.): 59–77.
Guenée, Bernard
1981   *L'Occident aux XIV siècles: Les états.* Paris: Presses univer-
               sitaires de France.
Hariss, G. L.
1975   *King, Parliament and medieval England to 1369.* Oxford: Clar-
               endon Press.

Hechter, Michael
 1975   *Internal colonialism.* Berkeley: University of California Press.
Hechter, Michael, and William Brustein
 1980   Regional modes of production and patterns of state formation
                 in Western Europe. *American Journal of Sociology* 85 (Mar.):
                 1061–94.
Henneman, John Bell
 1971   *Royal taxation in fourteenth century France: The development of
                 war financing, 1322–1356.* Princeton, N.J.: Princeton Univer-
                 sity Press.
Hirst, Derek
 1986   *Authority and conflict: England 1603–1658.* London: Edward
                 Arnold.
Homans, George C.
 1941   *English villagers of the thirteenth century.* New York: Norton.
Kantorowicz, Ernest H.
 1957   *The king's two bodies: A study of medieval political philosophy.*
                 Princeton, N.J.: Princeton University Press.
Keohane, Nannerl O.
 1984   *Philosophy and state in France.* Princeton, N.J.: Princeton
                 University Press.
Kiernan, V. G.
 1980   *State and society in Europe, 1550–1650.* Oxford: Blackwell.
Kiser, Edgar
 1986–87   The formation of state policy in Western European abso-
                 lutisms: A comparison of England and France. *Politics and
                 Society.*
Lodge, Eleanor C.
 1931   *Sully, Colbert, and Turgot.* London: Methuen.
Lyon, Bryce, and Adrian Verhulst
 1967   *Medieval finance: A comparison of financial institutions in north-
                 western Europe.* Brugge, Belgium: Tempel.
MacCaffrey, Wallace T.
 1981   *Queen Elizabeth and the making of policy, 1572–1588.* Prince-
                 ton, N.J.: Princeton University Press.
McDonald, John, and G. D. S. Snooks
 1985a   The determinants of manorial income in Domesday England:
                 Evidence from Essex. *Journal of Economic History* 45 (Sept.):
                 541–56.
 1985b   How artificial were the tax assessments of Domesday En-
                 gland? The case of Essex. *Economic History Review* 38 (3):
                 352–72.
Mann, Michael
 1980   State and society, 1130–1816: An analysis of English state
                 finances. In *Political power and social theory,* vol. 1, ed.
                 Maurice Zeitlin, 165–208. Greenwich, Conn.: JAI Press.

Miller, Edward
1975   War, taxation and the English economy in the late thirteenth and early fourteenth centuries. In *War and economic development: Essays in memory of David Joslin,* ed. J. M. Winter, 11–32. Cambridge: Cambridge University Press.
1981   Government economic policies and public finance, 1000–1500. In *The Fontana economic history of Europe: The Middle Ages,* ed. Carlo M. Cipollo, 339–73. Glasgow: William Collins.

Mitchell, Sydney Knox
1951   *Taxation in medieval England.* New Haven: Yale University Press.

Modelski, George
1978   The long cycle of global politics and the nation-state. *Comparative Studies in Society and History* 20:214–35.
1986   *Long cycles in world politics.* Seattle: University of Washington Press.

Morris, William A., and Joseph R. Strayer
1947   *The English government at work, 1327–1336.* Vol. 2, *Fiscal administration.* Cambridge, Mass.: Mediaeval Academy of America.

Mousnier, Roland E.
1979   *The institutions of France under the absolute monarch, 1598–1789.* Vol. 1, *Society and the state.* Trans. Brian Pearce. Chicago: University of Chicago Press.
1984   *The institutions of France under the absolute monarch, 1598–1789.* Vol. 2, *The organs of state and society.* Trans. Arthur Goldhammer. Chicago: University of Chicago Press.

North, Douglass C.
1981   *Structure and change in economic history.* New York: Norton.

North, Douglass C., and Robert Thomas
1973   *The rise of the Western world.* New York: Cambridge University Press.

Olson, Mancur
1982   *The rise and decline of nations.* New Haven, Conn.: Yale University Press.

Postan, M. M., E. E. Rich, and Edward Miller, eds.
1971   *The Cambridge economic history of Europe.* Vol. 3, *Economic organization and policies in the Middle Ages.* Cambridge: Cambridge University Press.

Prestwich, Michael
1972   *War, politics and finance under Edward I.* London: Faber and Faber.
1980   *The three Edwards: War and state in England, 1272–1377.* New York: St. Martin's Press.

Quinlan, Daniel C., and R. Clayton Fisk
    1982   Armies and taxes: The foundation of the absolute monarch. Paper presented to the American Political Science Association, Chicago.

Root, Hilton
    1987   *Peasants and kings: Agrarian foundations of French absolutism.* Berkeley: University of California Press.

Russell, Conrad
    1971   *The crisis of Parliaments.* Oxford: Oxford University Press.

Schofield, R. S.
    1963   Parliamentary lay taxation, 1485–1547. Ph.D. thesis, University of Cambridge.

Schumpeter, Joseph
    [1918] 1954   The crisis of the tax state. In *International economic papers: Translations prepared for the International Economic Association,* ed. A. Peacock and others, 5–38. New York: Macmillan.

Snooks, Graeme, and John MacDonald
    1986   *The Domesday economy.* Oxford: Oxford University Press.

Stone, Lawrence
    1947   State control in sixteenth-century England. *Economic History Review* 17:103–20.
    1967   *The crisis of the aristocracy, 1558–1641.* Oxford: Oxford University Press.

Strayer, Joseph R.
    1970   *On the medieval origins of the modern state.* Princeton, N.J.: Princeton University Press.
    1971   *Medieval statecraft and the perspectives of history.* Princeton, N.J.: Princeton University Press.

Strayer, Joseph R., and Charles H. Taylor
    1939   *Studies in early French taxation.* Cambridge, Mass.: Harvard University Press.

Tilly, Charles
    1985   Warmaking and statemaking as organized crime. In *Bringing the state back in,* ed. Peter B. Evans, Dietrich Rueschemeyer, and Theda Skocpol, 169–91. New York: Cambridge University Press.

Villers, Robert
    1984   Réflexions sur les premiers états généraux de France au début du XIVe siècle. *Parliaments, Estates and Representation* 4 (Dec.): 93–97.

Wallerstein, Immanuel
    1974   *The modern world-system.* New York: Academic Press.

Willard, James Field
    1934   *Parliamentary taxes on personal property, 1290 to 1334: A study in medieval English feudal administration.* Cambridge, Mass.: Mediaeval Academy of America.

Williams, Penry
    1979   *The Tudor regime*. Oxford: Clarendon Press.
Wolfe, Martin
    1972   *The fiscal system of Renaissance France*. New Haven, Conn.: Yale University Press.
Zagorin, Perez
    1982   *Rebels and rulers: 1500–1660*. 2 vols. New York: Cambridge University Press.
Zolberg, Aristide R.
    1980   Strategic interactions and the formation of modern states: France and England. *International Social Science Journal* 32:687–716.

EIGHTEENTH-CENTURY BRITAIN (Chapter 6)

Anderson, Gary M., William F. Shughart II, and Robert T. Tollison
    1985   Adam Smith in the customhouse. *Journal of Political Economy* 95 (41): 740–59.
Ashton, T. S.
    1959   *Economic fluctuations in England: 1700–1800*. Oxford: Clarendon Press.
Barnes, Donald Grove
    1939   *George III and William Pitt: 1783–1806*. Stanford, Calif.: Stanford University Press.
Binney, J. E. D.
    1959   *British public finance and administration*. Oxford: Oxford University Press.
Brewer, John
    1985   Unpublished book on the British state in the eighteenth century. Department of History and Literature, Harvard University, Cambridge, Mass.
    1988   The English state and fiscal appropriation: Taxes and public finance in England, 1688–1789. *Politics and Society*.
Brock, W. R.
    1967   *Lord Liverpool and liberal Toryism: 1820–1827*. London: Frank Cass.
Burke, Edmund
  [1790] 1888 Reflections on the revolution in France, and on the proceedings in certain societies in London relative to that event. In *The works of the Right Honourable Edmund Burke*, vol. 2, ed. James Prior, 277–518. London: George Bell and Sons.
Cannan, Edwin
    1912   *The history of local rates in England*. London: P. S. King.
Colley, Linda
    1986   Whose nation? Class and national consciousness in Britain, 1750–1830. *Past and Present*, no. 113 (Nov.): 97–117.

Cookson, J. E.
1975   *Lord Liverpool's administration: The crucial years, 1815–1822.*
                Hamden, Conn.: Archer Books.
Dietz, Vivien
1983   "Taxing Vanity": The history of assessed taxation in eigh-
                teenth-century Britain. An undergraduate thesis submitted to
                the Department of History, Harvard University.
Dinwiddy, J. R.
1985   Patriotism and national sentiment in England, 1790–1805.
                Mimeo.
Dowell, Stephen
1888   *A history of taxation and taxes in England.* Vols. 2–3. London:
                Longmans, Green.
Ehrman, John
1969   *The younger Pitt: The years of acclaim.* New York: Dutton.
1983   *The younger Pitt: The reluctant transition.* New York: Dutton.
Einzig, Paul
1959   *The control of the purse.* London: Secker and Warburg.
Feinstein, C. H.
1978   Capital formation in Great Britain. In *The Cambridge eco-
                nomic history of Europe,* Vol. 7, Part 1, *The industrial econo-
                mies,* ed. Peter Mathias and M. M. Postan, 28–96. New York:
                Cambridge University Press.
Foord, Archibald S.
1947   The waning of "The influence of the crown." *English Historical
                Review* 62:484–507. Reprinted in *The making of English his-
                tory,* ed. Robert L. Schuyler and Herman Ausubel, 401–13.
                New York: Dryden Press, 1952.
Gash, Norman
1984   *Lord Liverpool: The life and political career of Robert Banks
                Jenkinson, 2nd Earl of Liverpool, 1770–1828.* London:
                Weidenfeld and Nicolson.
Grice, J. Watson
1910   *National and local finance: A review of the relations between the
                central and local authorities in England, France, Belgium and
                Prussia during the nineteenth century.* London.
Hansard's Parliamentary History
1688–1800   Vols. 5, 21, 22, 24, 26. London: Her Majesty's Stationery
                Office.
Hirst, Derek
1986   *Authority and conflict: England 1603–1658.* London: Edward
                Arnold.
Holcroft, Thomas
[1780] 1944   *A plain and succinct narrative of the Gordon riots.* Ed. Garland
                Garvey. Atlanta: Emory University Press.
Hope-Jones, Arthur
1939   *Income tax in the Napoleonic Wars.* Cambridge: Cambridge
                University Press.

Hughes, Edward
  1934   *Studies in administration and finance, 1558–1825.* Manchester:
                  Manchester University Press.
Keith-Lucas, Bryan
  1977   *English local government in the 19th and 20th centuries.*
                  London: Historical Association.
Kennedy, William
  [1913] 1964   *English taxation: 1640–1799.* London: Frank Cass.
McCloskey, Donald N.
  1978   A mismeasurement of the incidence of taxation in Britain and
                  France, 1715–1810. *Journal of European Economic History*
                  7:209–10.
Mann, Michael
  1980   State and society, 1130–1816: An analysis of English state
                  finances. In *Political power and social theory,* vol. 1, ed.
                  Maurice Zeitlin, 165–208. Greenwich, Conn.: JAI Press.
Mathias, Peter
  1979   *The transformation of England.* New York: Columbia Univer-
                  sity Press.
  1983   *The first industrial nation: An economic history of Britain,
                  1700–1914.* 2d ed. London: Methuen.
Mathias, Peter, and Patrick O'Brien
  1976   Taxation in Britain and France, 1715–1810: A comparison of
                  the social incidence of taxes collected for the central govern-
                  ments. *Journal of European Economic History* 5 (Winter):
                  601–90.
  1978   The incidence of taxes and the burden of proof. *Journal of
                  European Economic History* 7:211–13.
North, Douglass C.
  1981   *Structure and change in economic history.* New York: Norton.
O'Brien, P. K.
  1959   British incomes and property in the early nineteenth century.
                  Economic History Review 12 (Dec.): 255–67.
Reilly, Robin
  1978   *Pitt the Younger: 1759–1806.* London: Cassell.
Reitan, E. A.
  1966   The Civil List in eighteenth-century British politics: Parlia-
                  mentary supremacy versus the independence of the crown.
                  Historical Journal 9 (3): 318–37.
Rose, George
  1810   Observations respecting the public expenditure and the influ-
                  ence of the crown. *Edinburgh Review* (April).
Sabine, B. E. V.
  1966   *A history of the income tax.* London: Allen and Unwin.
Seligman, Edwin
  1911   *The income tax: A study of the history, theory and practice of
                  income taxation at home and abroad.* London: Macmillan.

Shehab, F.
1953   *Progressive taxation.* Oxford: Clarendon Press.
Silberling, Norman J.
1924a   Financial and monetary policy of Great Britain during the
               Napoleonic Wars. I: Financial policy. *Quarterly Journal of
               Economics* 38:214–33.
1924b   Financial and monetary policy of Great Britain during the
               Napoleonic Wars. II: Ricardo and the Bullion Report. *Quar-
               terly Journal of Economics* 38:397–439.
Smith, Adam
[1776] 1937   *An inquiry into the nature and causes of the wealth of nations,* ed.
               Edwin Cannan. New York: The Modern Library.
Thompson, E. P.
1963   *The making of the English working class.* Middlesex, England:
               Pelican Books.
Ward, W. R.
1952   The administration of the window and assessed taxes, 1696–
               1798. *English Historical Review* 67:522–42.
Webb, R. K.
1968   *Modern England: From the 18th century to the present.* New
               York: Dodd, Mead.
Wiener, Joel H., ed.
1974   *Great Britain: The lion at home, A documentary history of
               domestic policy, 1689–1973.* New York: Chelsea House.
Wilson, Charles
1939   *Economic history and the historian.* London: Weidenfeld and
               Nicolson.

AUSTRALIA (Chapter 7)

The references in this section are divided into subsections. The first includes
general references; the second (pp. 243–44), Commonwealth Government documents; the third (pp. 244–46), newspaper articles; and the fourth (p. 246), press
releases by government officials.

Australian Society of Accountants and Institute of Chartered Accountants in
Australia
1982   Statement of taxation standards. *A.P.S.* 6:5029–34.
Bailey, K. H.
[1944] 1980   The Uniform Income Tax Plan (1942). In *The development of
               Australian fiscal federalism,* ed. W. Prest and R. L. Mathews,
               309–27. Canberra: Australian National University Press.
Barnard, Alan
1985   Australian government finances: A statistical overview, 1850–
               1982. Australian National University, Canberra. Working Pa-
               per no. 59.

Binns, K. J., and L. V. Bellis
[1956] 1980   Uniform taxation with states taxing incomes. In *The development of Australian fiscal federalism,* ed. W. Prest and R. L. Mathews, 361–76. Canberra: Australian National University Press.

Butlin, N. G., A. Barnard, and J. J. Pincus
1982   *Government and capitalism: Public and private choice in twentieth century Australia.* Sydney: Allen and Unwin.

Butlin, S. J.
1955   *War economy, 1939–42.* Canberra: Australian War Memorial.

Butlin, S. J., and C. B. Schevdin
1977   *War economy, 1942–1945.* Canberra: Australian War Memorial.

Carsten, A. R.
1977a   Challenging the commissioner. Lecture presented at Taxation Institute of Australia, Faculty of Law, Monash University, Melbourne.
1977b   Enforcement of payment in contested tax cases. *Australian Tax Review* 5–6:4–11.

Copland, D. B.
[1924] 1980   Some problems of taxation in Australia. In *The development of Australian fiscal federalism,* ed. W. Prest and R. L. Mathews, 35–45. Canberra: Australian National University Press.
1925   The Australian income tax. *Quarterly Journal of Economics* 39 (Nov.): 70–95.

Cranston, Ross
1979   From co-operative to coercive federalism and back? *Federal Law Review* 10 (June): 121–42.

Crisp, L. F.
1965   *Australian national government.* Croydon, Victoria: Longman Australia.

Crowley, Frank, ed.
1974   *A new history of Australia.* Melbourne: Heinemann.

Day, John
1982   Interview of the month: The Hon. John Howard, MP. *Australian Accountant* (Dec.): 702–3.

Downs, Anthony
1957   *An economic theory of democracy.* New York: Harper and Row.

Else-Mitchell, R.
1977a   Constitutional aspects of Commonwealth and state taxing laws. In *The politics of "new federalism,"* ed. Dean Jaensch, 35–42. Adelaide: Australian Politics Studies Association.
1977b   The rise and demise of coercive federalism. *Australian Journal of Public Administration* 36 (June): 109–21.

Encel, S.
1960   The concept of the state in Australian politics. *Australian Journal of Politics and History* 11 (May): 62–76.

Giblin, L. F.
[1926] 1980   Federation and finance. In *The development of Australian fiscal federalism*, ed. W. Prest and R. L. Mathews, 47–61. Canberra: Australian National University Press.

Gilbert, R. S.
1973   *The Australian Loan Council in federal fiscal adjustments, 1890–1965*. Canberra: Australian National University Press.

Grbich, Uri
1977   What the three sisters did to Section 260. Transactions and strategies for tax avoidance. Lecture presented at Taxation Institute of Australia, Faculty of Law, Monash University, Melbourne.

1983   Problems of tax avoidance. In *Taxation issues of the 1980's*, ed. John G. Head, 413–32. Sydney: Australian Taxation Research Foundation.

Greenwood, G.
1976   *The future of Australian federalism*. 2d ed. St. Lucia: University of Queensland Press.

Groenewegen, P. D.
1979   Federalism. In *From Whitlam to Fraser*, ed. Allan Patience and Brian Head, 51–69. Melbourne: Oxford University Press.

1983   The political economy of federalism, 1901–81. In *State and economy in Australia*, ed. Brian Head, 169–95. Melbourne: Oxford University Press.

1985   The National Taxation Summit: Success or failure? An overview of the major issues. Department of Economics, University of Sydney. Mimeo.

Gyles, R. V.
1984   Conspiracy to defraud the revenue. *Australian Law Journal* 58 (Oct.): 567–72.

Hamilton, R.
1984   Taxpayers' rights in the commissioner's quest for information. *Australian Accountant* (Dec.): 942–50.

Harding, Ann
1983   Who benefits? An exploratory study of the Australian welfare state and redistribution. Fourth year honours thesis, Department of Government and Public Administration, University of Sydney.

Head, John G.
1977   Tax reform in Australia. Lecture presented at Taxation Institute of Australia, Faculty of Law, Monash University, Melbourne.

1983   Issues in Australian taxation policy in the 1980's. In *Taxation issues of the 1980's*, ed. John G. Head, chap. 1. Sydney: Australian Tax Research Foundation.

Kakwani, Nanak
1983   The impact of personal income taxation and government transfers on income distribution and poverty in Australia. In *Taxation issues of the 1980's*, ed. John G. Head, chap. 9, 153–80. Sydney: Australian Tax Research Foundation.

Keane, P. A.
1983   Investigations and rights of access. *Taxation in Australia* 18 (Oct.): 405–19.

Laffer, K. M.
[1942] 1980   Taxation reform in Australia. In *The development of Australian fiscal federalism*, ed. W. Prest and R. L. Mathews, 297–308. Canberra: Australian National University Press.

Lehmann, Geoffrey
1983   The income tax judgments of Sir Garfield Barwick: A study in the failure of the new legalism. *Monash University Law Review* 9 (Mar.): 115–56.

Liebler, M. M.
1983   The taxation (unpaid company tax) legislation: A practical analysis. *Australian Tax Review* 12 (1): 29–44.

McCabe, Patrick, and David LaFranci
1982   Report of inspectors appointed to investigate the particular affairs of Navillus Pty Ltd and 922 other companies. Melbourne: Government Printer.

Macintyre, Stuart
1985   *Winners and losers*. Sydney: Allen and Unwin.

Maddock, Rodney
1982   Unification of income taxes in Australia. *Australian Journal of Politics and History* 28 (3): 354–66.

Maddock, Rodney, and Janet Penny
1983   Economists at war: The Financial and Economic Committee, 1939–44. *Australian Economic Review* 23 (Mar.): 28–49.

Marr, David
1980   *Barwick*. Sydney: Allen and Unwin.

Martin, A. W.
1982   Australian federation and nationalism: Historical notes. In *Public policies in two federal countries: Canada and Australia*, ed. R. L. Mathews, 27–46. Canberra: Centre for Research on Federal Financial Relations.

Mathews, Russell
1976   *The changing pattern of Australian federalism*. Reprint no. 17. Canberra: Centre for Research on Federal Financial Relations, Australian National University.

1978   *Issues in Australian federalism*. Reprint no. 24. Canberra: Centre for Research on Federal Financial Relations, Australian National University.

1980   *The structure of taxation*. Reprint no. 34. Canberra: Centre for Research on Federal Financial Relations, Australian National University.

1982   *Tax effectiveness and tax equity in federal countries*. Reprint no. 51. Canberra: Centre for Research on Federal Financial Relations, Australian National University.

1983   *The case for indirect taxation*. Reprint no. 54. Canberra: Centre for Research on Federal Financial Relations, Australian National University.

Menzies, Robert
1967   *Central power in the Australian Commonwealth*. London: Cassell.

Mills, R. C.
[1928] 1980   The financial relations of the Commonwealth and the states. In *The development of Australian fiscal federalism*, ed. W. Prest and R. L. Mathews, 63–76. Canberra: Australian National University Press.

Morgan, David R.
1983   Personal income tax indexation: The Australian experience. In *Taxation issues of the 1980's*, ed. John G. Head, chap. 5, 71–97. Sydney: Australian Tax Research Foundation.

Munn, G. D.
1981   Part IVA: I.T.A.A.: A practitioner's view. *Australian Accountant* (Oct.): 506–8.

Nevile, J. W.
1983   Macro-economic effects of tax avoidance. Centre for Applied Economic Research, University of New South Wales, Sydney. Unpublished paper.

Norman, Neville R.
1985   *The economics of personal tax escalation in Australia*. Sydney: Allen and Unwin.

Parsons, R. W.
1966   The control of tax avoidance. Lecture 12 presented at Income taxation (series 2), 1–11. Committee for Post Graduate Studies in the Department of Law, University of Sydney, Sydney.

Prest, W.
1977   Fiscal significance of the "new federalism." In *The politics of the "new federalism,"* ed. Dean Jaensch, 55–63. Adelaide: Australian Political Studies Association.

Prest, W., and R. L. Mathews, eds.
1980   *The development of Australian fiscal federalism*. Canberra: Australian National University Press.

Sawer, Geoffrey
1977a   New federalism. In *The politics of the "new federalism,"* ed. Dean Jaensch, 15–20. Adelaide: Australian Political Studies Association.

1977b   Seventy-five years of Australian federalism. *Australian Journal of Public Administration* 36 (Mar.): 1–11.

Scotton, R. B., and Helen Ferber, eds.

1978   *Public expenditures and social policy in Australia.* Vol. I: *The Whitlam years, 1972–75.* Melbourne: Longman Cheshire.

1980   *Public expenditures and social policy in Australia.* Vol. II: *The first Fraser years, 1976–78.* Melbourne: Longman Cheshire.

Staples, Jim

1985   Taxes: The dissenters. *Australian Society* (June): 13–19.

Stilwell, Frank

1985   Where to lay tax emphasis. *Australian Society* (June): 19–22.

Stretton, Hugh

1980   Future patterns for taxation and public expenditure in Australia. In *The politics of taxation,* ed. John Wilkes, 43–81. Sydney: Hodder and Stoughton.

Telfer, J.

1984   Professional obligations of tax agents. *Australian Accountant* (June): 331–35.

Troy, Patrick N.

1969   An example of urban road planning in Australia. *Australian Planning Institute Journal* (Jan.): 11–17.

Troy, Patrick N., ed.

1978   *Federal power in Australia's cities.* Sydney: Hale and Icemonger.

Wallschutzky, I. G.

1982   Results of a survey on some aspects of tax avoidance. *Taxation in Australia* 17 (July): 282–97.

Wilkes, John, ed.

1980   *The politics of taxation.* Sydney: Hodder and Stoughton.

Wilkins, D. C.

1981   Tax avoidance—Section 260 replaced. *Australian Accountant* (July): 402–6.

1982   Tax avoidance. *Australian Accountant* (Dec.): 707–12.

1983   Recovery of tax. *Australian Accountant* (Dec.): 199–200.

GOVERNMENT DOCUMENTS
(Papers produced under the auspices of the Parliament
of the Commonwealth of Australia)

Advisory Committee on Prices and Incomes

1984   Prices and income policies: The third progress report on government initiatives.

Commissioner of Taxation

1950–85   Annual reports.

Committee on Taxation and Inflation

1975   Report (Mathews report).

Committee on Uniform Taxation
    1942   Report to the treasurer on uniform taxation.
Commonwealth Committee on Taxation
    1953a   Report on collections by installments. Reference no. 29.
    1953b   Report on penal provisions and prosecutions. Reference no. 34.
    1953c   Report on provisional tax. Reference no. 27.
    1953d   Report on returns and assessments. Reference no. 31.
Draft White Paper
    1985   Reform of the Australian tax system.
Legislative Research Service, Department of the Parliamentary Library
    1982   Tax evasion and avoidance. Basic Paper no. 4.
Senate Standing Committee on Finance and Government Operations
    1983   Income tax regulations (amendment). Official Standard Report for 7 Sept. 1983.
    1983   Report on the income tax regulations (amendment) contained in Statutory Rules 1983 no. 111 (Prescribed Payments System).
Special Prosecutor R. V. Gyles, Q.C.
    1984   Annual report 1983–84.
Taxation Review Committee
    1975   Full report 31 Jan. 1975 (Asprey report).

NEWSPAPER ARTICLES
(1969–85, listed chronologically)

Dixon, D. A. Privileges in the A.C.T. *Nation*, 8 Mar. 1969, 10.

Unions combine to press for tax reform. *Canberra Times*, 7 July 1970, 1.

Smith, Vincent. How the rich avoid tax. *National Times*, 12–17 June 1972, 1, 4.

Smith, Vincent. Closing down on those short lives. *National Times*, 19–24 June 1972, 45.

Dale, Brian. 320 submissions to Tax Review Committee. *Australian Financial Review*, 6 Apr. 1973, 10.

Tax review "could take two years." *Canberra Times*, 16 Apr. 1973, 3.

Ackland, Richard. Court's tax shock. *Australian Financial Review*, 7 Mar. 1974, 1, 10.

Mining "abuse" denied. *The Advertiser*, 26 June 1974, 3.

Bell, Glenys. Moonlighting tax cheats lose a good "lurk." *National Times*, 9–14 Feb. 1976, 3.

Farthing, Joe. A small honest raid on federal treasury. *Nation Review*, 23–29 July 1976, 993.

Murray, Brian. Roving tax man to catch two job cheats. *The Australian*, 3 Nov. 1976, 1.

Webb, Christopher. How to outwit the taxman with the charity man. *National Times*, 8–13 Aug. 1977, 3.

Freeman, Pete. Trusts: How a tax loophole was closed. *Sydney Morning Herald*, 29 Aug. 1977, 3.

Tax justice for self-employed. *The Mercury*, 31 Jan. 1978, 4.

Sawer, Geoffrey. The ancient art of dodging tax lawfully. *Canberra Times*, 17 May 1978, 2.

Crackdown on $20 million tax cheats. *Sunday Telegraph*, 25 Feb. 1979, 26.

Some tax cuts, bigger penalties. *Canberra Times*, 28 May 1981, 1.

Mills, Stephen. New move on tax law. *The Age*, 28 May 1981, 1.

QLD law tax loophole. *The Sun*, 3 June 1981, 13.

Police seize papers in tax-dodge swoop. *Canberra Times*, 21 May 1982, 1.

Chadwick, Paul, and others. Tax avoidance report. *The Age*, 27 May 1982, 1–4.

Chubb, Philip, and Richard Guilliat. Hundreds in tax list. *The Age*, 28 May 1982, 1, 4.

Freeman, Peter. Accountants join fight against tax avoidance. *Sydney Morning Herald*, 15 June 1982, 15.

Crock, Susan. Law group supports taxation reforms. *The Age*, 16 June 1982, 3.

Legge, Kate. Unions move on tax dodgers. *The Age*, 16 June 1982, 3.

Waterford, Jack. ACT seen as a $100 million-a-year tax haven. *Canberra Times*, 18 July 1982, 1.

Holberton, Simon. Tax guidelines on super could benefit companies. *The Age*, 6 Aug. 1982, 15.

Elias, David. Paintings the key to success. *The Age*, 29 Sept. 1982, 2.

Investment tax dodge overseas uncovered. *Canberra Times*, 13 Oct. 1982, 1.

Mannix, Teresa. Former ministers named in tax-payment report. *Canberra Times*, 29 Oct. 1982, 1.

Report names politicians for understating income. *Australian Financial Review*, 29 Oct. 1982, 2.

Solomon, David. "Scientology's" status challenged in court. *Australian Financial Review*, 10 Nov. 1982, 7.

Crook, Susan, and Simon Holberton. Financial levy move to combat tax avoidance. *The Age*, 27 Nov. 1982, 3.

Retrospectivity and tax recoupment. *Law Society Journal*, Dec. 1982, 745–47.

Campaign on cash payments. *Canberra Times*, 19 Apr. 1983, 10.

Hickie, David, and Wendy Bacon. The great tax dodge. *National Times*, 22–28 July 1983, 25–28.

Innes, Prue. Bank fights $17 million claim over tax schemes. *The Age*, 12 Aug. 1983, 3.

Sturgess, Gary. Professionals hit by $5 million tax claim. *The Age*, 13 Aug. 1983, 3.

Chubb, Philip. ALP councillor pushed tax avoidance: MP. *The Age*, 19 Aug. 1983, 3.

Ramsey, Alan. Bank fights $17 million claim over tax schemes. *The Age*, 2–8 Sept. 1983, 3.

Windham, Susan. 1984 — The year of the guilty conscience. *Sydney Morning Herald*, 21 Jan. 1984, 2.

Wasiliev, John. Capital gains: Last tax game in town. *Australian Financial Review*, 6 Mar. 1984, 12, 13, 22.

McCathie, Andrew. Tax Act: A toothless tiger for super fund avoidance. *Australian Financial Review,* 9 Mar. 1984, 6.

McCathie, Andrew. Prosecutor blasts Tax Office over "inaction" on avoidance. *Australian Financial Review,* 28 Mar. 1984, 3.

Court opens a floodgate of tax. *Western Australian,* 11 Apr. 1984, 3.

McCathie, Andrew. Tax legislation's validity upheld. *Australian Financial Review,* 11 Apr. 1984, 19.

Moral crusade signalled on tax avoiders. *Canberra Times,* 20 Apr. 1984, 3.

Ryan, Colleen. Tax avoidance initiatives: Not with a bang but a whimper. *National Times,* 4–10 May 1984, 38.

Ryan, Colleen. Section 260: An unexploded bomb... *National Times,* 12–18 Oct. 1984, 44.

Waterford, Jack. Crackdown on common family dodge. *Canberra Times,* 18 Dec. 1984, 1.

20,000 face playback over family tax rule. *Canberra Times,* 19 Dec. 1984, 9.

Ryan, Colleen. Family trust tax blitz. *National Times,* 18–24 Jan. 1985, 38–39.

Short, John. Tax and you, part I. *Sydney Morning Herald,* 27 Mar. 1985, 1–4.

Short, John. Tax and you, part II. *Sydney Morning Herald,* 28 Mar. 1985, 1–4.

PRESS RELEASES

Dawkins, J. S. (Minister for Finance)
  Retrospective legislation against tax avoidance. 28 Apr. 1983.
  Measures against tax evasion. 2 May 1983.
Howard, John (Treasurer)
  Tax avoidance — cash payments. 15 Aug. 1978. Press release no. 78.
  Schemes to avoid income tax. 24 Sept. 1978. Press release no. 98.
  Tax avoidance: Bonus shares. 3 Oct. 1978. Press release no. 103.
  Carry-forward of paper losses generated under tax avoidance schemes. 24 May 1979. Press release no. 41.
  Income tax: Tax avoidance through trusts and income of dependent children. 26 July 1979. Press release no. 75.
  Tax avoidance by trust stripping. 5 Mar. 1980. Press release no. 26.
  Tax avoidance: Exploitation of the states of bodies whose income is exempt from tax. 24 June 1980. Press release no. 66.
  Expenditure recoupment schemes of tax avoidance. 30 Jan. 1981. Press release no. 98.
  Tax avoidance on profits from short-term property transactions. 10 Sept. 1981.
  Expenditure recoupment schemes of tax avoidance. 9 Feb. 1982. Press release no. 16.
  Avoidance of income tax: Trust stripping. 11 May 1982. Press release no. 59.
  Measures against tax evasion. 17 Aug. 1982. Press release no. 154.
O'Reilly, W. J. (Commissioner of Taxation)
  Penalties for evasion of income tax. 25 Jan. 1983. Press release no. 1.

Index